# SPATIALIZA-TION TAKES COMMAND

NOTES ON THE FUTURE OF
URBANISM, THE INTERNET,
AND LIFE AS WE LIVE IT

## METAVERSE URBANISM

FIRAS SAFIEDDINE

**Spatialization Takes Commnand.
Metaverse Urbanism**

**Author**
Firas Safieddine

**Published by**
Actar Publishers
New York, Barcelona
www.actar.com

**Distribution**
Actar D
New York, Barcelona

New York
440 Park Avenue South,
17th Floor
New York, NY 10016, USA
T +1 2129662207
salesnewyork@actar-d.com

Barcelona
Roca i Batlle 2-4
08023 Barcelona, Spain
T +34 933 282 183
eurosales@actar-d.com

**Indexing**
English ISBN: 978-1-63840-147-6
Library of Congress Control Number:
2024936424

**Publication date**
Spring 2024

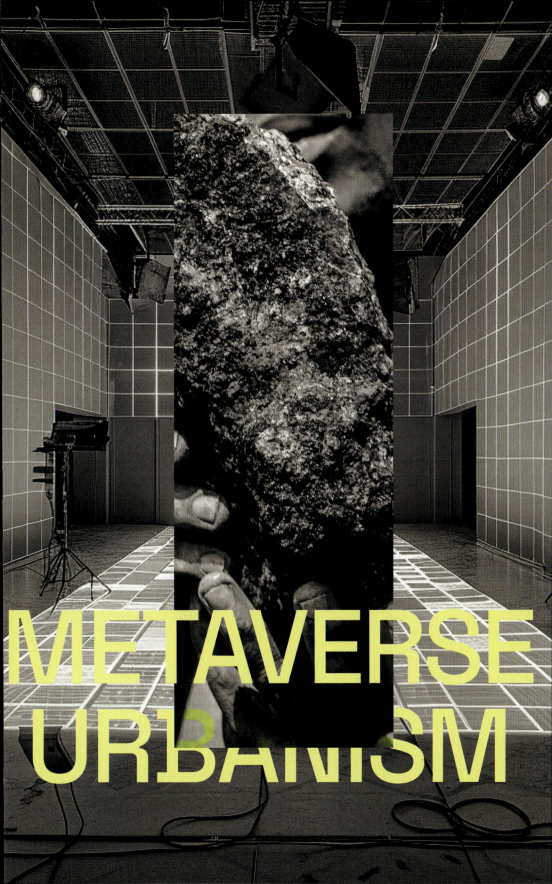

# METAVERSE URBANISM

**Content Curation:** Firas Safieddine
**Graphic Designer:** Lina Salamanca
**Editor:** Reine Al Ariss
**Chapter V content:** Spatial Forces

**Content Guide:**
→ Within the chapters, the
   GoogleSheets linked through QR
   codes as mostly compilations
   of online content as part of the
   author's readings.
→ All references are listed in Harvard
   Style, arranged by chapter
   title, and organized alongside
   accessible URLs.
→ The full Bibliography is accessible
   through the QR code at the end of
   the book.
→ This book does not intend to list
   facts and figures about the topic,
   nor act as an objective explanation
   of the phenomena at stake. It
   combines both speculation and
   current facts.

**Acknowledgement:**
The Gamium City-world project,
showcased in Chapter V is a project
by "Spatial Forces"
The Gamium City-world project was
commissioned by "Gamium"

**Date of Writing:**
Major content produced between
March and June of 2023

# SPATIALIZA-TION TAKES COMMAND

**FIRAS SAFIEDDINE**

# METAVERSE URBANISM

NOTES ON THE FUTURE OF
URBANISM, THE INTERNET,
AND LIFE AS WE LIVE IT

# SPATIALIZA-TION TAKES COMMAND

# Spatialization
## takes
## command

**F. SAFIEDDINE**

SPACE, TIME AND ARCHITECTURE

# chanization
# takes
# command

## S. GIEDION

author of SPACE, TIME AND ARCHITECTURE

POSITION

**Spatialization takes command. The infinite stack, encompassing and bound by the physical and virtual realms, undergoes a process of densification propelled by the latest technological innovations.**

As the internet evolves into its spatial iteration, contextual awareness becomes more pertinent than ever before. Media geology assumes the mantle of the new archeology. Everything becomes bio. The biologization of all things opens up a fresh frontier: the neural domain, an almost uncharted territory ripe for interfacing, from the cerebral to the planetary.

The metaverse, the spatial internet, is a work in progress. An evolutionary step for the world as we live it, a transformative and expansive internet that shapes everything. A reordering of governance systems, emergent cloud economies, and the birth of a world of perceptual significance beckon forth.

The Metaverse is the Spatial internet and all that it takes to make it happen, it is the convergence of the internet of spaces and ownership; a shift towards a mass-personalized, experiential, and gamified internet and stakeholder economy, expanding a global financial agency that expands the market plane

# TLDR;

Metaverse Urbanism is a seminal work that explores the spatial internet and its implications, touching on the future of architecture, urbanism, and spatial design. The book is structured into five parts, beginning with an introduction that provides an overview of the evolution of the internet and the concept of the spatial internet, as well as an examination of key topics such as content creation, digital identity, cyberspace, neurotechnology, ecology, and new practice models.

The second chapter provides readers with some of the the jargon, current landscape, and technosphere enabling them to gain a better understanding of the concepts explored in the book.

The third part of the book, "Letters from ~~Tomorrow~~ Today," delves into cutting-edge topics such as Electrical Ecologies, Media Geology, The Network State, gamified parenthood, technobiophilia, spatiology, augmented browsing, digital graveyards, promptism, and mineral intelligence, among others. These concepts provide a glimpse into the future of social, economic, technological, cultural, and urban phenomena that will shape and will be shaped by the metaverse.

The fourth chapter, "A Hitchhiker's Guide to Metaverse Urbanism," lays out a blueprint for metaverse cities, and puts forward a didactic structure to metaverse urbanism. This section explores topics such as virtual world-building, automated urban morphologies, planning, the DAO stack, virtual urban economies, data, and metaverse lands.

Finally, "The Gamium City-World," defines a new concept, the City-world, through a specific project that demonstrates a realized example of virtual cities. This project includes 10 neighborhoods with unique designs, including Genesis, SAT, Ilios, Kaban, Panthera, Egea, Sena, Khala Tua, OX, Rei, and Noa.

The book offers a sophisticated exploration of the metaverse as the natural evolution of the Internet into the Internet of ownership and places. It argues that architects, urbanists, and spatial designers shall be the driving force behind metaverse urbanism and that the metaverse is a phygital space that will change everything. The book's comprehensive structure and in-depth exploration of concepts make it an invaluable resource for anyone interested in the future of technology and its impact on urban design.

# I.
# INTRODUCTION
## SPATIALIZATION
# TAKES COMMAND

# III.
# LETTERS FROM
## ~~TOMORROW~~
## ———— TODAY

# II.
# GETTING YOU ALL CAUGHT-UP

1.Metaverse Jargon

# IV.
# A HITCHHIKER'S GUIDE TO METAVERSE URBANISM

# V.
# THE GAMIUM CITY-WORLD

SPATIAL

TAKES

CO

      0:07 / 0:08

**Who let the dogs out?** #apple #visionpro

Chit2am ♪

  Subscribe

ZATION

MMAND

# 1. THE EVOLUTION OF THE INTERNET, A GENEALOGY OF WEB 3.0

"We are those who have wrapped the planet in wire. This is the signal accomplishment of our time. Our pyramids are gossamer shaped."

BENJAMIN BRATTON

**The Internet is relatively new, emerging out of ARPANET, a 1969 Cold War operation of the U.S. Defense Department that combined the computers of four universities. Network Fever**

Wires wrap the planet. The network infrastructure for our digital life is physical. In the post-World War II era, when communication and computing merged, the internet was actually born. This decade was a time of building the internet itself, inventing and deploying technologies that enabled it, and setting the stage for mass adoption. The modern era of the internet kicked off in the early 1990s, starting from basic packet switching decades before, and peaked markedly with the creation of the first webpage and the release of the World Wide Web (WWW) by CERN in 1991.

Initially non-graphic- text-based, until MOSAIC, 1993, the internet disrupted multiple sectors and domains and continued to evolve to become what we know today.

Multimedia changed the face of the internet in 1992 when the number of hosts broke one million. Shortly after, in 1993, the number of hosts peaked at 2 Million with 600 WWW sites. This trend continued upward, hitting over 12 million users by the time WIFI was invented in 1997, and Google emerged in 1998.

On January 1, 1983, in what is known as a flag day, NCP was officially rendered obsolete when the ARPANET changed its core networking protocols from NCP to the more flexible and powerful TCP/IP protocol suite, marking the start of the modern Internet.

**While the beginnings and ends of the internet iterations, Web1.0, 2.0, and 3.0 have been thoroughly studied and marked by events, arguably, Web2.0 starting in 2007, and web3.0 starting in 2016 or 2017. The aim here is not to go through this classification, but rather to create a simple understanding of the last 30 years of the internet, and how we're moving forward to Web4.0. In this chapter, Web 4.0 is not referred to, as it's dealt with along Web 3.0 as what is coming next. The same applies to the Internet of People or the Internet of Things. While one might argue which was massively deployed first, or when IoT actually started, I am here referring to when it became largely relevant and adopted at global scales.**

Early in the 1980s and for over/the next twenty years, the internet heavily relied on big desktop computers, wired internet connections, technically challenging interfaces, and no ecosystem or intuitive interface for democratic content creation.

While the 90s marked the emergence of Web1.0, the beginnings of the 2000s marked the end of it.

The year 2000 was a pivotal moment with the .com bubble burst, defining a new age within the internet's timeline. Darcy DiNucci's "Web 2.0", coined a year before the bubble burst, perhaps served as a just-on-time term to close gates on the previous decade. The term became widely used in 2004 with the emergence of new platforms, websites, and Rich Internet Applications (RIA) that were highly interactive and user-driven.

Wikipedia, Facebook, and Twitter, coupled with the smartphone were the beginning of a snowball, signaling an era of social media. The internet became a platform-based digital place that connected people, attracting Hillary Clinton to get on board early with YouTube campaign videos, and Ron Paul to set a fundraising record of $4.3 Million in a single day.

This was the second decade of the internet, where platforms pioneered the scene, and the internet became an internet of people. A landmark event we might all remember is the iPhone reveal of 2007. That's where the ball started rolling.

# "There's an app for that!"

A 2009 iconic campaign catchphrase by Apple played a pivotal role, and in 2010 the word 'App' was voted "Word of the Year". Pocket-sized "Black Mirrors" took over the world, transforming how we interact, see, and use the world. With the mass adoption of smartphones, the "There's an app for that!" became a self-fulfilling prophecy that dominated the third decade of the internet.

The smartphone app combo took over address books, pocket watches, loyalty cards, cash, keys, IDs, portrait photos of loved ones, pocketbooks, small notepads, and maps. It dematerialized a lot of what was thought to be forever physical. Most importantly, it changed how we interacted with our world presence. The combo served purposes beyond playing a game or looking at a map or making a transaction.

At a more complex level, Apps offered a solution for anything –almost.

Apps then evolved from "functional" to interactive. Now, users can share information, and the smartphones themselves collect data. The smartphone-user network became a sensing mesh almost covering the planet. Smartphones were not only connected to the internet but to other devices and objects. Similarly, other devices within the same network were connected, from homes to satellites.

The Internet of Things was born. With that, a third layer of connectivity, interactivity, and complexity was built and added to the Internet.

With hyper-connected users and smart homes now came "smart cities"; moving the dial-up producing a brand name for tech-heavy hyperconnected urban environments.

Now the puzzle pieces came together with a mature infrastructure, well-established platforms, killer apps on one hand, record adoption, online communities, and capacity for monetization on the other. Democratization of content creation tools through the platforms and Apps was a glue that brought everything together.

While users were able to feed in basic information, publicly share an image, or add a place on a Map, with the emergence of the creator's economy, a new type of user emerged. The prosumers: A user base that is simultaneously a consumer and a producer of content.

Web 2.0 is the shift where the internet became a platform, a read-write platform. Web 2.0 gave users more interaction with less control.

# Web 2.0 gave users more interaction with less control.

# THE INTERNET WILL ONLY BECOME INCREASINGLY SPATIAL.

( THE FOUNDATIONAL
STATIC WEB )

## WEB 1.0

### The Internet of Databases and Documents.

Mainly connects nodes of databases, in a simple manner, and moves from the Internet to the Internet. HTTP, HTML, Websites, emails, etc.

( THE MASS-ADOPTED
INTERACTIVE WEB )

## WEB 2.0

### Seamless connections of information and applications
### The Internet of People & Internet of Things

With the emergence of platforms, not only people got better connected with databases but also with each other, creating the Internet of people and social media. The other frontier was things, once that got connected, be it phones, energy generators, cars, and even thermostats.

## WEB 3.0 / 4.0

### The Internet of Places and Ownership

The next 10 years will be the next shift in the Internet's history, towards an Internet of places, or spaces. The promise brings with it the internet of ownership too, with blockchain technologies and identity social innovation taking place. Ultra-intelligent, symbiotic web, read-write concurrency, and new interfaces change how we interact. Blockchain, Edge, Ai, XR, etc.

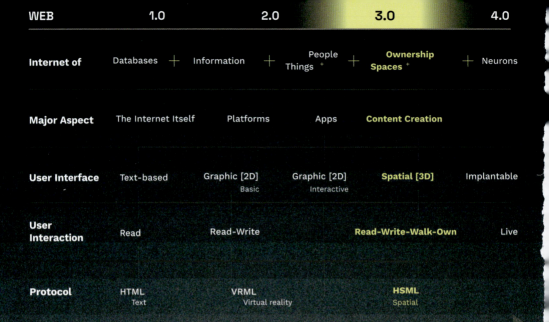

| WEB | 1.0 | 2.0 | 3.0 | 4.0 |
|---|---|---|---|---|
| **Internet of** | Databases + | Information + | People Things + + | Ownership Spaces + | + Neurons |
| **Major Aspect** | The Internet Itself | Platforms | Apps | Content Creation | |
| **User Interface** | Text-based | Graphic [2D] Basic | Graphic [2D] Interactive | Spatial [3D] | Implantable |
| **User Interaction** | Read | Read-Write | | Read-Write-Walk-Own | Live |
| **Protocol** | HTML Text | VRML Virtual reality | | HSML Spatial | |

"Web 4.0 will be a read-write concurrency web. It ensures global transparency, governance, distribution, participation, collaboration into key communities such as industry, political, social and other communities. WebOS will be such as a middleware in which will start functioning like an operating system. WebOS will be parallel to the human brain and implies a massive web of highly intelligent interactions. World Wide Web and Its Journey from Web 1.0 to Web 4.0"

NUPUR CHOUDHURY

The second and third decades examined - 2000-2020- mark the Web 2.0 phase of the internet. One that is powered by wireless internet connection, growing cloud infrastructure, and smaller and more mobile computers; the phase ends with these accomplishments enabling versatile interfacing, a new creator economy, and an abundance of data.

Looking back at the macro scale, the creators' economy had reached a peak in tandem with breakthroughs in high-speed internet, advances in graphics technology, development of virtual reality technology, and increased computing power. These main enablers made it possible to transmit large amounts of data. quickly and efficiently. It became possible to create advanced graphics and even 3d animations, to create virtual environments that can be experienced in a more immersive way, and to produce more complex and sophisticated ones.

The fourth decade of the internet and the WWW is an era of content, fueled by a creators' economy that responds to an attention economy that is only growing.

"The Semantic Web provides a common framework that allows data to be shared and reused across application, enterprise, and community boundaries" JOHN MARKOFF

Web 3.0 appeared in John Markoff's 2006 article, as a third generation of the internet, where the web becomes executable and semantic.

As we examine the 4th decade, we can track an evolution where the internet and the WWW grew to an increasingly interactive, visual, and immersive realm. It progressed on all levels and moved from text-based to technical to graphical, reaching interactive 2d and finally, 3d.

The ultimate engaging and immersive experience, in other words, the most natural and holistic one, is the spatial experience.

# 2- DIGITAL COLONIALISM / TECHNO FEUDALISM

- YANIS VAROUFAKIS

With cloud-based Alexa-like devices or apps in the role once occupied by Don Draper, we find ourselves in the most dialectical of infinite regresses: We train the algorithm to train us to serve the interests of its owners. The more we do this, the faster the algorithm learns how to help us train it to command us. As a result, the owners of this algorithmic cloud-based command capital deserve a term to distinguish them from traditional capitalists.

Within the era of digital connectivity, an unsettling reality has emerged, one where a perpetual asymmetry of power grows with time.

It's a peculiar paradox: the information we generate and the value we create is essentially ours, yet we find ourselves in a position bombarded by targeted advertisements curated based on analyzing the data collected.

This predicament extends beyond mere inconvenience as it borders on a form of economic enslavement. We are unwittingly bound to a system that thrives on our data while we receive little or no return, and most importantly, we have no say in it.

The asymmetry of this relationship is striking: we provide the fuel that powers the digital economy, yet we often find ourselves on the receiving end of targeted ads, manipulative algorithms, and questionable privacy practices.

The legal construct that once offered a semblance of protection, the infamous "terms of service," has become outdated and inadequate. It fails to address the fundamental questions surrounding ownership, control, and fair compensation when it comes to data. We are navigating a complex and ambiguous landscape where our rights and agency are increasingly eroded.

However, it's important to recognize that the issue at hand goes beyond the mere commodification of data. It is not about the strings of ones and zeros; it is the predictions made on the basis of biases, thoughts, experiences, and identities. Data is an intrinsic part of who we are in the digital space.

More and more, online presence is becoming denser, and therefore, more representative.

When data is lost, more than just data is lost.

Companies at the scale of Facebook and Twitter can now influence election results in the world's most powerful country. Manipulation of public opinion and electoral processes have underscored a clear image of how important data is. The ability of platforms like Facebook to shape narratives, influence decisions, and sway outcomes highlights the urgency of re-evaluating the current state of affairs.

Web 3.0 is a pivotal moment in our relationship with information and the online landscape. A shift in the ownership of the produced data is fundamental to avoid a future of digital enslavement.

# 3- PROPERTY RIGHTS

- DARA BIRNBAUM

## "RUMOR AS NETWORK'S NET WORTH"

Property rights and freedom are intricately intertwined, forming the foundation of a prosperous society- in a democratic capitalist system. The ability to own and control property grants individuals the freedom to engage in transactions at various levels, empowering them to create value; and therefore, to create chances for third parties to contribute.

The concept of property rights incentivizes vision, predictability, and agency; and therefore, enables the network effect to flourish, opening up new economic opportunities. It is through ownership that companies emerge, with individuals and organizations leveraging their commodities to generate value. Without property rights, long-term valuation becomes challenging, hindering investment and growth.

The correlation between strong property rights and high GDP is evident across countries. Nations that prioritize and protect property rights tend to experience greater economic prosperity. This link underscores the importance of establishing a legal framework that upholds and defends individuals' rights to own and control their assets.

But how do property rights actually work? The essence of ownership lies not in the physical attributes of a property, but in the virtual contract backed by the government. It is this contract that grants legitimacy and makes ownership tangible. Property rights are intertwined with democratic values and stability, as seen in examples like South Korea's transformation in the 1980s. Despite having a lower GDP than North Korea at the time, South Korea's embrace of property rights and capitalism propelled its economic growth.

The significance of property rights is further exemplified by the behaviors of certain communities. For instance, the Chinese diaspora, a population that is nearly as big as that of France, often displays a strong inclination to invest in property abroad. This behavior stems from the desire to mitigate the insecurities they face in their home country, emphasizing the psychological and economic importance of property rights.

In the realm of Web 3.0, there is an opportunity to reshape ownership dynamics, enabling everyone to become an owner. This includes exploring models of partial ownership and establishing frameworks to support such arrangements. Existing systems like 401K and S&P500 were intended to address these issues, but they largely hold cash rather than providing true ownership opportunities.

In today's economy, stakeholders are people affected by a company, whether shareholders or not. Shareholders on the other hand are de facto stakeholders. The aim is to move away from shareholder capitalism to stakeholder capitalism. Therefore, fostering an economy that capitalizes on agency, involvement, and network value.

The sharing models that dominate today, where ownership is obscured or absent, are essentially deceptive arrangements for which we pay a price. True stakeholder capitalism recognizes that stake is not merely cash but represents actual ownership, aligning incentives and distributing value more equitably.

Tokenization offers a pathway to embrace stakeholder capitalism, where individuals can have a tangible stake in the assets they support, fostering greater inclusivity and shared prosperity.

Property rights are the bedrock of a flourishing society today, empowering individuals with the freedom to transact, create value, and invite contributions. By embracing and safeguarding property rights, nations can unlock economic potential, foster democratic values, and pave the way for stakeholder capitalism, ensuring a more equitable and prosperous future.

Up until the 90s, property rights in China were on shaky grounds, physically and intellectually. During the 90s, within its transition period, China moved from a hub for production factories of piracy and copycat products to making the first quantum call, with a vision to realize the quantum space-based internet.

The shift in vision has played a pivotal role in protecting intellectual property. Leading to a robust software industry and growing innovation.

China has become a major producer of patents, with 4.21 million in 2022, surpassing the United States in certain areas. This shift reflects the impact that intellectual property rights can have in fostering innovation and technological advancements.

The historical trajectory of copyright laws and intellectual property in the United States and China illustrates the correlation between strong intellectual property rights, and property rights in general, and large and powerful economies.

# 4- THE NEXT INTERNET

# Life is an immersive game

The next Internet is an Internet of places and ownership, perhaps the two most important pillars of the transition. Financial literacy, network effects, spatial technologies, property rights, and augmented cognition are central to this transition.

The internet of spaces and ownership is at stake and will be driven by the gamification of everything.

**History of the Internet**

# THE SPATIAL INTERNET

It has become a widely repeated phrase that if you get 10 experts in a room, you might get 11 definitions of what the Metaverse is. The Metaverse is not a predefined concept that lands with its hidden definitions that need to be uncovered. Passive attitudes towards the topic avoid definitions by avoiding clear positions and safeguarding any possible future scenarios.

The Metaverse is a work in progress, and its end is definitely undefined yet. Pursuing a vision is in itself an endeavor of practicing a vision of what the Metaverse could be.

AR is not the Metaverse.
VR is not the Metaverse.
Cool AI is not the Metaverse.

**The next internet connects information, people, things, places, and property.**

As the term Metaverse might be problematic, a definition in this context is useful to move on. For the lack of any better term, I'm using the term Metaverse to describe an emerging ecosystem of online virtual experiences, therefore understood as a 3-dimensional iteration of the internet as we know it. It is unlike "3d models on a computer", and it is not what designers and architects have been doing in the last 20 years designing virtual spaces. There are more developments that will enable the Metaverse, other foundational technologies, and some features that will emerge eventually such as interoperability and more.

The Metaverse is more than just a technical feat - it is a technocultural phenomenon that is poised to reshape the way we live, work, and interact with one another. As the Metaverse evolves, we can expect to see it become more accessible, user-friendly, and inclusive - just as the internet did before it.

As definitions vary, I find Mathew Ball's take on what the Metaverse is to be the clearest and most sharp. While incomplete, as it is biased to a virtual iteration of it, this book stands firm in the position that the Metaverse, or the next internet, is going to outgrow the virtual world into the physical world. A complementary augmentation and phygital interfacing.

The Metaverse is the Spatial Internet and all that it takes to make it happen; it is the convergence of the internet of spaces and ownership, a shift towards a mass-personalized, experiential, and gamified internet and stakeholder economy, expanding a global financial agency that expands the market plane.

"A massively scaled and interoperable network of real-time rendered 3D virtual worlds that can be experienced synchronously and persistently by an effectively unlimited number of users with an individual sense of presence, and with continuity of data, such as identity, history, entitlements, objects, communications, and payments."

- THE METAVERSE BOOK BY MATTHEW BALL, 2022.

While I find this definition precise in its majority, the "end product" attitude is one that I don't align with. The definition sets finite thresholds that the development might cross to attain the phase defined as the Metaverse. No Technology is floating in the air. all technologies, social innovations, and paradigm shifts have their roots within history and precedents and will have their yield affect other movements.

Throughout the internet's evolution, milestone breakthroughs have defined epochs, such as the mass adoption of the smartphone, the invention of the App, social media platforms, etc.

The Spatial Internet or the Metaverse is a phase transition and a process, rather than a final state.

**MAIN FEATURES**

→ **Massively scaled,** not only regarding the volume of adoption but also the hierarchy produced as a consequence of massive scaling. Worlds, galaxies, and verse(s).

→ **Interoperable,** a taken-for-granted state of the internet today, is still a challenge. The Metaverse will be the largest collection of massively adopted verses, but there will always be Metaverses, just like the internets.

→ **Network,** underlining the importance of it as a connected system.

→ **Real-time rendered 3d virtual worlds,** otherwise a gigantic amount of data to be stored and used. Real-time rendering offers an on-demand-like solution for rendering only what is needed.

→ **Experienced synchronously and persistently,** the unique feature that makes the Metaverse a shared place, not only experienced individually but also as a shared online experience.

→ **Experiences by an effectively unlimited number of users,** a demanding requirement, that is confined to the technical capacity. The volume of users simultaneously occupying certain spaces will grow.

→ **The individual sense of presence** is a foundational element to qualify the next internet as spatial. The sense of spatiality is connected to embodiment and presence.

→ **Continuity of data** (identity, history, entitlements, objects, communities, and payments), just like the internet today, is another vital element to the adoption and implementation of the Metaverse.

While all these defining features will render a Metaverse, the path towards that is viable, and Metaverses will form first, before becoming a single entity. The transition is gradual.

**The Internet carries a vast range of information resources and services, such as the interlinked hypertext documents and applications of the World Wide Web (WWW), electronic mail, telephony, and file sharing."**

# Metaverse = Metavearth

On another note, the Metaverse does not merely consist of virtual worlds. Augmented worlds and virtual extensions of real-world scenarios are Metaverses too. The spatial internet will be diffused through numerous applications, the most interesting being the phygital ones.

Threshold-based definitions for identifying The Metaverse are not to be confused with all the production that leads to a single Metaverse. The current phase is a beginning that draws the path for what's next. Metaverses will become The Metaverse, with Worlds, Galaxies, and Verses.

Treating the Metaverse as the evolution of the WWW is not sufficient. The next iteration of the internet will change both the infrastructure, platform and the circulating content.

**The Internet's definition from Wikipedia:**

**"The Internet is the global system of interconnected computer networks that uses the Internet protocol suite (TCP/IP) to communicate between networks and devices.**

**It is a network of networks that consists of private, public, academic, business, and government networks of local to global scope, linked by a broad array of electronic, wireless, and optical networking technologies.**

**The World Wide Web definition from Wikipedia:**

**"The World Wide Web (WWW), commonly known as the Web, is an information system enabling documents and other web resources to be accessed over the Internet."**

In a word, the internet is the network of interconnected computers and servers that act as infrastructure for the WWW. The WWW is a collection of websites, pages, and other web resources to be accessed and operated upon.

The next generation of the internet will witness a change in both the internet and the WWW; and a change in the hardware infrastructure and the information system that forms the WWW. The Spatial Internet as used within this book, refers to the next generation of internet and WWW to be precise. It is a bidirectional evolution of simultaneous causal emergence. Current technologies enable the first steps of a new world wide web, which drives demand for better infrastructure and so on.

Probably the most trivial, high-speed internet connectivity is critical infrastructure for the Metaverse. It enables seamless and real-time communication, and faster data transfer of larger packets, leading to smooth interaction between users across different virtual spaces across the network.

The next hype is AR. It is the foundational step for massively adopted VR. The next generation of the internet is phygital. Augmented Reality (AR), Virtual Reality (VR), and Extended Reality (XR) technologies provide the infrastructure for immersive experiences, enabling users to interact with digital content in physical and virtual environments in a more natural and intuitive way.

While not foundational, **Artificial Intelligence (AI)** plays a central role in the Metaverse by enabling operations at various scales. Its role can be seen in and traced from intelligent virtual characters, and avatars, to virtual AI-powered co-pilots, language models, and creative production pipelines. AI-powered applications help generate and control virtual content, simulate realistic behaviors, and enable dynamic intelligent -augmented- interactions within the Metaverse.

the Metaverse a highly interactive environment. Collaborative, no-code, and generative are the adjectives of future 3d content creation.

**Spatial computing technologies** such as spatial mapping, tracking, and localization, have reached new heights within the development of the infrastructure, allowing for seamless integration of virtual content with the physical world. This perhaps makes it/them the most interesting and the most foundational to my vision of the Spatial Internet. A shift that enables users to interact with virtual objects and spaces in a spatially-aware manner, blurring the boundaries between the physical and virtual worlds.

Moreover, **cloud and edge computing technologies** are used as the computational infrastructure necessary to store, process,

# AI is a symptom of data abundance.

**Blockchain and Distributed Ledger Technology (DLT)** are foundational for decentralized and secure digital asset ownership, transactions, and governance within the Metaverse. Enabling digital property rights, tokenized economies, and decentralized governance models is essential for creating a decentralized and user-centric Metaverse.

Advanced, **democratized 3D modeling and design tools** are essential for creating virtual environments, objects, and characters within the Metaverse. The emergence of open-source, easy-to-access tools, whether online or offline, empowers a generation of creators and makes

and deliver enormous amounts of data and content within the new verse. Making scalability and performance required for a seamless and immersive user experience in the Metaverse a feasible objective.

Just like any technology, things start to be very technical and require highly skilled people to use them. The internet was the same, moving from an expert-only domain to a wider "average" user domain, becoming more interactive, user-friendly, and open with the introduction of complex UI/UX integrations.

# The volumetricization of the WWW

What I bet on next is the internet's evolution, moving from being 2-dimensional to 3-dimensional, transforming websites into web spaces. The volumetricization of the WWW is on its way, as new technologies augment the Internet itself.

The Metaverse represents the next stage in the evolution of the internet. Where once the internet was a purely 2-dimensional medium, the Metaverse offers the potential to transform websites into fully-realized web spaces that can be explored, inhabited, and shaped by users.

→ "Snow Crash" by Neal Stephenson
→ "The Metaverse Roadmap" by the Acceleration Studies Foundation
→ "Virtual Worlds: A First-Hand Account of Market and Society on the Cyberian Frontier" by Edward Castronova

The notion of Web 3.0 does not necessarily hinge upon the presence of 3D, real-time rendered, or synchronous experiences. While the Metaverse, as virtual worlds, may encompass such elements, Web 3.0 is a broader concept that encompasses decentralization, without being strictly tied to specific technological features. Similarly, the Metaverse does not inherently demand decentralization, distributed databases, blockchains, or a relative shift of online power or value from platforms to users.

While these elements may be relevant in certain Metaverse implementations, the essence of the Metaverse lies in real-time rendered virtual world space itself, rather than specific technological infrastructures. It is imperative to consider that Web 3.0 and the Metaverse can exist independently or in various combinations, and their true essence lies in their underlying principles and concepts, rather than specific technological requirements.

## CHARACTER TO WORLD

The shift in narrative building has been from character to world. Worlds have moved to a central position, where they became the essential component. Characters have been pivotal in cinema, theatre, and society probably, where the narrative revolves.

Character journeys are past, and world-building-based narration is present. This shift reflects a new market-responsive attitude towards a plural narrative rooted in a foundational element, and this narrative can be merchandised in a million ways.

**History of the WWW**

# THE OWNERSHIP INTERNET

## Ownership in the next internet is not just important, it is foundational.

Within the next phase of change, ownership, and property rights undergo significant transformations compared to traditional systems. Web 3.0 is the decentralized web or the blockchain-based web. It is characterized by its decentralized nature, cryptographic security, and smart contracts. These features bring about novel approaches to ownership and property rights, empowering individuals with greater control over their digital assets.

Digital Asset Ownership is key.

The new economy allows individuals the ability to own their digital assets, such as cryptocurrencies, non-fungible tokens (NFTs), digital collectibles, and most importantly, intellectual property. Through the use of blockchain technology, ownership is recorded on a public ledger that is transparent, immutable, and accessible to all participants. This empowers individuals with a greater sense of control and ownership over their digital possessions.

Within the Web 3.0 ecosystem, not only ownership is acknowledged, but also property rights. It enables self-custody, which allows individuals to have direct control over their digital assets without relying on intermediaries. Through the use of cryptographic keys, users can securely store and manage their assets in personal wallets or hardware devices. This gives them full ownership and the ability to transact directly, without the need for trusted third parties.

Smart contracts, which are self-executing agreements coded on the blockchain, play a crucial role in Web 3.0 ownership. The code does the work. These contracts automate and enforce contractual terms, removing the need for intermediaries. Smart contracts can also facilitate ownership transfers, establish conditions for property rights, and enable decentralized applications (dApps) to interact with digital assets securely and transparently.

Web 3.0's perhaps most vital aspect to grow is tokenization, which guarantees a network effect based on agency and education. Tokenization is essentially the shift towards stakeholder economics and tokenomics that involve all affected parties. It is a transformative upgrade to the financial landscape, one that adds layers of richness, transparency, and equity to the ecosystem. Tokenization can be applied to digital assets and physical assets, such as transforming real-world assets into digital representations on the blockchain. This allows for fractional ownership and increased liquidity, making it easier to transfer and trade ownership rights. Tokenization, thus, expands the accessibility and potential uses of assets while maintaining verifiable ownership records. Mass Tokenization enriches the financial plane.

Decentralized transactions are another key component of Web 3.0, enabling direct peer-to-peer transactions of digital assets and accelerating money. These marketplaces are often powered by blockchain technology, transparency, security, and verifiability of ownership.

Authorization and authentication are key.

Individuals can buy, sell, and trade assets directly with each other, eliminating the need for intermediaries and fostering a more inclusive and open ecosystem.

Governance and decentralized autonomous organizations (DAOs) are integral to Web 3.0 ownership. DAOs are entities governed by smart contracts and community participation. They enable collective decision-making regarding the management, use, and ownership of digital assets. Token holders often have voting rights and influence over the direction of the organization and its associated assets. It pushes the boundaries of ownership and grants token holders agency by playing an active role.

Lastly, the open Metaverse can only thrive if motivated by interoperability, allowing digital assets to be seamlessly transferred and utilized across different platforms and blockchains. This enhances the portability and transferability of ownership rights, enabling assets to be accessed and utilized in various decentralized applications and ecosystems.

## Ownership in the next internet is foundational, not only ownership but ownership rights as well.

Ownership drives engagement, attention, and agency. It drives involvement, which then drives knowledge, a secondary economy, and financial literacy through gamification globally.

Web 3.0 ownership is the single most important element in the Metaverse transformation, alongside the spatialization of the interface.

### History of Blockchain

# 5- CONTENT CREATION

The evolution of the internet can be simplistically divided into 3 epochs.

In the first 10 years, from 1990 until 2000, it was the time the internet was actually being built.
To understand the evolution of the internet, we can divide it into three distinct epochs. In the first decade, from 1990 to 2000, the internet was in its nascent stages - a time of building the foundational infrastructure that would enable the global network we know today. This was a period of experimentation and innovation as pioneers laid the groundwork for what would become a revolutionary technology.

The following 10 years, it was about building the platforms, Facebook, Twitter, etc.
The last 10 years, from 2010 until 2020, it was all about getting the Apps, maximizing outreach, and infiltrating everyday life.

The second decade, from 2000 to 2010, was characterized by the emergence of social media platforms like Facebook and Twitter. These platforms transformed the internet from a static, one-way communication medium to a dynamic, interactive space where people could connect, share, and collaborate in real-time.

In the third decade, from 2010 to 2020, the focus shifted to mobile devices and apps, as companies like Apple and Google revolutionized the way we interact with the internet on the go. The rise of smartphones and tablets made the internet more accessible and integrated into our daily lives than ever before.

In the next few years, as we pierce through the fourth decade within our timeframe, reaching 2030, I suspect is when content creation peaks. More so than where it is now. With a massively connected audience and easy-to-access creation tools, content creation is going to be a huge thing to look at.

Looking ahead to the next decade, roughly 2020 through 2030 onwards, we can expect to see a new wave of innovation centered around content creation. With a growing and increasingly connected global audience and an abundance of easy-to-use tools and platforms for content creation, we are likely to see a surge in creativity and innovation across a range of mediums, from video and photography to music and art.

The rise of the internet has brought about a fundamental shift in the way we consume and produce content. In the past, the line between content creators and consumers was clear-cut: there were those who made things and those who consumed them. However, with the advent of powerful content creation tools and the rise of social media platforms like Facebook, YouTube, and TikTok, this distinction has become increasingly blurry.

## Prosumer: a person who is "part of a new 'wikinomics' model where businesses put consumers to work"

(RITZER & JURGENSON, 2010, P.17).

Today, we are seeing the emergence of a new type of digital actor: the "prosumer". Prosumers are individuals who both consume and produce content, blurring the traditional line between these two roles. Users wear two hats. In addition to engaging with content, they are empowered by the accessibility and ease of use of modern content creation tools. These tools allow them to quickly and easily create and share their own content with a global audience.

The possibilities for creative expression are limitless-almost, and the barriers to entry are lower than ever before. As more and more people become content creators in their own right, the spatial internet epoch is to be a vibrant and diverse ecosystem of digital content emerging.

This new paradigm has far-reaching implications for the way we think about creativity, culture, and innovation. By breaking down the traditional barriers between content creators and consumers, prosumers democratize the creation and dissemination of new ideas and perspectives, leading to an ultra-dense flow of content.

The digital content prosumer phenomena will accelerate even further, as the boundary between the physical and digital worlds becomes increasingly porous. New forms of content creation and consumption emerge, and with that, they erase the once-clear boundaries between these two activities even further.

Production is no longer the exclusive province of a small elite of tech-savvy professional creators. It is now accessible to anyone with the know-how for making and sharing. Content creation happens with minimal requirements, and it is an adaptive learning experience that virtually everyone gets exposed to.

The content creation landscape is expanding on a daily basis, with a trend to create the best no-code online builder for users to create their own content, from worlds to any digital assets.

YouTube is the world's largest educational platform, and most community-backed content creators provide value, knowledge, entertainment, monetization, and know-how/that.

# THE CURRENT LANDSCAPE

A new creator's economy is taking shape, revolutionizing how individuals participate in digital ecosystems. Platforms like Meta, Epic Games, Unity Technologies, Decentraland, Roblox, and Fortnite, amongst a long list, are at the forefront of this transformation, offering tools and spaces for users to build, monetize, and share content and experiences.

This creator-centric paradigm allows for the democratization of content creation, enabling artists, developers, and entrepreneurs to thrive. Virtual worlds, decentralized applications, and blockchain technology are fostering innovative ways to create, trade, socialize, own digital assets, and monetize online presence.

Blockchain-based platforms like Decentraland and The Sandbox are empowering users to build, buy, and sell virtual assets within decentralized virtual spaces. Decentraland being amongst the oldest, demonstrates how token holders - MANA in this case - can be stakeholders. In-game economies are emerging rapidly, microeconomies within the larger economic landscape.

Tech giants such as Google, Microsoft, Tencent and Meta have also entered the Metaverse landscape. While the Metaverse hype might have been created by the campaign released by Meta and Marc Zuckerberg, Meta continues to be a major player, bringing forward Horizon Worlds, a Facebook linked Metaverse platform.

Platforms like Spatial.io and Mona offer users a space to host Unity-built experiences.

These platform, require creators to be minimally skilled in game design, and game-engine development.

The need for content, identity integrations, community building and on-chain monetization is driving a new generation of metaverse platforms, that are capable of leveraging both the spatial aspect, building on top of well established game engines, and simultaneously, embedding all the tokenization, identity, creation and ownership layers. The democratization of Metaverse-building.

Gamium, a project I have been part

### List of Metaverse Platforms

of brings together the above-mentioned aspects, celebrating DeSo (Decentralized Social) blockchain applications, and its MST ( Metaverse Social Token ) applicable in the 3d environments. While creators can use the online, browser-based, no-code toolkit to build their gamified worlds, the identity and ownership layer of the platform offers robust mechanics for communities and creators to earn simultaneously. With a Create-Socialize-Earn moto, Gamium aims at becoming the go-to platform of the next internet.

What Wordpress did to creating websites, is GMetri's mission to creating Metaverses. A lightwight, easy-to-use, utility-first, low-fi, device agnostic online platform for creating and gamifying virtual environments. A platform we've used extensively, as it offers out-of-the-box VR and AR solutions, and rapid way to deploy environments.

While I might be biased to the last two platforms mentioned, here is another platform that is the elephant in the room. Roblox, a platform that is gaining traction with peaks at over 40 million daily users. A low-fi metaverse platform that demonstrates the value of utility and community, where graphics are secondary. Roblox is where GenZ and GenAlpha hangout. It is the new public space.

The list is endless, with great projects, that vary on the main characteristics, from open to closed, hi-fi to low-fi, VR first, PC first, Mobile-first, or cross devices, and varying across the spectrum when it comes to ownership, monetization, ease of use, NFT integrations, marketplaces, identity, monetization and more. Mozilla Hubs, Sansar, Omniverse,

CryptoVoxel, Blocktopia, Polyland, etc. By the time you read this book, we might have an extra line-up of new platforms.

A platform that came in recently, Bezzle, rebranded to Bezi. While not a metaverse platform yet, it is one to look at, a collaborative 3d creation space, where realtime modeling and design can happen. With AR and ai-integrations the platform has some unlocked potential.

This is a quick walkthrough several of the major platforms. The current landscape is broad, not to mention the other layers, beyond platforms. Entities that offer the infrastructure, and other enabling technologies.

## Metaverse platforms

From sources across the web

 Decentraland ⌄

 Sandbox ⌄

 Roblox ⌄

 Upland ⌄

 Axie Infinity ⌄

Bloktopia ⌄

 Metahero ⌄

 Star Atlas ⌄

Fortnite ⌄

 Somnium Space ⌄

 Cryptovoxels ⌄

 Illuvium ⌄

 Spatial ⌄

 Horizon Worlds ⌄

 NVIDIA Omniverse ⌄

 Meta ⌄

 NeosVR ⌄

 Second Life ⌄

 Sorare ⌄

 Stageverse ⌄

 Microsoft ⌄

 Microsoft Mesh ⌄

 VIVERSE ⌄

 Voxels metaverse ⌄

Show less ⌃

Feedback

# 6- DIGITAL IDENTITY

Digital identity is a crucial component of the internet and will be more so as we approach the new era of digital presence and ownership. Digital presence is no longer limited to mere information. Packaged as a digital identity, digital presence in the Metaverse is one with digital embodiment. They are seamlessly integrated.

Digital identity is not restricted to humans but also encompasses entities such as organizations, devices, and bots. Being digital in nature, it can be used in the physical world for 'real' applications.

The internet, corporations, and the market are cross-border. Yet many identities are border-constraint.

**A Simple, basic, and brief timeline of Identity evolution:**

1. **Pre-digital Era (Analog Identity):** Identity was primarily physical, tied to tangible documents like passports and driver's licenses.

2. **Early Digital Identity (1990s):** Introduction of digital identities with email addresses and usernames for online services. Limited personal information is shared online.

3. **Social Media Era (2000s):** The proliferation of social media platforms led to the creation of online profiles and personas. Users shared personal information and interacted with a global audience.

4. **Mobile and App-Based Identity (the 2010s):** Integration of mobile devices and apps for identity verification and authentication. The emergence of biometric authentication methods like fingerprint and facial recognition.

5. **Blockchain and Self-sovereign Identity (2010s-2020s):** The development of blockchain technology offered secure and decentralized identity management. Self-sovereign identity models allow individuals to have greater control over their digital identity.

6. **Metaverse and Extended Reality Identity (2020s and Beyond):** Evolving identity concepts within the Metaverse, where avatars and virtual personas become significant. Identity is increasingly tied to digital interactions in immersive virtual environments. Advancements in artificial intelligence and biometrics continue to shape identity verification and security.

Enhanced personalization and security measures are integrated into digital identity solutions. Focus is growing on privacy and data protection in digital identity management.

Decentralized identity systems aim to give individuals more control and ownership over their data. Digital wallets and NFTs introduce new ways to represent and verify ownership of digital assets and identity.

Identity increasingly transcends borders and platforms, as digital identity systems become more interconnected and global. Globalization has consumed identity and flattened it at the local level. It will throw it back at the global level, with a new locality that belongs to new communities.

**Who needs an identity, a single proof of identity, controlled by a single authority?**

What is next will challenge traditional concepts of identity management. Where can centralized identity systems go?

2017 hosted the Equifax data breach jeopardizing the identities of millions. 2018 witnessed the Cambridge Analytica scandal poking centralized control of user data on social media platforms like Facebook.

# When evil is going on, how do identified victims escape?

Bot wallets dominate the web. There is only a digital identity for identities that exist in physical

While identity is not property in the traditional sense, there is a compelling connection between identity rights and property rights. Identity is a deeply personal and intangible aspect of an individual, encompassing their self-expression, culture, and beliefs.

In the next internet, a person's identity, especially in the form of personal data, is linked to property. Massive amounts of data are produced by users, and for organizations, this data is precious property. Therefore, property rights and the freedom to manage, safeguard, and own one's digital identity and data become entwined.

# Human rights are universal and indivisible, identities must also be as such.

When discussing digital identity, it is important to highlight the work of **Christopher Allen** on the topic and the scheme towards Self-Sovereign Identity.

PHASE ONE:
**Centralized Identity (administrative control by a single authority or hierarchy)**

In the early days of the Internet, centralized authorities controlled digital identity, like IANA and ICANN for IP addresses and domain names. Certificate authorities (CAs) emerged to verify online identities for commerce. Some of these authorities created hierarchies, but centralization caused issues, as users were locked into a single authority, leading to fragmented identities across different websites. Today, digital identities are still mostly centralized or hierarchical, owned by entities like CAs and domain registrars. However, there has been a growing movement to give users more control over their identities in the past two decades.

PHASE TWO:
**Federated Identity (administrative control by multiple, federated authorities)**

With the dawn of the new millennium, the landscape of digital identities witnessed a paradigm shift in the management of online identities and how they were freed from the bonds of balkanization. Microsoft's Passport program, which was revealed in 1999, was one of many that spearheaded this shift. It visualized a framework for federated identities, allowing individuals to utilize one identity on several websites. However, by placing Microsoft at the core of the federation, this innovative strategy covertly maintained a certain level of centralization, diminishing the potential benefits of decentralization.

The emergence of a federated identity undoubtedly minimized the impacts of balkanization by allowing users to move freely between different websites inside the system. However, it was unable to give up the authority vested in individual sites, maintaining their status as autonomous centers of power.

### PHASE THREE:
**User-Centric Identity (individual or administrative control across multiple authorities without requiring a federation)**

The Augmented Social Network proposed a new digital identity concept, emphasizing individual control in the early 2000s. The Identity Commons and the Internet Identity Workshop continued this work, introducing the idea of user-centric identity, aiming to empower users with control.

**The work of the IIW has supported many new methods for creating digital identity, including OpenID (2005), OpenID 2.0 (2006), OpenID Connect (2014), OAuth (2010), and FIDO (2013). As implemented, user-centric methodologies tend to focus on two elements: user consent and interoperability. By adopting them, a user can decide to share an identity from one service to another and thus de-balkanize his digital self.**

However, despite efforts like OpenID, powerful entities still largely control these identities.

Facebook Connect, while user-friendly, limits choice and control, and brings back Facebook as the central authority.

### PHASE FOUR:
**Self-Sovereign Identity (individual control across any number of authorities)**

# The time to move toward self-sovereign identity is now.

- Christopher Allen

Initially, designs aimed for user-centricity with centralized control but some user consent. Now, self-sovereign identity emphasizes user autonomy completely.

It heated up In 2012, with ideas such as Devon Loffretto's SSA and initiatives like Open Mustard Seed, focusing on giving users control over their digital identities. Various approaches have since been developed, including cryptographic methods and legal frameworks. This concept has also gained attention in international policy discussions, particularly in addressing issues like the refugee crisis and the rights of foreign workers.

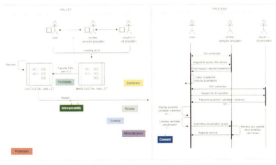

FIGURE 1. The general SSI process flow and connected properties proposed by Allen [4]

It is made by and between Individuals. Within any Society, Individuals have an established Right to an "identity", and to all of the benefits and responsibilities of some form of "Nationally Sovereign Structure" of governance and administration. Sovereign Source Authority (SSA) refers to the actual default design parameter of Human identity, prior to the "registration" process used to inaugurate participation in Society.

- Devon Loffreto

What happens once users gain full control over the sharing of their personal data away from systems of centralized identity?

# "Existence: Users must have an independent existence."

Here is a walk through the 10 initial principles drafted by Allen:

Self-sovereign identity is based on the core essence of the individual,- the "I," which cannot exist solely in digital form. It is the authentic self that is made public and accessible through limited aspects of the identity.

**"Control: Users must control their identities."**
Users must have authority over their identities, with secure algorithms ensuring their validity. They should have the ability to refer to, update, or conceal their identity as desired. While others can make claims about a user, these claims should not define the identity itself.

**"Access: Users must have access to their own data"**
Users should have easy access to their own data, retrieving all claims and related information within their identity. There should be no hidden data or gatekeepers. However, this doesn't grant them equal access to the data of others, only to one's own.

**"Transparency: Systems and algorithms must be transparent"**
The systems and algorithms governing identity networks must be transparent. They should be open, well-known, and independent of specific architectures, allowing anyone to examine their function and management.

**"Persistence: Identities must be long-lived."**
Identities should ideally last indefinitely or for as long as the user wishes. While private keys and data may need periodic updates, the identity itself remains. However, the right to be forgotten should be respected, allowing users to dispose of an identity if and when desired.

**"Portability: Information and services about identity must be transportable."**
Identity information and services should be transportable and not dependent on a single third-party entity. This ensures user control, even if entities disappear or circumstances change, enhancing identity's persistence.

**"Interoperability: Identities should be as widely usable as possible."**
Identities should be widely usable across various contexts, transcending borders and facilitating global identities without compromising user control. Persistence and autonomy contribute to their continuous availability.

**"Consent: Users must agree to the use of their identity."**
Users must provide consent for the use of their identity. While interoperability increases data sharing, it should only occur with the user's consent, even if others present claims on their behalf. Consent may not always be interactive but must be deliberate and well-understood. Informed consent is key.

**"Minimalization: Disclosure of claims must be minimized."**
Disclosure of claims should be minimized, sharing only the necessary data for specific purposes. For privacy protection, selective disclosure, range proofs, and other techniques can be employed. Yet, achieving non-correlatability remains challenging.

**"Protection: The rights of users must be protected."**
User rights must be safeguarded, prioritizing individual freedoms over the network's requirements. To ensure decentralization, Identity authentication should be conducted through independent algorithms that are resistant to censorship and coercion.

The internet has arguably changed everything, almost.

The next move will continue to do so as well.

Potentially, no facet of our lives will be left untouched or unaltered.

How identity can be affected by the metaverse is one of the areas worth dedicating a full chapter to in this opening segment.

The internet has revolutionized the way we live, work, and communicate, connecting us to a vast and constantly expanding digital universe of information, resources, and experiences. But the internet is far from static. And as technology continues to advance, we can expect to see even more dramatic changes that could transform our daily lives in ways we can hardly imagine.

What is the potential impact of the Metaverse on our sense of identity? The Metaverse promises to be a fully realized and immersive digital world. One where we can explore and interact with vast and intricate virtual environments that rival the complexity and richness of the physical world. As we live through this, we are likely to see new forms of social, cultural, and economic dynamics emerge, reshaping the way we perceive ourselves and our place in the world.

Here, as we navigate a complex and constantly evolving digital landscape, questions about identity and self-expression will take on a whole new dimension. How will our digital personas intersect with our physical identities? What new forms of community and belonging will emerge in this new space? And how will we reconcile the freedom and fluidity of the Metaverse with the constraints and responsibilities of the physical world?

# KEY ASPECTS OF SELF-SOVEREIGN IDENTITY IN THE METAVERSE:

**User Ownership and Control:** With SSI, users have ownership and control over their digital identities and personal data. They can create, manage, and use their digital identities across different virtual worlds and platforms. they have the ability to control what information is shared, with whom, and for what purpose.

**Privacy and Security:** SSI emphasizes privacy and security, allowing users to share their personal information only when necessary and with explicit consent. SSI uses cryptographic techniques to ensure that the information is securely stored and shared and that it can be verified without revealing unnecessary details.

**Trust and Verifiability:** SSI provides a framework for establishing trust and verifiability in the digital world. Through the use of decentralized and distributed technologies, SSI allows users to verify the authenticity of their digital identities and the information they share, without relying on centralized authorities.

**User Empowerment:** SSI empowers users by giving them more control and autonomy over their digital identities, allowing them to manage their online presence and interactions in a self-determined manner.

**"The Path to Self-Sovereign Identity" by Christopher Allen and Shannon Appelcline, 2016**
This paper, published in 2016, is often regarded as one of the foundational works on SSI. It outlines the principles, concepts, and technical components of SSI, providing a comprehensive overview of the topic. http://www.lifewithalacrity.com/2016/04/the-path-to-self-soverereign-identity.html

**"W3C Verifiable Credentials Data Model 1.0" by the World Wide Web Consortium (W3C)**
This specification provides a technical standard for representing verifiable credentials, which are a key component of SSI. It defines a data model and a set of JSON-LD-based formats for expressing verifiable credentials. Both can be used to create and exchange verifiable information in a decentralized and privacy-preserving manner.

Decentralized Identifiers (DIDs) https://www.w3.org/TR/did-core/

# "A Comprehensive Guide to Self-Sovereign Identity" by Drummond Reed, Heather Vescent, and Kaliya Young

This book provides a comprehensive overview of SSI, covering its historical background, principles, technical components, use cases, and potential impact. It also delves into related topics such as decentralized identifiers, verifiable credentials, and consent management.
https://www.amazon.com/Comprehensive-Guide-Self-Sovereign-Identity-ebook/dp/B07Q3TXLDP/
https://lists.w3.org/Archives/Public/public-credentials/2021Mar/0147.html

The new type of identifier, Decentralized identification - AKA DIDs, enables a verifiable decentralized digital identity. A DID can be any person, organization, data model, entity, or subject based on how it is assigned by the DID controller. Unlike classic federated identifiers, DIDs are made to be independent of centralized registries, identity providers, and certificate authorities. The design of the DID serves a particular purpose; other parties may assist in finding data on DIDs, but its controller does not need third-party authorization to show control over it. Reliable interactions with this subject are allowed with DIDs being URLs that link the DID subject with a DID document. Every DID document can provide cryptographic material, verification methods, or services that offer a set of mechanisms that allow the controller to prove DID control.
https://www.w3.org/TR/did-core/

Self-Sovereign Identity: Decentralized Digital Identity and Verifiable Credentials - Book by Alex Preukschat and Drummond Reed
https://www.amazon.es/Self-Sovereign-Identity-Decentralized-verifiable-credentials/dp/1617296597

"The Sovrin Foundation: Sovrin Protocol and Token" by the Sovrin Foundation
This whitepaper provides an overview of the Sovrin protocol, which is a decentralized identity platform that aims to enable SSI. It outlines the technical architecture, principles, and features of the Sovrin protocol, which is designed to provide a decentralized and interoperable infrastructure for self-sovereign digital identities.
https://sovrin.org/wp-content/uploads/Sovrin-Protocol-and-Token-White-Paper.pdf

# 7-
# CYBERSPACE

"Even A Brick Wants
To Be Something"

- LOUIS KAHN

# How about bits,
# what does a bit want to be?

Within discourse, Norbert Wiener coined "Cybernetics" in 1948, a new theory that shaped things from warfare to everyday technologies. Most importantly, it was a new notion within architecture and marked the emergence of cyberspace.

Arising in the post-WWII era, cybernetics was initially employed by scientists, engineers, and the Air Force. It embodies the study of feedback, communication, and control within living beings and machines. Thus, it serves as the foundational underpinning through which we seek to comprehend the intricacies of cyberspace.

While Cybernetics is the study of communication and control in systems, Cyberspace is the virtual - now mixed - environment where digital communication occurs. The relationship between the two lies in applying cybernetic principles to analyze and enhance the systems within the digital sphere. Cybernetics enable Cyberspace.

Cyberspace emerged as a concept in the late 20th century as computers and communication technologies advanced. The concept gained prominence with the publication of William Gibson's science fiction novel "Neuromancer" in 1984. Gibson used the term "cyberspace" to describe a virtual realm accessed through computer networks.

Drawing upon the ideas of cybernetics, cyberspace became a manifestation of the interconnectedness of computers, communication channels, and human-machine interactions. It represented a conceptual extension of cybernetics' focus on control, communication, and information processing systems to experience and interactions.

As the internet expands and technology advances, the concept of cyberspace gains practical relevance. It encompasses the interconnected global network of computers, data, and digital interactions that constitute the emerging digital landscape. Cyberspace became a space where individuals could communicate, exchange information, and engage in virtual experiences.

Cyberspace, thus, reflects the application of cybernetic principles to the digital domain. It explores the dynamic interplay between information, control systems, human-computer interfaces, and the networked nature of digital communication. It examines the flow of information, feedback loops, and the complex interactions between humans and machines within the virtual realm. With that, it became fundamentally a space where all of that happens.

Cyberspace is the spatial and conceptual extension of cybernetics, reflecting the interconnectedness of computers and communication systems. It became a virtual realm where individuals could engage in digital interactions and navigate through virtual environments, fueled by advances in technology and visionary thinking.

Numerously defined and explored by leading minds within the space of architecture, the term is indeed fluid., in its connotations, nevertheless, there is a clear longing for an architecture beyond architecture. Cyberspace is an attempt to overthrow the drawing, an implosion of dimensions that renders classical architectural media obsolete, from buildings to books.

**Burning Chrome:** https://archive.org/details/burningchrome0000gibs/page/n7/mode/2up

The term first appeared in the 1960s as the name of an atelier. But it wasn't until the 1980s that William Gibson popularized the term with his description of it as "a consensual hallucination experienced daily by billions of legitimate operators, in every nation, by children being taught mathematical concepts."

While Gibson's definition resonates more closely with our current understanding of cyberspace, he himself admitted that he coined the term simply because it was an "effective buzzword" and "essentially meaningless".

Fast Forwarding to a more relevant definition and usage of the term, the widely understood connotation is the place where things like video calls, websites, online transactions, etc. happen. Put more precisely, "the internet is considered as an imaginary space without a physical location in which communication over computer networks takes place." Cyberspace is exactly that "imaginary" space.

There have been a number of works that highlight the term. To list a few, "Neuromancer" by William Gibson (1984), "Snow Crash" by Neal Stephenson (1992), Virtual Reality: The Revolutionary Technology of Computer-Generated Artificial Worlds - and How It Promises to Transform Society by Howard Rheingold (1991), " Cyberspace: First Steps" (1991), "The Hacker Crackdown" by Bruce Sterling (1992), "Being Digital" by Nicholas Negroponte (1995), and eventually, AD - Architects in Cyberspace.

Our intuitive longing for a spatial image of the internet is intriguing. Equally as compelling, and even more importantly, is the conceptual need for a space to host social interaction through an online network.

Despite its lack of physicality, there is a persistent desire for a spatial conception of the Internet. It heightens as social interactions occur through online networks.

# The internet is not just a tool for communication, but a new type of space that is fundamentally changing the way we live the world around us.

**Cyberspace is a fully visualized spatialization of all information within global information processing systems. It operates through pathways established by current and future communication networks, facilitating the simultaneous presence and interaction of multiple users. It allows input and output from and to "the human sensorium" as a whole. Cyberspace, thus, enables simulations of both real and virtual realities. It also goes a step further and enables remote data collection and control through telepresence, and promotes total integration and communication with a total and diverse range of intelligent products and environments in real space.**

## MARKOS NOVAK - 1991 - "CYBERSPACE: FIRST STEPS":

Cyberspace is a new domain that exists as a result of the convergence of information technology and telecommunications. It has the potential to transform the way we communicate, work, travel, shop, and pray. Cyberspace has transformative power in the way we live.

The design of cyberspace, like that of physical spaces, has a profound impact on how we interact with it. Cyberspace yields new social interaction; translating to new societies.

The lack of physical constraints in cyberspace means that it is an open, flexible, and dynamic environment. The emergence of cyberspace requires us to rethink traditional concepts of property, identity, and authority. The boundary between physical and virtual spaces is becoming increasingly blurred, and new hybrid spaces are emerging.

Cyberspace is a new opportunity for creative expression and experimentation. It is a political space with values, biases, and interests of its designers and users. Having said that, the future of cyberspace is uncertain and will depend on how we choose to design and use it.

### The Spatial internet is a new and hybrid space
The wired world is a new environment for humanity to move in, a new geography that will require new concepts and ideas to become fully understood.

### Cyberspace is a social and cultural phenomenon
Cultural expression and social interactions are the core of cyberspace. It is a deeply social and cultural phenomenon, like language itself. Cyberspace serves as a medium for expression, sharing, connection, and production. In its own light, it is a means of "saying, being, and doing.

### Architecture and urbanism will adapt to cyberspace
There is no runway from the new 'contamination' as it has already leaked to every part of our economy. Cyberspace is a reality. Urbanism has become phygital already, and architecture too.

### The design of cyberspace is important
Experience is the ultimate goal. As social life expands to the virtual, electronic environments become the new way we frame such ecosystems. Designing environments in the metaverse will be as important as designing environments in the 'real world'.

### The Metaverse is a continuation of cyberspace
It is the end goal, as it goes beyond the web and into more sensorial experiences. The metaverse is cyberspace's path to realization.

"We are transitioning from a world of atoms to a world of bits...this transition, while gradual, is profound--and not optional."

"What is different about being digital, compared with being analog? Simply this: Whereas an analog signal is continuous, a digital signal is discrete.

"The digital age...is all about liberation, about cutting loose from those dark satanic mills we call offices and going back to the land, the land of the mind, the land of cyberspace."

"Cyberspace is a metaphor that allows us to grasp this place where since about the time of the second world war we've increasingly done so many of the things that we think of as civilization."

"In cyberspace, physical distance becomes irrelevant. A person in Japan can read a newspaper from New York as easily as someone in Manhattan. Indeed, the newspaper can be published in Japan, typeset in Hong Kong, and sent electronically to New York for printing."

"Cyberspace offers the opportunity to bring us together without bringing us together. It offers us a community without geography."

The 90s offered a new zeitgeist, where an overlapping of evolving curves of computers, the internet, interfaces, and new questions in architecture occurred.

**Size matters.** Computers slimmed down from 30 tons in the late 1940s - ENIAC- to 3 kg in the late 1980s. The shrink represents the transformation from the first computer as we know it, to the last computer as we use it. New technologies are often dressed with a promise, technology becomes an exploration medium to find answers and to formalize new questions.

In this digital arena, architects navigate virtual spaces, manipulating elements with the precision of code. Architecture that is made on a computer and always accessible from it is a hands-off practice. A new causal structure is illusionary to the hands-on believers.

Within cyberspace, variables make architecture infinite. It is no longer confined to fixed numbers, but to placeholder variables that, when altered, produce new outcomes. Architecture becomes reconfigurable, abundant, and agile.

Cyberspace is the answer to the gap between what architecture can do at a moment in time, and what architecture was intended to do at that moment. It offered an open world of potential and new possible dimensions. Essentially, it expands on what architecture can do.

Cyberspace is the portal to the body-avatar-cyborg continuum, a realm of interconnectedness and expansion. It is a new conception of cyber-reality and fiction. The movement is a new grassroots technoculture that adopts an ontology open attitude to perception and the world, and essentially, the real.

The 90s witnessed a new file format, the VRML - Virtual Reality Markup Language- as a shift from HTML - to HyperText Markup Language. The spatial overthrows the graphic, after the graphic overthrew the text-based. A new paradigm of interfacing.

### HSML -Hyper Space Modeling Language *( Verses )*

Powered by the latest technologies, communications, and futurist thinking, space is, therefore, the machine, and not "the house". Space is the machine, and it can be intelligent. Architecture is the craft of creating spatial intelligence. Just like all intelligent formations, architecture too is a material assemblage, with material and nonmaterial effects. Now with a virtual dimension, architecture lives within computers and is only accessible through the machine. Architecture is computed, transmitted, rendered, and reprogrammed.

The new paradigm is hands-off. Space is modifiable as such. All is algorithm, and algorithms must be reconfigured. Technology is the interface between the architecture and its effect. Architecture is text again, experienced through digital interfaces.

Spatial intelligence within this context is a capacity of space, an emergent property of environments, physical, virtual, or phygital. With infinite theories, responsiveness, and autonomy, kinetic theories of architecture seem to scratch the right surface. They touch on sensing, perception, and action, on embedded systems and machine intelligence, and most importantly, on environmental interactions. Space becomes the medium.

Howard Gardner characterizes intelligent environments through seven major possibilities: Visual Verbal, Kinesthetic, Musical, Mathematic, Personal, and intrapersonal. Today the list expands to potentially neverending areas of intelligence. The spatial internet is a new digital frontier through which we are redefining spatial narratives.

The Spatial Internet is essentially a convergence of realms.

The next decade of cyberspace is the age of architectural digital phenomenology. Interactive interfaces, gestural interactions, and sensory stimuli converge to engender multisensory environments that elicit profound emotional and cognitive responses.

# The spatial internet is cyberspace's highest aspiration.

# 8- MINERAL INTELLIGENCE, ELECTRICAL ECOLOGIES, AND THE METAVERSE

The chronology of our comprehension of the emergence of all things can be summarized as geology first, then biology, and technology. Biology owes its genesis to geology, which is attributable to contextual variances and friction.

Geology is a precondition for Biology

The most important factor in this process is the transformation in the intrinsic arrangement of material assemblages and their internal landscapes.

While the geology to biology is a linear process, what comes next is not.

As biology emerges, it creates technology whereafter the sequence becomes nonlinear, it consumes all the above generating new geologies, biologies, and intelligences simultaneously.

# Intelligence is an emergent property of material assemblages

Intelligence is an emergent property of material assemblages, as a property that arises from the ecological interactions within material configurations, and might have arisen initially from biological circuitry.

We have not always been the only human species, nor has our intelligence. Human intelligence is a phase in the evolution of intelligence at large. Intelligence, by definition, predates humans and shall outlive them.

The current technosphere demands a shift in design theory comprehension, and consequently, in the action moving forward across the design discourse from the atom to the territory. More specifically, advancements in neurotechnology, planetary-scale sensing, big data, territorial surveillance, and artificial intelligence can be drivers to a new design discourse amidst ecological challenges currently at play.

Mineral Intelligence is a comprehensive term for AI. Synthetic intelligence manifests in various forms through synthesis. The term artificial is obsolete. All is natural, and all is real.

Processes of emergent properties based on holes that come together as an assemblage of parts.

From the very first machines created until today, breakthroughs in AI come to accelerate the pace of things. Amidst the AI revolution, a tremendous disruption in several fields is about to occur. But unlike most other AI models, the current models have finally gained access to human language.

Since I learned about code and programming, I've always had a deep curiosity, are we going to learn how to code before computers learn how to speak English?

AI today is at a decisive moment. It has rapidly become impossible to think about the digital world without AI, considering the number of creation models built on AI, and the number of services and companies built on top of AI models.

As Harari points out, the difference between nukes and AI is that nukes cannot make better nukes, but AI can make better AI.

Intelligence encompasses a broad range, bound by the electrical and the neural. This understanding is the foundation of my notion of "Electrical Ecologies." This entails the process of streamlining operational mechanisms to facilitate comprehension and manipulation at the electrical level, with the ultimate aim of converting electrical objects into neural ones, from the cerebral to the planetary.

The electrical is conceived as an advanced state of the charged, and the neural as an advanced state of the electrical. Hence recognizing that all neural ecologies are electrical ecologies, while not all electrical ecologies are neural ecologies, yet.

# All neural ecologies are electrical ecologies, but not all electrical ecologies are neural ecologies, yet.

### What is "Electrical Ecologies"?

It is a method to both comprehend ecosystems by ontologically flattening them to their "electrical layer", and operate at that layer due to its quantitative and workable nature. Given the planet's sensing and processing capabilities, Electrical Ecologies aims at conceptualizing a framework for closing the loop: sensing, processing, and automated action, at the scale of the planet. Hence it is a planetary-scale nervous system.

"Electrical Ecologies" is an ecological concept that examines the world through its electrical layer - infrastructure, from charged matter to the intricacies of cortices - neural objects. Its pluralistic outlook acknowledges the existence of sub-ecologies, nested within each other, within a complex, multi-layered system of electrical domains.

Complementary to "Dark Ecology", which proposes a comprehensive model, "Electrical Ecologies" adopts a pragmatic lens with an operational attitude, emphasizing the possibility of action at the electrical layer and the formation of emergent networks of intelligence. On the macro, it provides insight into the emergence of planetary-scale computation as a phenomenon that lives upon "Electrical Ecologies."

Electrical Ecologies is Dark Ecology comprehended as to where sub-ecologies fall on the charged-to-neural spectrum being functionally hackable through manipulating the electrical layer. It is a form of putting Dark Ecologies into action.

### Electrical Ecologies is Dark Ecology in action.

The second Copernican turn has not sufficiently changed the design discourse yet. Thus there is a new raison d'être to be operated upon, a pressing need for a design agenda grounded in a projective entanglement with the present elephants-in-the-room- bio-computation, artificial [designable] intelligence, data at scale, and eventually IoN.

We stand upon unprecedented access to designing the neural [both mineral and biological]. Complementary to the material component -and operating at the electrical layer- interactions with neural ecologies, or other sub-ecologies, are rather read-write mechanisms. Not only do they allow data mining from electrically active neural environments but also writing back, by changing physical features such as the spatial layout, or wiring. Hence an approach that performs on the spatial distributions of material assemblages to construct intelligence.

As neurotechnology continues to evolve, the human brain itself is gradually being transformed into a workable medium. IoT becomes IoN.

## IoT becomes IoN.

Brain-computer interfaces enable a new agency for brains, as they enable a direct link between our nervous system and the Internet of Things. The upshot is a revolutionary shift towards an Internet of Neurons, or IoN, a medium in which the biological nervous systems are on-grid.

Neurons, biological or synthetic, are interconnected using advanced iterations of technologies such as brain-computer interfaces (BCIs), neuroprosthetics, or neural implants. These interconnected neurons exchange information, process data, and collaborate to perform complex tasks or solve problems collectively.

At their core, both Electrical Ecologies and the Internet of Neurons are concerned with understanding the world through its electrical layer. The emergence of the IoN creates a new kind of networked ecosystem that synergizes both synthetic and biological systems, creating a space in which electronic devices interact directly with the human nervous system.

Electrical Ecologies, the Internet of Neurons, and the Metaverse converging represent a new paradigm in which the boundaries between the physical and digital, synthetic and biological, are put to coexistence. This highlights the material foundations of both intelligence and the virtual and provides a framework for an

ecology that can house both in a single system.

The internet of neurons is the spatial internet's paradigmatic shift, where users and the internet are connected bidirectionally. IoN is a feasible application within the Internet's next milestones, allowing simultaneous bidirectional communication between brains and the web.

Due to the potentiality the current landscape holds, the projection is towards a framework for augmenting the sensing -and processing- layer with an automation layer; similarly at the scale of the planet, and therefore the argument calls for a planetary scale nervous system. A system at that scale does not imply a center, but rather a coexistence of multiple centralities that co-occur and change constantly at all scales.

# GETTING YOU ALL CAUGHT UP

...celerates digital transformation through immersive en...

Subscribe

...have partnered to create technology designed to combine the real and digital worlds to acce...
...ngineering goes beyond traditional 2D practices by creating a fully integrated, user cent...

...averse identity?

PORSCHE

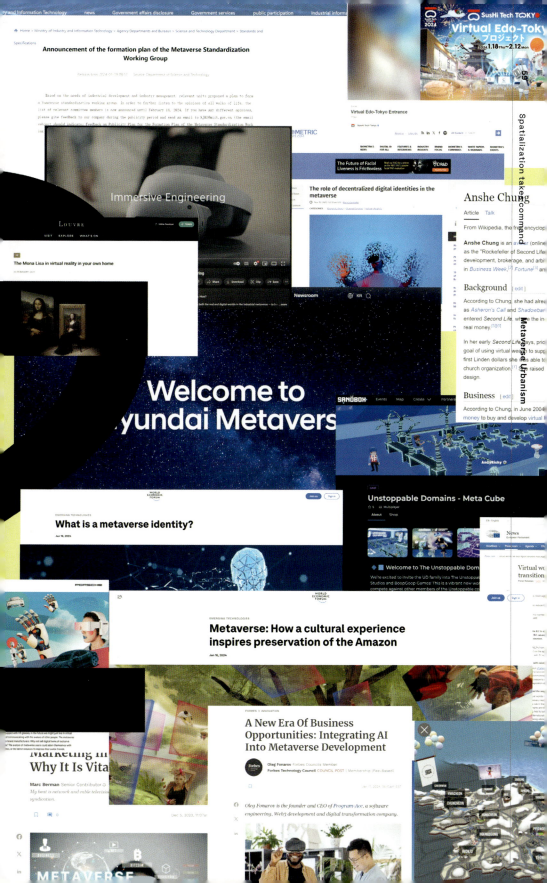

City-world, I thought it was a unic... ...diated through our senses...

*Correct your spelling*

**city world**

🗑 Dismiss

...ce, it is now possible to revisuali...

*Verb problem*

**revisit**

🗑 Dismiss

ⓖ See more

A decentralized economy in the metaverse utilizing blockch... ...ntent will be ai-genera... ...d in a passive manner, to create a peer-to-peer economic system where users have... control over their digital assets, transactions, and interactio...

The coexistence of cloudalists and a decentralized econom... reality that is opt... ...atures of...

*Correct your spelling*

Interoperability w... **cloudless** virtual wo...
allowing users to... ...tities acro...

⌷ Add to dictionary

User empowerme... ...l over their
transactions. An i... 🗑 Dismiss ...n the meta...

Collaborative spaces. **The *volumetricization* of the WWW** is on

...oving from being 2-dimensional to

...net itself.

*Unknown word:* **volumetricization**

...e evolution

...e Metaver... ⌷ Add to dictionary m

...n be explo... ...rs.

🗑 Dismiss

ⓖ See more in Grammarly

...eration Studies Foundation

...standing digital embodiment within this...

The new
Real-tim...
and the...
techno...
subject...

...e same frame, cyberception - Ray Ascot...

...tting Architec... ...vak's...

*Correct your spelling*

**perception**

⌷ Add to dictionary ...was...

🗑 Dismiss

ⓖ See more in Grammarly

...e after Being...

...future-manuf... ...nform...
...regarded as material instar... From p...
electro...

The real-time revolution transforms physical space into tempo...
teletopia, atopia, and utopia. Telepresence and optoelectroni...
while urb... ...moves activities to interfaces.

*Correct your spelling*

**utopia**

Paradoxe... ...ance us from the immediate, an...
augment... ⌷ Add to dictionary ...n to reduce our notions of reali...
presence... 🗑 Dismiss

ⓖ See more in Grammarly

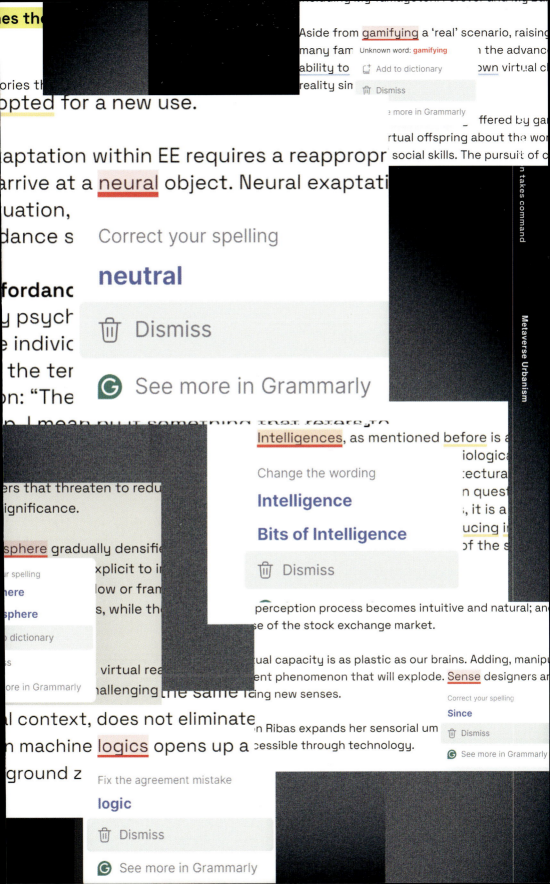

Here is a short list of Metaverse jargon that you might want to Google. While some of them might sound general, they have different connotations within the context of the metaverse.

| | | |
|---|---|---|
| Altcoin | DAS | Anon |
| MILEs | DApp | ANCAP |
| Minting | ERC | API |
| PFP | EVM | ATL |
| Ledger | FOMO | Bridge |
| Play2Earn Models | FUD | BTD |
| Rug pull | Gas | Bull |
| Pump and Dump | Interoperability | Bear |
| Scarcity | IPFS | Bitcoin |
| Seed phrase | IRL | Satoshi |
| Tokens | Land | Creator Economy |
| Token-gated | MaaS | DD - Due Diligence |
| Tokenomics | Metazens | Collateral |
| Defi | NFT | Winter |
| Crypto | Spatial Audio | DEX |
| Crypto Currency | Spatial Computing | CEX |
| Crypto Evangelist | Smart Contract | ETH |
| Decentralization | AGI | Ethereum 2.0 |

| GPT | Shitcoin |
| Haptic Suit | Singularity |
| HBA - Human Biometric | Stablecoin |
| Avatar | VRO - Virtual Room Object |
| Genesis block | TXN Hash |
| HFSP | Utility Token |
| ICO - Initial Coin Offering | Wallet Address |
| Cap | BCI |
| Metamask | HMI |
| Moon | AI |
| Node | Digital Assets |
| On/Off-Chain | Holder |
| PFP | Web3 |
| Post-scarcity Economy | DAO |
| Private key | Airdrop |
| Public Key | Floor |
| Authentication | SSI |
| Authorization | IoT |

# LETTERS

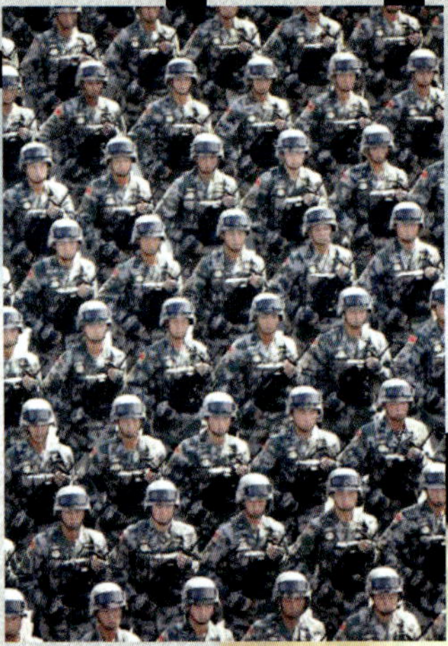

# FR

# TOMOR

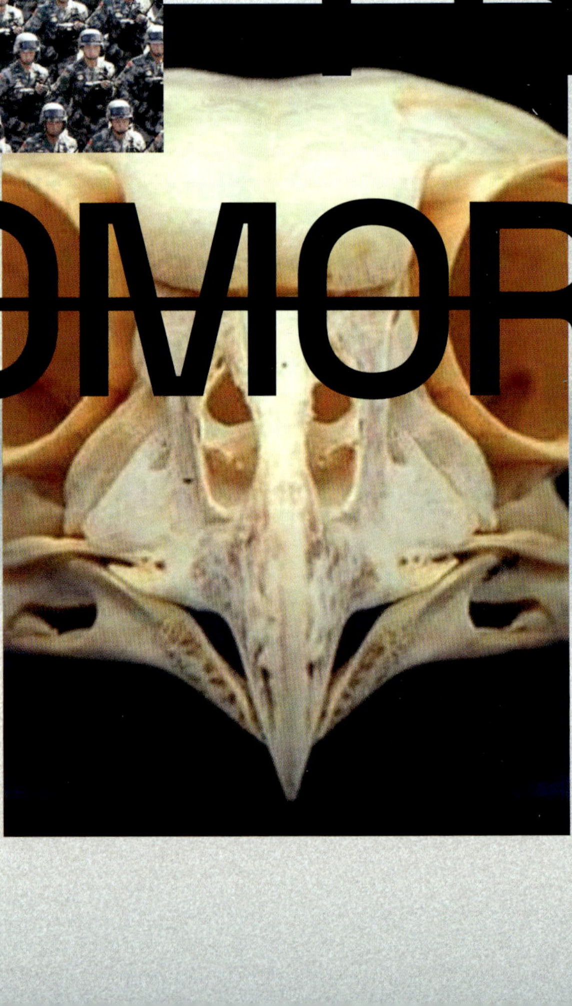

OM
ROW
TODAY

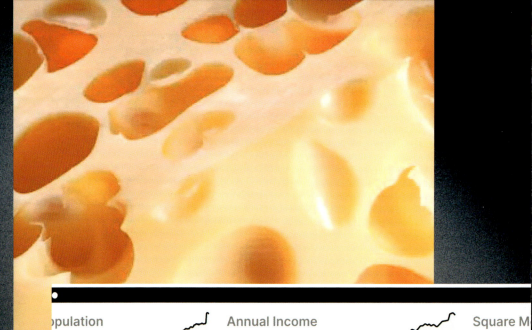

| | | |
|---|---|---|
| opulation | Annual Income | Square M |
| **729,314** | **$157,651,814,346** | **136,794,** |

 Tokyo     🧑 166,842

 Mumbai     🧑 127,415

Delhi     🧑 109,777

 São Paulo     🧑 100,105

New York     🧑 86,002

 Lima     🧑 85,227

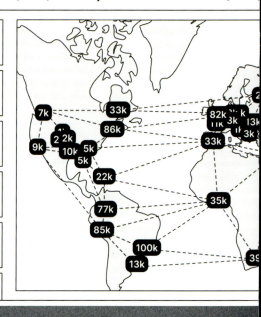

# THE NETWORK STATE

995 BEING DIGITAL - NICOLAS NEGROPONTE

"Cyberspace offers the opportunity to bring us together without bringing us together. It offers us a community without geography."

The shifting tides of history have witnessed the demise of empires, giving way to the rise of sovereign states or nations. Yet, the landscape of nations has undergone a profound transformation in the past century, with the number of nations multiplying from a humble 70 to a staggering 195 today, averaging more than one new country per year. As nations continue to splinter into smaller entities, borders that were once considered immutable, have become volatile. Identity and culture are no longer bound by geography, and the traditional model of governance is being challenged.

Todays's borders are surreal.
Today's nation-states will become obsolete.
What is a nation-state anyway?
At the center of it, it is a common culture, language, and history.

The basis for forming distinct social, cultural, and political communities.

The concept of nations with fixed borders has been repeatedly violated as the pursuit of resources and surplus reshaped the geopolitical landscape.

**Geography was always on the side of power.**

HTTPS://WWW.NEWSINLEVELS.COM/
WP-CONTENT/UPLOADS/2020/06/DE-
POSITPHOTOS_4059533_S.JPG

The rise of nationalism and calls for independence from both left and right blocks across the political spectrums further signify a growing trend toward an increasing number of nations. There is a shift in perspective to reject geography-based clustering, an attempt to design a new system of nations, based on a common drive, albeit still within the confines of physical land.

HTTPS://WWW.RESEARCHGATE.
NET/PUBLICATION/291166291_THE_
FOLLOWING_GAME_-_GAME_THEORY_
AND_RATIONALITY/FIGURES

**There will soon be a million reasons to create a state.**

The post-Cold War era, coupled with the proliferation of the internet and widespread telecommunications, has given rise to a new social possibility, the network society, as coined by Manuel Castells. The network society is a direct implication of information technologies and communication networks, heralding the advent of the "internet of people" in the second decade of the internet, as described in Castells' seminal book "The Rise of the Network Society" published in 1996. This transition in communication and networking technologies inevitably leads to a shift in governance, organization, and hierarchies.

The rise of the network society foreshadows the emergence of a new type of state, the network state. It represents a dissolution of the modern state under the influence of global networks of communication and information, replacing hierarchical and

Balaji Srinivasan revitalized the concept of the network state, presenting a manifesto and a framework for a new archetype of state. It is one based on a "book", a constitution, and physical land acquisition in tandem with a clear governance system, and online community infrastructure. Citizenship will be redefined in terms of voluntary affiliation with a particular network rather than a particular nation-state. Borders are no longer intact. States are composed of lands across the planet in a distributed layout manner.

If there is any socio-political form regarding the evolution of states that the metaverse can accelerate, it is the network state as it is built on the notion of community, and runs through protocols at the core and foundation of what makes the metaverse.

Geography >> Community
Community >> Geography

"We are moving from the industrial era, built around the manufacturing of goods, to a new era in which knowledge and information are the primary sources of value creation. This new society is built around the networks that connect us, and these networks are changing the way we live, work, and relate to one another. The network society is emerging as the dominant form of social organization in the 21st century."

"THE RISE OF THE NETWORK SOCIETY, 1996

bureaucratic structures with decentralized, networked forms of organization. The inevitable implication of information and communication technologies enables new forms of coordination and control that are less reliant on traditional bureaucratic structures.

Online hyperconnectivity, blockchain, new community-building platforms, cryptocurrencies, and the diminishing relevance of geographical physical borders, have provided the groundwork for the network state as a new form of political organization. A new form of state that is a decentralized opt-in political entity that would provide a range of services to its members such as dispute resolution, security, and identity verification. The network state operates on a global scale, with members joining and leaving as they see fit, and would be resistant to the capture or co-option by any particular interest group.

Network states are states of the spatial age of the internet. While becoming the internet of places and ownership, the spatial internet comes along as an enabler.

**Network states are startup nations.**

The network state embodies state-building in the spatial age of the internet. Startup nations, DAO Nations etc., names will vary, but the phenomena is slowly crawling in.

The fourth decade of the internet has witnessed social innovation, redefining othering and community, identity and embodiment, financial and economic activity, and most definitely a readiness for a new order that will change the map.

"The network state is the next stage in the evolution of human society. As cryptocurrencies, smart contracts, and other blockchain technologies come to maturity, they will enable the creation of a new kind of state—one that is more decentralized, more autonomous, and more secure than any that has existed before." "The network state is the next stage in the evolution of human society. As cryptocurrencies, smart contracts, and other blockchain technologies come to maturity, they will enable the creation of a new kind of state—one that is more decentralized, more autonomous, and more secure than any that has existed before."

Nintendogs
Video game

Overview | Gameplay | Guides | Characters | Rules | Unlockables | Tips and tricks | Reviews

Includes:
Miniature Dachshund
Golden Retriever
Beagle
Pug
Siberian Husky
Shih Tzu

nintendögs

YouTube • Japancommercials4U2
Gameplay • 32:02

NINTENDODS.
nintendögs

YouTube • RTGame
I Haven't Checked My Nintendogs in 14 Years
Sorry i was gone so long, I had to get some milk Watch more videos like this: ...
1 Jun 2019
10:40

| Platform | Initial release date |
|---|---|
| Nintendo DS | April 21, 2005 |

Nintendo
Warum erscheinen bei meinem "Nintendogs"-Spiel nicht alle ...

| | New York | 86,002 |
|---|---|---|
| | Lima | 85,227 |

85k
100k
13k

# GAMIFIED PARENTHOOD

In the evolving landscape of parenting, it is the incremental yet transformative changes that often hold the most profound impact on society. In our modern era, a wave of intelligent systems and wearables crafted for children are promising to optimize the parenting experience through the novel concepts of quantification and gamification of daily routines.

Looking forward, it seems evident that even more sophisticated systems are on the horizon, poised to revolutionize the fabric of parenting as we know it. Picture smart homes with ambient sensors that vigilantly monitor a child's well-being, while augmented reality systems immerse young minds in unparalleled educational experiences.

Parents will leverage the power of cutting-edge algorithms that analyze their child's behavior and personality, generating tailored recommendations for educational content and social interactions.

Marketing campaigns promise personalized insights that will empower parents to sculpt their child's development with surgical precision, unlocking their full potential in previously unimaginable ways.

The integration of artificial intelligence into the communication ground is primed to change parenting into a data-driven, game-like experience.

With children enthusiastically engaging with smart toys and educational games, their progress will be monitored and rewarded in real time, fueling their motivation to learn and grow through the constant positive reinforcement of digital badges and virtual rewards.

This evolution in the two-sided 'game' is gradually changing the relationship between both sides, the parents and the kids. Most importantly, it is also changing the relationship between parents and parenthood, and between kids and how they navigate that 'parenting' authority.

Drawing inspiration from learn-to-earn models and game theory, the reward system has been woven into the essence of modern parenting. Data monitoring, an obsession with optimization, and an interface-mediated relationship have become hallmarks of this new paradigm.

The seemingly not trivial nature of the interaction shifts from one where the representation of the other side is tightly connected to the digital representation. A new interface slides in between. The Raise-to-earn model is here.

# A GLIMPSE INTO THE ANCESTORS OF GAMIFIED PARENTHOOD, A BLUEPRINT.

| | | |
|---|---|---|
| 1996 | → | Tamagotchi, a small handheld digital pet game, is released by Bandai in Japan. |
| 1997 | → | Tamagotchi is released worldwide and becomes a cultural phenomenon. |
| 1998 | → | Digimon, a virtual pet game featuring digital monsters, is released by Bandai. |
| 2000 | → | The Sims, a life simulation game where players create and control virtual people, is released by Maxis. |
| 2004 | → | Nintendogs, a virtual pet game featuring dogs, is released for the Nintendo DS. |
| 2007 | → | Babyz, a virtual child-raising game, is released by Ubisoft. |
| 2008 | → | Spore, a game where players create and evolve their own creatures, is released by Maxis. |
| 2010 | → | My Virtual Child, a virtual child-raising game designed for parents, is released by Pearson. |
| 2011 | → | Skylanders, a game that combines physical toy figures with a virtual world, is released by Activision. |
| 2013 | → | Disney Infinity, another game that combines physical toys with a virtual world, is released by Disney Interactive Studios. |
| 2014 | → | Tomodachi Life, a life simulation game where players control a group of virtual friends, is released for the Nintendo 3DS. |
| 2015 | → | Minecraft: Story Mode, a game where players make choices that affect the story, is released by Telltale Games. |
| 2017 | → | A new version of Tamagotchi, called Tamagotchi On, is released in Japan and later worldwide. |
| 2020 | → | The pandemic leads to a surge in the popularity of virtual child-raising games, including My Tamagotchi Forever and My Baby Unicorn. |

myvirtualchild.com/landing/
irtualChild

Raise a
MyVirtualChild is
the effects of you
learning in class

Aside from gamifying a 'real' scenario, raising virtual kids will become a popular trend among many families in the future. With the advancement of technology, parents now have the ability to create and raise their own virtual children through artificial intelligence and virtual reality simulations.

With unparalleled interactivity offered by games and simulations, parents are empowered to educate their virtual offspring about the world, instill essential values, and foster emotional intelligence and social skills. The pursuit of creating the most advanced and successful virtual children turns virtual parenting into a highly competitive field, where parents strive to outdo each other in raising the perfect digital progeny.

Virtual parenting communities emerge, where they can exchange tips and techniques for raising their virtual kids and compete with one another in virtual parenting competitions.

## If partners can have virtual children, why can't children have virtual parents?

It's a thought-provoking concept that challenges traditional notions of parenthood and underscores the transformative power of gamified parenthood in reshaping the way we perceive and approach the art of raising children.

The rise of gamified parenthood may usher a new era. One where children are crafted with unique personalities and abilities and are nurtured by virtual parents through artificial intelligence and extended reality interfaces.

Gamified parenthood is a powerful force that is redefining the landscape of parenting, paving the way for virtual children and virtual parents to coexist in a sphere where technology and imagination intertwine. The future of parenting is being shaped by the gamification of daily routines, the integration of artificial intelligence, and the endless possibilities of virtual reality, ushering in a new era of parenting that is both extraordinary and unparalleled.

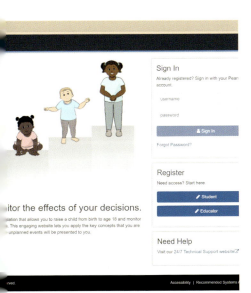

itor the effects of your decisions.

lation that allows you to raise a child from birth to age 18 and monitor
. This engaging website lets you apply the key concepts that you are
unplanned events will be presented to you.

## 2.5- Digital Fertility

Gamified parenthood in its new form is parenthood by design. It is already old news that scientists have successfully produced "designed" offspring by manipulating genes and biological codes. The genetic architecture is indirectly gamified through medical institutions. A parent or a group of parents can select features they want to have in a baby, be it a digital or a biological one.

Digital fertility becomes a new index, one that is built on the convergence of technology and reproductive possibilities of genetic engineering and its adoption.

**Digital fertility is a new social status.**

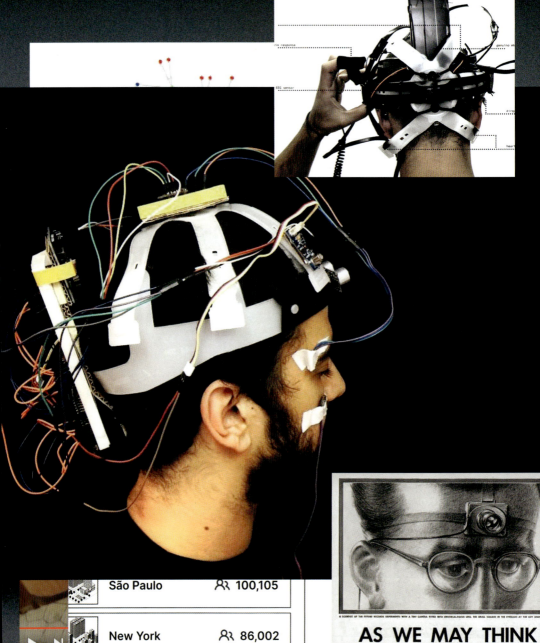

| | São Paulo | 🥷 100,105 |
| | New York | 🥷 86,002 |
| | Lima | 🥷 85,227 |

A SCIENTIST OF THE FUTURE RECORDS EXPERIMENTS WITH A TINY CAMERA FITTED WITH UNIVERSAL-FOCUS LENS. THE SMALL SQUARE IN THE EYEGLASS AT THE LEFT SIGHTS...

# AS WE MAY THINK

### A TOP U. S. SCIENTIST FORESEES A POSSIBLE FUTURE WO
### IN WHICH MAN-MADE MACHINES WILL START TO TH

**by VANNEVAR BUSH**

DIRECTOR OF THE OFFICE OF SCIENTIFIC RESEARCH AND DEVELOPMENT

Condensed from the Atlantic Monthly, July 1945

# 3- SPATIOLOGY

Architecture oscillates within the bounds of "The Spatial". An augmented spatial cognition, characterized by a heightened demand for and receptivity to spatial heterogeneity, necessitates a hybridity that captures attention and lays the groundwork for a new paradigm.

"All is Architecture" marked the dawn of spatiology.

## "All is Architecture" was the death of Architecture. Spatiology is its resurrection.

The genesis of architecture beyond Architecture itself is a new discourse, one of all things spatial. A paradoxical reset that, while expanding the discourse, only magnifies the essential object of architecture: spatial structures, and the production of interiorities, worlds within worlds.

As the etymology of Spatiology suggests, it's both the study of "the spatial" and its states of becoming and affecting events. Architecture is no longer an envelope that hosts space. The void becomes the content charged with stimuli, and the experience is understood as content. There is a dynamic relationship between the three. The structure is virtual, "The plan is not on the floor. architecture grows beyond the drawings, the drawing evolves further, to the reality of the virtual, and in Deleuzian terms, to a structure.

Peter Eisenman: The "real architecture" only exists in the drawings. The "real building" exists outside the drawings. The difference here is that "architecture" and "building" are not the same.

Buildings are to Architecture what a drawing is to art. It is a fundamental part of it, but it is not it.

here ⓘ info

DOUBLE POINTS FOR
THE NEXT 2 MINUTES

RICE

ou deserve to look fabulous
LOSE WEIGHT
FEEL GREAT!

try it

TOTAL
$0.00

éxito

POINTS
level 99

MY SHOPPING LIST

☐ Half watermelon
☐ Alpinette yoghurt
☐ 200g cream cheese
☐ 1 Quart milk

recipes

MY SHOPP

☐ Half watermelon
☐ Alpinette yoghu
☐ 200g cream che
☐ 1 Quart milk

2:18 / 6:15

▶ ▶| ◀)) 2:18 / 6:15

Lima        ஃ 85.227

A SCIENTIST OF THE FUTURE RECORDS EXPERIMENTS WITH A TINY CAMERA FITTED WITH UNIVERSAL-FOCUS LENS. THE SMALL SQUARE IN THE EYEGLASS AT THE LEFT SIGHTS T

# AS WE MAY THINK

A TOP U. S. SCIENTIST FORESEES A POSSIBLE FUTURE WO
IN WHICH MAN-MADE MACHINES WILL START TO TH

DIRECTOR OF THE OFFICE OF SCIENTIFIC RESEARCH AND DEVELOPMENT
by VANNEVAR BUSH
Condensed from the Atlantic Monthly, July 1945

# AUGMENTED BROWSING

Both, the fear of the mundane and eternal fetishization of what glitters, thrive to continuously present a new image that cannot afford getting old. The relentless pursuit of novelty and the allure of strobe-like distractions drive a perpetual cycle of presenting ever-changing images. It is a skin-deep surfing of an effervescent environment of disposable events.

An exponentially growing consumption reality presents a new form of social unification.

A short life span is always advantageous for impressing: bursts of energy that enthrall the senses and then fade, yielding to the next stimuli. It is not only about the singular event, but the context where it survives, a curated environment where "more" is always available.

Grids of tiling in supermarkets deliberately amplify the noise of our trolleys as we speed through, intentionally extending our journey. Commodities and products are meticulously curated in sections and shelves. Every placement is guided by consumer psychologists and neuro-marketing specialists, crafting an enticing path to the desired product.

HTTPS://WWW.YOUTUBE.COM/
WATCH?V=YJGO2IVYZSS

The journey to the product is a gold mine to be seized. We have all been in a store, or even a supermarket, where we buy stuff on the way to our destination (the thing we were going to buy). We make predestination purchases and call it impulse buying.

The incessant scrolling and endless feeds on social media platforms epitomize this phenomenon. There is an endless stream of personalized content, based on the user's browsing history, likes, and dislikes.

Infinite content, reinforced with content-aware algorithms, is a recipe for developing a shorter attention span while consuming bite-sized content.

Augmented browsing takes this experience to a new level: akin to the souvenir shop at the end of a museum tour, the pop-up ads on a webpage, or the street vendors en route to the movies.

With more interaction media, smartphones, and XR, augmented browsing leaps forward. It expands the field of operation by introducing new layers into the existing virtual and physical fabric. A world of overlays that maintains an infinite feed of possibilities. It is one that perpetually feeds our appetite for endless content.

Searching, browsing, and navigating collapse into one seamless experience. "Looking for," "looking at," and "finding the way" become interchange-able, as the traffic of content guarantees that all these actions happen simultaneously, fueling an insatiable quest for more.

1.  According to a study by Microsoft, the average human attention span has dropped from 12 seconds in 2000 to 8 seconds in 2015.
    **Microsoft Corp. "Attention Spans." (2015).**

2.  A survey of 2,000 participants by the Statistic Brain Research Institute found that the average attention span for adults in 2015 was 8.25 seconds.
    **Statistic Brain Research Institute survey: Statistic Brain**
    **Research Institute. "Attention Span Statistics." (2015).**

3.  A 2016 study by the National Center for Biotechnology Information found that people's attention spans have decreased by 33% in the last 15 years.
    **National Center for Biotechnology Information study: Junco, Reynol, and Fabio. "The relationship between frequency of Facebook use, participation in Facebook activities, and student engagement." Computers & Education 58, no. 1 (2012): 162-171.**

4.  A 2017 study by Prezi found that 42% of respondents said they lost interest in a presentation within the first 15 minutes, and 19% said they lost interest within the first 5 minutes.
    **Prezi study: Prezi Inc. "The Science of Attention." (2017).**

# The mass murder of attention spans.

# DIGITAL GRAVEYARDS

## The best graveyards are those that don't need to exist.

Here is a timeline of the evolution of death, how we deal with it, and how death is going to be digitized.

→ **Ancient Egypt** - Death was seen as a journey to the afterlife, and elaborate funerary rituals were performed to ensure a smooth transition. The dead were mummified and buried in tombs filled with grave goods, and their names were inscribed on monuments to ensure their memory would live on.

→ **Ancient Greece and Rome** - Death was seen as a natural part of life, and funerary rites were performed to honor the dead and ensure their peaceful passage to the underworld. Otherwise the dead were cremated, and their ashes were placed in urns.

→ **Industrial Revolution** - Death became more medicalized and less of a natural process. More diverse and secular practices and attitudes toward death emerged. The dead were often buried or cremated, and the invention of the camera led to the rise of post-mortem photography as a way to remember the dead, moving from physical memory - tomb or ashes - to an image of the dead person.

→ **20th Century** - Death became increasingly privatized, with many people dying in hospitals rather than at home. The funeral industry became more commercialized, and cremation became a more popular alternative to traditional burial.

→ **Digital Age (Current)** - With the rise of the internet, social media, and virtual reality, new ways of memorializing and remembering the dead have emerged. Digital graveyards, online memorials, and virtual reality experiences are all examples of how technology is changing how we deal with death.

HTTPS://THEPLAIDZEBRA.
COM/JAPANS-ANSWER-TO-A-
SHORTAGE-OF-GRAVEYARD-
SPACE-IS-LITERALLY-A-
STAIRWAY-TO-HEAVEN/

→ **Cyberspace ( Next )** - The trend will only grow, and death will become more privatized, experience-based, and interactive. Generative AI-Language models, machine learning, and generative visualization technologies for VR and AR, coupled with a bank of data about any person will be able to create a virtual avatar that can outlive the physical person - post-death.

HTTPS://WWW.WIONEWS.
COM/PHOTOS/JAPAN-SUP-
PORTS-MODERN-CEMETER-
IES-WITH-QR-CODES-AND-
CRANES-472600

Character building - not to be confused with character design as a graphical endeavor - is building a digital underlying structure for an avatar that is achieved by running the user's data through machine learning and Ai models. This means that all decisions made afterward by the machines are qualified as "real" decisions. Real here refers to answers, actions, etc. that hold together when tested against the training information i.e. has all the features that make the user who they are.

In the metaverse, the dead can dance. Personalized avatars built on real human data will live in these virtual environments.

The dead are dead...it's only the virtual avatar that is represented. But how significant is that?

An evaluation of interactions since COVID-19 became a pandemic, quantifies the increasingly virtual and digital nature of communication be it through phone or video calls. In parallel, a series of telecommunication enhancement devices take over more space, and a utility-oriented communication ethic makes geography less relevant.

Advanced Telecommunications Research Institute International (ATR) has developed a "human presence" transfer media called "Hugvie®" that enables users to strongly feel the presence of remote partners while interacting with them."

Dead or away might become the same; to have a relationship with a dead person's avatar can be almost like having a long-distance relationship.

With a play/pause button on the AR interface, it is now possible to revisualize memories that have been captured. Adding to that, the content will be ai-generated, and avatars will be autonomous. Scenes will not only be replayed in a passive manner, the characters will be responsive. A model that learns by going through online data, daily monitoring, and manual input of information through questions, preference mapping, 3d scanning, etc.

That model will be at a certain readiness that would qualify as an assistant, or an auto-response message box when people are not available.

At the next phase, as its learning gets reinforced and its results become sharper, it can now simply replace the person for a lot of virtual tasks, from playing games to making calls, etc. Task-based identical replicas will be extensions to our image. They will slowly take over our online presence and we will fade into data.

### Digital graveyards are the ideal graveyards.
They are storages of models, rather than pure data, models of characters ( personalities ), and an online archive of immortal avatars. Personal.ai by Human Labs Inc. creates a user-owned and user-controlled "digital extension" of a person or an entity based on traits, knowledge, and memories. It is an AI that learns from user input and generates outputs in alignment with the given data.

Interacting with virtual elements, mediated through our senses defines the trend.

Mama, where have you been?
Have you been thinking of me?

HTTPS://WWW.YOUTUBE.COM/
WATCH?V=MU38AXHHZXM

s' with dead daughter in virtual reality

fucking Architecture

then it'll slide out to the t.

▶ ▶| 🔊   1:27 / 3:04

Stanford researchers develop brain-controlled typing for people with paralysis

Stanford

All   From Stanford

Will we learn code first?
Or will machines learn English first?

# PROMPTISM

**A new era of human-computer interaction.**

This paradigm-shifting approach has transformed the way non-experts communicate with artificial intelligence (AI), surpassing the perennial question of whether computers can outperform humans in English proficiency before we master coding.

With the emergence of language models like ChatGPT and text-to-image model-based applications such as MidJourney or Dalle, a new "ism" has taken center stage, revolutionizing our perception of AI and redefining our creative capacities.

Promtism goes beyond basic web prompts or the Discord server of MidJourney, evolving into a domain that encompasses entire businesses and services that govern social life. Creative production is at stake, with designers donning a new hat - that of prompt engineers, recognizing the critical correlation between the prompt and the output.

Understanding how the AI model functions becomes a key advantage for artists and authors, as prompt engineering clinically curates the right terminology and word choice to produce desired outcomes through the model. At its pinnacle, it entails reverse engineering the model in real-time, harnessing its complexity and relevance to create intentional content.

Promtism is fast content, and just like fast food, it is mostly junk. The prompt culture is an interesting one, where in general, no understanding of the model is needed to create content. It is only needed to create intentional content. All computational models work with the input and the processing capacity they have. Whatever the input is, there will be output. GIGO is inevitable.

Promtism moves us from fast content to instant content. Its instinctivity gives no space for thought and reflection. Consequently, all generated content looks interesting.

Wandering in augmented cityscapes, content overlaying the environment becomes on-demand and instantaneous, and generated with minimal input. It takes a prompt entry to cover the city in vegetation, to transform cards into spaceships, and to watch the stock exchange on the building facade.

This is a shift in human-computer interaction that redefines using and interacting with the world.

In a parallel field, Brain-computer-interfaces - BCI - the communication with the machine is through a direct highway that connects brain activity with computing processors. Prompting becomes diverse and possible through thought alone.

HTTPS://WWW.BBC.COM/
NEWS/WORLD-US-CANA-
DA-65069316

fucking Architecture

☑ Show Vertex Normals

# THE MESH POLICE

## The new virtual budget is geometrical/technical.

### Polycount, texturing and the Metaverse police

Engineers are left behind when designing the virtual arena. No gravity, no mechanics, and no sewage.

A new context that suggests a new type of budget, new technical requirements, and an understanding of the foundational aspects of virtual world-building.

The metaverse context holds access to a long-awaited dream, that of breaking free from gravity and reducing noise to produce 'pure' design. But scratching the surface, the reality is more complex.

While metaverse spaces escape real-world constraints, such as gravity, having the building structurally sound, etc. Geometry, from a computational perspective, comes to replace that. To describe it in a straightforward way, geometry is an important and decisive feature. It's a make-it-or-break-it kind of thing. Great design, bad geometry, you're out.
Geometry here refers to the quantitative aspect of things, the number of polygons, face-normals, texturing, light maps, etc.

Geometry becomes a virtual budget, where it's almost the only project constraint, almost.
In the case of browser-based game engines, polycount is a central issue, as platforms can host a not-so-generous file size with polycounts of around a 200K average at best. So, this makes the potential for open worlds far-fetched.

A new form of budget, new game rules that underlie new form-making strategies.

The lighter the model, the smoother the experience.

With a more online presence comes the increasing importance of efficient geometry and low polycount in virtual environments. The need for consequent regulation and oversight in the development of the metaverse is also peaking in significance. Limits are set by the host platforms and engines.

### Performance
It impacts the performance and rendering speed of the virtual world. Complex and inefficient geometry can slow down the rendering process, causing lag and decreased performance. This can lead to a poor user experience, particularly in an environment where real-time synchronized interaction is key.

### Storage
Efficient geometry can also have an impact on storage and bandwidth requirements. Storing and streaming large amounts of data for complex geometry can be expensive and impractical, especially for online applications that need to be accessible to a wide range of users.

### Scalability
Efficient geometry has the ability to impact the scalability of virtual environments. As the size and complexity of virtual worlds increase, efficient geometry can allow for more detailed and immersive environments without sacrificing performance or requiring excessive resources.

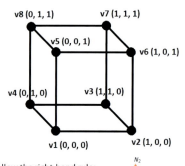

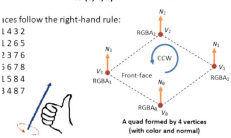

Faces follow the right-hand rule:
1 4 3 2
1 2 6 5
2 3 7 6
5 6 7 8
1 5 8 4
3 4 8 7

A quad formed by 4 vertices
(with color and normal)

## For example, Decentraland:

"Scene limitation rules #
Below are the maximum number of elements that a scene is allowed to render at the same time:

**n represents the number of parcels that a scene occupies.**

→ Triangles: **n x 10000** Total amount of triangles for all the models in the scene.

→ Entities: **n x 200** Amount of entities in the scene.

→ Bodies: **n x 300** Amount of meshes in the scene.

→ Materials: **log2(n+1) x 20** Amount of materials in the scene. It includes materials imported as part of models.

→ Textures: **log2(n+1) x 10** Amount of textures in the scene. It includes textures imported as part of models.

→ Height: **log2(n+1) x 20** Height in meters.
Important: Only entities that are currently being rendered in the scene are counted for these limits. If your scene switches between 3D models, what matters is the rendered models at any point in time, not the total sum. Player avatars and any items brought by a player from outside the scene don't count for calculating these limits either.

→ File size: **15 MB per parcel - 300 MB max** Total size of the files uploaded to the content server. Includes 3D models and audio. Doesn't include files that aren't uploaded, such as node.js packages.

→ File count: **200 files per parcel** Total count of the files uploaded. Includes 3D models and audio. Doesn't include files that aren't uploaded, such as node.js packages.

→ Max file size **50 MB per file** No individual file of any type in the scene can exceed 50 MB, no matter how many parcels the scene has."

Retrieved from *https://docs.decentraland.org/creator/development-guide/scene-limitations/*

Level of Detail ( LOD ) features, Nanites, and other factors help builders go a step further on engines such as Unity and Unreal Engine. Having said that, the technical challenge still stays the same. Good geometry and texturing are essential.
*https://docs.monaverse.com/create/building-spaces/building-in-the-metaverse*

fucking Architecture

# Resolution in the virtual world is key.

## The World's Water

All water on, in, and above the Earth
- Liquid fresh water
- Fresh-water lakes and rivers

Howard Perlman, USGS;
Jack Cook, Woods Hole Oceanographic Instit
Adam Nieman.
Data source: Igor Shiklomanov
http://ga.water.usgs.gov.edu/earthhowmuch.h

# RESOLUTION VS SCALE

Let's get to basics, and write down a box,
A cube can be represented in so many ways.
V stands for vertex and F stands for face:

V 0 0 0 255 0 0

V 1 0 0 255 0 0

V 1 1 0 0 0 255

V 0 1 0 0 0 255

V 0 0 1 0 255 0

V 1 0 1 0 255 0

V 1 1 1 255 0 0

V 0 1 1 255 0 0

F 1 4 3 2

F 1 2 6 5

F 2 3 7 6

F 5 6 7 8

F 1 5 8 4

F 3 4 8 7

Describing the vertices and then the faces is
enough to draw the cube.

Size does not matter, as the information is still the
same. And here is an illustration of how it works.

While resolution is more concerned with the level
of detail, scale might be a misleading way to think
about the impact if resolution is not taken into
account.

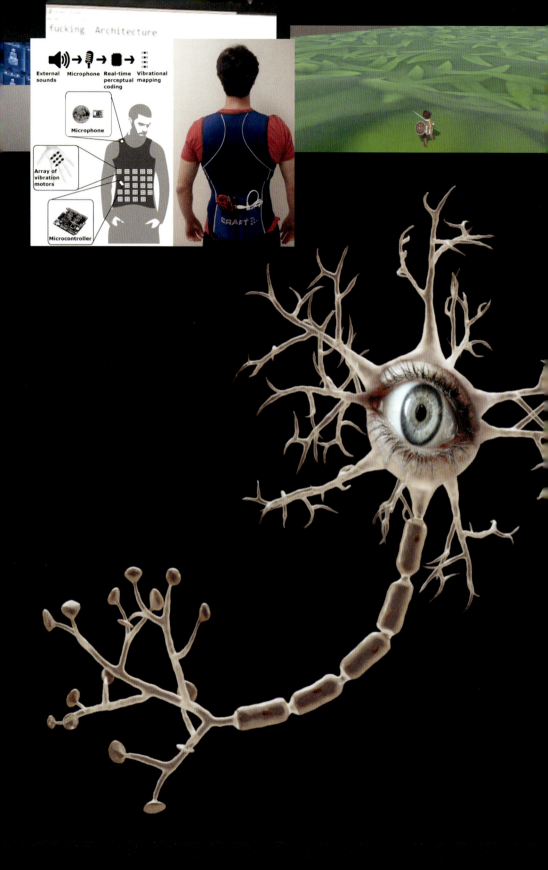

External sounds → Microphone → Real-time perceptual coding → Vibrational mapping

Microphone

Array of vibration motors

Microcontroller

# DISPOSABLE SENSES

### SENSING AND PERCEPTION

Sensing is the capacity to funnel information and data about the world.

Perception is the process of making sense of this information. For example, our eyes sense light, our brain perceives a scene. We see from our brains. The construction of an image out of the neural input signals sent to the brain from the eyes ( while arguably they are part of it ) is called perception.

While it seems very straightforward, a number of other senses also play a role in constructing any mental image, and, thus, our perception of it. We have the tendency to perceive things differently, and with biases based on whether our senses are on a low or high. Attention, hunger, balance, and heat, among many other things we sense, can easily affect how other senses work.

### SENSORY SUBSTITUTION

The brain's cross-modal plasticity, its capacity to reorganize and adapt in response to changes in sensory input, is key to sensory remapping. The latter is the process of rewiring the neural circuits in the brain to accommodate sensory input from a non-traditional sensory modality.

This plasticity, where the brain adaptively processes sensory input from different modalities and learns to interpret and make sense of the information presented through unconventional sensory channels, is what enables a game abounding with yet-to-be-realized opportunities.

If sense-making is a brain trade, the promise of sensory substitution is to divorce the sensing instrument from the perceived type. Sensory substitution is based on using one sensory modality to convey information typically processed by another sensory modality. In other words, it is a technique that allows information from one sensory channel to be presented through a different sensory channel.

FIRAS SAFIEDDINE

For example, using sound to convey visual information or touch to convey auditory information becomes possible.

Perceptual transduction, or the process of converting sensory information from one modality to another, has been a theme of experimentation since the 1960s. It was perhaps triggered by Paul Bach-y-Rita's "tactile vision", a device that converted visual information into tactile stimulation for the blind. The 1967 paper laid the foundation for Sensory Plasticity.

Neil Harbisson is a living example of someone who listens to color. His brain has acquired new sensory skills and abilities through training or practice. Neil's skull-implantable is an example of perceptual transduction that operates within the bounds of the 5 senses. It is a device that translates optical information-color hues -into intricate frequency soundscapes, which he has learned to perceive as color. Perceptual learning is a native skill, it is the brain's natural state of adaptation. It is the foundation of synesthetic perception, the phenomenon of experiencing sensory perceptions in one modality as a result of intentional stimulation in a different modality.

Sensory substitution devices (SSDs) are designed to provide sensory input to an individual through an alternative channel to compensate for a sensory loss, sensory substitution, or to augment sensory perception.

## SENSORY AUGMENTATION

In his 2011 book "Incognito: The Secret Lives of the Brain", David Eagleman exposed the sensory augmentation experiment where a participant wore a specially designed vest equipped with vibratory actuators. These actuators translated stock market data into patterns of vibrations that were then transmitted to the participant's torso through the vest. The participant was trained to interpret these vibrations as information about stock prices and make decisions based on the patterns of vibrations they felt in their body.

Over time, the participant's brain adapted to the new sensory input and learned to associate specific patterns of vibrations with different stock market conditions, such as rising or falling prices. The participants were able to use this information to make trading decisions, even though they were not receiving any visual or auditory cues which are typically used in traditional stock trading.

On a larger timescale, the perception process becomes intuitive and natural; and the subject grows a new sense, a sense of the stock exchange market.

The sensorial and perceptual capacity is as plastic as our brains. Adding, manipulating, or replacing senses is a present phenomenon that will explode. Sense designers are the new thing, with designers prototyping new senses.

The Seismic Sense of Moon Ribas expands her sensorial umwelt, it unlocks layers of the world and makes them accessible through technology.

▶ Barry C Smith: We Have Far More T... 🗍
youtube.com

IN SIGHT
5:36

— Aristotle was wrong and so are we: there are far
more than five senses Subscribe to the Aeon Vid...

"In 2013, Moon developed a sensor that vibrates whenever there's an earthquake on the planet. The sensor, which is permanently implanted in her feet, vibrates at different levels depending on the intensity of each earthquake and is wirelessly connected to online seismographs... Moon has been wearing the sensor permanently since March 2013 and has used her seismic sense to create dance pieces...The choreography depends on the earthquakes felt during the duration of the performance and the intensity of the dancer's movements depends on the magnitude of each earthquake (which can be felt from 1.0 on the Richter Scale). If there are no earthquakes during the time of performance the dancer will not dance."

**If we can add any sense, what would it be?**

Haptic feedback from virtual environments is shaping an emerging niche industry of wearables, bringing a virtual touch to physical bodies in the world. From handshakes to affectionate cuddles, the fusion of the virtual and the real becomes increasingly seamless.

Between the physical and the virtual, sensory augmentation becomes a plug-and-play paradigm to unlock features of our environment and expand our umwelt, which is simultaneously virtual and physical. The virtual world becomes an extension of the physical one.

New senses give people the capacity to sense the number of users within their metaverse store, the sense of atmospheric pressure in a remote location on the planet, or even the temperature of the oceans at the poles. It creates a new paradigm of senses on demand.

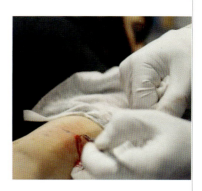

**Milei calls for "market mechanisms" to solve lack of organ donors**

*His comments were repudiated by the Argentine transplant regulator*

# ORGANS
# ON-DEMAND

Metaverse Urbanism

'In Defense of Capitalism' speculates on the future of human skin and its evolution to an augmented tissue as it grows the ability to show graphics. It is a critique that operates within the friction space between the future implications of current technological breakthroughs and the social innovation around it.

The bioplastic wearables suggest a series of skin implants, from bioluminescent tattoos to glowing implantables, that will render the forever interface with the world a profitable and publicly consumed estate. Once implanted, brands start renting human skins, rendering them walking billboards.

Ultimately, some become immortal, and start using the skin as an interface to promote self-owned unneeded organs.

Futuristic yet rooted in a real current technosphere, it's an invitation to explore the landscape around its territory.

HTTPS://WWW.YOUTUBE.COM/
WATCH?V=BD1YOAGLFVG

Technologies and techniques to lab-grow and produce human organs and tissues will solve immense problems, and cause a shift in how we understand life itself. This is a new form of survival mechanism that is designed by humans. Similar to all breakthroughs, what starts as a necessity, becomes available for luxury. Organs on demand won't forever be for survival, but for enhancing healthy lives too.

HTTPS://WWW.YOUTUBE.COM/WATCH?V=-
RGI_BCETKM

Groundbreaking technologies at the base of a new industry make it a plausible one. 3D bioprinting enables the production of three-dimensional structures using living cells.

## Living cells are the new ink.

A layered disposition of cells, biomaterials, and growth factors creates complex tissue structures; and the precise placement of cells in specific patterns and configurations, allows the fabrication of functional tissues with desired properties.

Scaffold-based Tissue Engineering that uses biocompatible materials - synthetic polymers or natural extracellular matrix (ECM) components - yields a framework or scaffold that structurally supports cells to grow and differentiate into functional tissue. The scaffold is a template for tissue formation. It holds the potential to be designed to mimic the native tissue's architecture and properties.

Decellularization and Recellularization remove cellular components from an organ or tissue, leaving behind a natural ECM scaffold.A scaffold that can then be repopulated with new cells through recellularization. Decellularization and recellularization techniques regenerate functional tissues from donated organs or tissues, allowing for the creation of custom-made tissues with a reduced risk of rejection.

Stem Cell Technologies, spanning the isolation, culture, and differentiation of stem cells into specific cell types, are then used to regenerate damaged or diseased tissues. Undifferentiated cells are generated with the potential to differentiate into various cell types. Stem cells play a crucial role in tissue engineering. Different types of stem cells, such as embryonic stem cells, induced pluripotent stem cells (iPSCs), and adult stem cells, are used to generate different tissues or organs.

Biofabrication is a multidisciplinary field that encompasses various technologies - including 3D bioprinting - to create functional tissues and organs. It involves the precise deposition of living cells, biomaterials, and other components to create complex tissue structures with desired properties. Biofabrication techniques allow for the creation of tissues with specific shapes, sizes, and functionalities, tailored to the needs of individual patients.

Organ-on-a-chip is a microscale technology that uses microfabrication techniques to create small, functional models of human organs on microchips. These chip-based models mimic the structure and function of human organs, providing a platform for studying tissue development, disease modeling, and drug testing. Organ-on-a-chip technology enables the generation of functional tissue models for testing and validation before translating to larger-scale tissue engineering approaches.

An avalanche of emerging science, biocomputation, and bioengineering advancements is blooming a startup scene, a new industry of organs-on-demand.

1. **Organovo** - focuses on developing 3D bioprinting technology to create living tissues for medical research and transplant purposes.

2. **Prellis Biologics** - uses holographic printing technology to create microvasculature and other components of human organs.

3. **Aether** - is a startup that is developing a system to produce transplantable lungs using stem cells and a bioreactor.

4. **Lung Biotechnology** - part of United Therapeutics, which is developing techniques to grow human lungs for transplantation.

5. **Tissue Engineering and Regenerative Medicine International Society** (TERMIS) - an organization that brings together scientists, clinicians, and industry partners to advance the field of tissue engineering and regenerative medicine.

Tissues are a new asset type, owned and monitored in virtual telemedicine facilities. Blockchain is used to keep track. With telemedicine being revolutionized through the metaverse, body enhancements and monitoring take the lead.

Virtual Reality Simulation for Tissue Engineering is used in the design and development of lab-grown tissues. Scientists and researchers use VR simulations to model and test different tissue engineering approaches, including 3D bioprinting, scaffold-based tissue engineering, and organ-on-a-chip technologies. VR simulations could allow for virtual experimentation and optimization of tissue engineering processes, helping to streamline and accelerate the development of lab-grown tissues.

Simulations provide immersive and interactive experiences for learning about tissue engineering principles, techniques, and best practices. It brings forth a new form of virtual training on how to handle and manipulate lab-grown tissues, perform surgical procedures, or optimize tissue culture conditions. The user-base simulations, too, are used to educate users about tissue engineering and regenerative medicine, helping them understand the potential benefits and limitations of lab-grown tissues.

Patient engagement is used to engage patients who are undergoing tissue engineering treatments or receiving lab-grown tissues. Virtual tours of the tissue engineering facilities show patients how their lab-grown tissues are being cultured or 3D printed, or allow them to virtually explore and interact with their own virtual tissues. This could help patients feel more connected and engaged with their tissue engineering treatments, enhancing their understanding and acceptance of the technology.

On the other hand, lab-grown tissues potentially have applications within the metaverse itself. Lab-grown tissues are used to create virtual avatars with more realistic and functional organs, muscles, and tissues, enhancing the immersive experience in the metaverse.

_Instagram_  **Log In** Sign Up

**bebiselis** ✔  Follow  Message  •••

92 posts  4,758 followers  194 following

**Elis**
Blogger
Tips och råd för småbarnsföräldrar 👶 🦐 ICA-familjens yngsta och mest nyfikna medlem.
🔗 www.ica.se/recept/barnmat

Elis favorit  Recept  #SommarMe...  Dietist-tips II  Elis mythbustar  Recept  Recept

⊞ POSTS  ⌖ TAGGED

"Just 36% of Gen Z have an optimistic outlook on the state of the world today, while less than 30% believe the economic and political state of their country will improve." A 70% readiness to engage in building a new world, or at least consuming it.

# METAVERSE NATIVES

Just a generation or two ago, houses of the average population in most of the world had no access to a stable electricity supply. I do not know the world without computers, phones, and the internet. I am almost as old as the modern internet (1990 onward).

The third and fourth decades of internet history have the internet and its ways of revealing in the world deeply rooted in our identity propositions, our social life, and how we see the world. The next generation will be one that does not know the world pre-metaverse. The spatial internet is ground zero; it is the reference. In retrospect, the fourth decade in the internet is a basic prototypical romantic genesis of "the world" as it becomes.

Today's metaverse to the Metaverse Natives is what the internet is to today's generation: natural, trivial, and an essential part of the world.

Metaverse natives are innately talented world-makers. Worldbuilding will be the craft of the century, when designing is possible through available tools, all become designers.

Metaverse natives are natural virtual socializers, building communities and navigating a landscape of diverse identity archetypes.

Virtual and augmented sports have become mainstream. Metaverse natives are virtual sports champions.

Metaverse natives live in a singular world of the fused virtual and physical. Drawing a line between both becomes retro art. Metaverse natives occupy the pinnacle of a social evolution toward financial literacy. They are economic pioneers.

HTTPS://WWW.INSTAGRAM.COM/
BEBISELIS/?UTM_SOURCE=IG_
EMBED&IG_RID=8F1D5D0E-9702-
4EFF-AF45-14524638670A

To quote a 22-year-old from the UK in the Deloitte report, "The metaverse is about relaxing and forgetting about the world." The capacity for hyper-personalized realities in the metaverse within the hyper-connected world manifests as poles to a new reality. It is not a reality that strikes, it is a reality that people willingly step into.

Money, identity, and socializing amongst an almost infinite list of how Gen-Z engages with the metaverse is presented in a dedicated report by Nokia. Like the majority of the brands racing into the metaverse, Nokia is betting to capture a new audience. Their bet is on a new age group that has never seen the pre-internet world, and that will be the main driver for the next economy.

# REASONS TO CHOOSE ARTIFICIAL PLANTS FOR OUTDOORS

MAY 12, 2020   ARTIFICIAL PLANTS & TREES BLOGS

0:41 / 2:28

elaxation Walking in Virtual Reality android

# TECHNO-BIO-PHILIA

## "Transposition of biophilia into the digital"

A teammate confronted me with an interesting question, why on earth would you put trees in a virtual environment when they seem to be practically useless?

'Virtual chlorophyll' is perceptually valid. Studies unveil that as clinical patients find solace in virtual nature through immersive VR wearables, thus, experiencing increased relaxation. The forest, a vital element of life, is reduced to its aesthetics and perceptual qualities. Technobiophilic environments are the new green.

Ecological Urbanism, Biocities, and other concepts have been catalyzing avant-garde urban theory, and have ecology at its core. The functional aspect of vegetation from biodiversity, to ecological balance and public space enhancement, curates a leading number of city design proposals.

The metaverse has trees too, and greenery that can overpower architecture itself. From virtual scenes of extreme, pristine, rain-forest-dense, virgin-ecology of flora to "green filters", a real built environment is a greenscreen for augmented flora.

My 2016 neuroscience research opened the way to understanding the phenomena from a different standpoint.

New quantifiable processes to understand emerging concepts were key to examining how the built environment influences the brain, physically, and consequently our perception.

Biophilia, the innate human affinity to chlorophyll in specific and nature in general,, was one to project to the metaverse.

While trees and vegetation in the metaverse do no photosynthesis and produce no gas, the perceptual aspect of trees is partially maintained.

Biophilia is the innate human affinity to chlorophyll or nature, whereas technobiophilia is the innate human affinity for nature and how it can be enhanced or mediated through visual technology. It is a concept that naturally came out and was etymologically traced back to 2013 in Sue Thomas' "Technobiophilia: Nature and Cyberspace".

Technobiophilia in the metaverse will drive the design of spaces for applications like virtual forest explorations, healing, meditation, yoga, and psychedelic trips. It is poised to be integrated into future hospitals and patient engagement centers, and with that, transform the healthcare landscape.

There is a body of research that supports and backs up the claim but simultaneously shows its insufficiency. With scientific work now exposing NDD - "nature deficit disorder"- even more disorders are to be stacked on top of the rest in a rapidly evolving cyberpsychology era.

The symbiotic relationship between humans and their virtual environments creates a new nature, perhaps an augmented nature.

YouTube
Yaroslav Petryk · 2:29

VR Forest Relaxation Walking in Virtual Reality android

Watch >

Uploaded: Apr 13, 2020 · 992 Views · 5 Likes

VR Forest Relaxation Walking in Virtual Reality, Paweł Patrzek, Virtual Reality Relax Forest Walk is a place where you can spend your free time and relax after the hardships of the whole week and ...

1. "Virtual Nature Environments Enhance Affectionate Touching Behavior" by Merlijn Jocque and colleagues was published in Cyberpsychology, Behavior, and Social Networking in 2018. This study found that exposure to virtual nature environments increased affectionate touching behavior in romantic couples.

2. "The Potential of Virtual Reality for the Investigation of Awe" by Alex J. Taylor and colleagues was published in Frontiers in Psychology in 2017. This study explores how virtual reality can be used to induce feelings of awe and wonder, which can have positive correlations with and effects on mental health and well-being.

3. "The Effects of Virtual Nature on Anxiety and Aggression" by Rachelle J. Doorley and colleagues was published in Cyberpsychology, Behavior, and Social Networking in 2013. This study found that exposure to virtual nature environments reduces anxiety and aggression in participants.

4. "The Restorative Benefits of Nature: Toward an Integrative Framework" by Rachel Kaplan and Stephen Kaplan was published in the Journal of Environmental Psychology in 1989. This article proposes an integrative framework for understanding the restorative benefits of nature on human well-being, which includes attention restoration, stress reduction, and mood enhancement.

5. "View through a window may influence recovery from surgery" by Roger S. Ulrich was published in Science in 1984. This study found that patients who had a view of nature outside their hospital window recovered more quickly from surgery and required fewer pain medications than patients who had a view of a brick wall.

6. "Virtual reality forest therapy for the improvement of mental health in elderly populations": Virtual reality forest therapy can improve the mental health of elderly individuals.

7. "The Restorative Effects of Virtual Nature Experience on Mental Fatigue": Virtual nature experiences can help increase cognitive performance, reduce stress, and aid in perceived restorativeness .

8. "Physical Activity and Virtual Nature: Perspectives on the Health and Behavioral Benefits of Virtual Green Exercise published in the book: Nature and Health - Physical Activity in Nature in 2021. ": Virtual nature experiences are used as a strategy for exercise and health benefits.

9. "The Psychological Benefits of a Virtual Forest Experience": Virtual forest experiences can provide psychological benefits such as stress reduction and positive emotions.

10. "Natural environments and subjective well-being: Different types of exposure are associated with different aspects of well-being": Different types of exposure to natural environments can have varying impacts on subjective well-being.

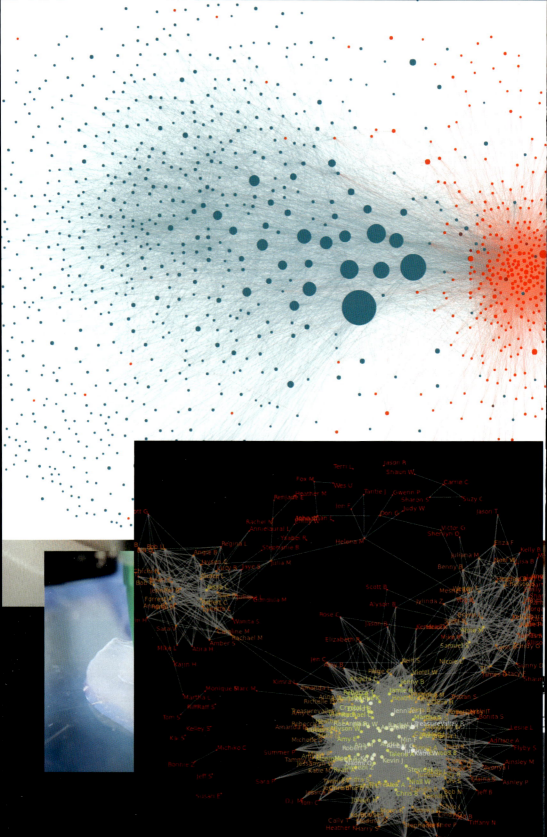

# DIGITAL TRIBALISM

Slight divisions expand into profound fissures, leading to an increasing divergence between two ideological poles.
Subsequently, with mirroring, and an echo chamber effect, both poles become more and more self-similar.

## The polarity between the poles amplifies. People within these bubbles progressively converge.

### Ecochambers and Filter Bubbles.

Throughout the unfolding of the last decade of social media, the world has witnessed a phenomenon that now shapes social media and society in general. Individuals developed the tendency to form echo chambers, self-similar communities, and identities based on shared interests, values, visions, and beliefs.

We have seen a large part of its occurrence in digital spaces such as social media, forums, and online gaming. Technology has made it easier than ever for people to connect with like-minded individuals regardless of their geographical location.

Pre-internet, the social context was almost inevitable. However, now, within online echo chambers, "pure contexts" are now possible and incentivized with algorithms that show users more of what they would like.

Mark Federman defines it as "the natural evolution of social groups in the digital age, where the boundaries of the group are defined by its digital presence, and the group is held together by its shared interests, values, and beliefs. Digital tribalism creates new possibilities for connection, collaboration, and social innovation, but it also has the potential to reinforce social divisions and perpetuate inequalities."

Seth Godin, in his book "Tribes: We Need You to Lead Us," argues that in the digital age, people are searching for connection and community and that technology has enabled the formation of new tribes based on shared interests and passions.

Similarly, Douglas Rushkoff, in his book "Cyberia: Life in the Trenches of Hyperspace," discusses how the internet has allowed individuals to form digital tribes based on shared interests, ideologies, and values. He argues that digital tribalism has the potential to be both positive and negative, as it can promote solidarity and a sense of belonging, but it can also lead to polarization, conflict, and the reinforcement of narrow worldviews.

"Digital tribalism is the phenomenon where people form groups around shared ideas, interests, or beliefs, and use digital tools to connect and communicate. The internet has made it easier than ever to form and participate in tribes, and as a result, we are seeing a proliferation of niche communities that are reshaping our culture and society."

- SETH GODIN

It is a phenomenon that reflects the changing nature of identity, community, and belonging in the digital age.

The Digital Anthropology Report of 2009, which shows the outcome of surveying 2000 UK "users of technology" and identifies six tribes, categorized on the basis of internet usage and relative savvy:

**Digital extroverts (9%*):** Unsurprisingly, these are the early adopters or advanced users of technology.

**Timid technophobes (23%):** People with limited technology skills, who are generally suspicious of all things digital.

**Social secretaries (13%):** Those who use technology, particularly for social means and ends.

**First lifers (12%):** Those who are neither for or against technology per se and will only use a few applications that they find particularly useful.

**E-ager beavers (29%):** Those who use technology a lot, but are less confident in creating digital artifacts than the digital extroverts.

**Web boomers (8%):** An older group of Internet users who mainly use the Internet to access information online. [* percentages refer to the numbers of survey participants who made up each 'tribe'] (Hockly, 2011, para 4)

In 2017, Environics Research, a Canadian research firm, published a survey of Millennials. Bradley Cooper describes the six (Canadian) millennial tribes identified in this research as follows:

**Lone Wolves** tend to live alone and closely mirror Gen Xers' desire for independence. They usually have a "live and let live" attitude.

**Engaged Idealists** wish to engage in meaningful careers. They want to contribute as much as possible to their work, environment, and communities. 70 percent are women and 45 percent are single women.

**Bros and Brittanys** work hard and play harder. They like to be on top of fashion and technology trends and tend to have more defined gender roles. They represent one-quarter of Canadian millennials.

**Diverse Strivers** long to be successful in many ways and value respect and status. They are the most likely to have a household income of six figures or more. They also happen to be big spenders.

"Digital tribalism is the process by which our mediated interactions have redefined and recontextualized human relationships into new and stranger forms. Our online identities and relationships are increasingly fragmented, with people inhabiting multiple, conflicting communities and contexts at once."

- DOUGLAS RUSHKOFF, "PROGRAM OR BE PROGRAMMED"

**Critical Counterculturalists** tend to be progressive-minded. They value diversity and gender equality and heavily oppose what they view as illegitimate or superficial status and authority. They long for authentic relationships. Almost half are single men and 83 percent have no religion.

**New Traditionalists** tend to be more religious than other tribes; 61 percent espouse conservative Protestantism. They are more likely to be married and tend to respect authority more than millennials. They value duty and some traditional values, but they are also environmentally conscious and often purchase green products. (2017, para 3).

Social Media Echo Chambers is the natural evolution of virtual social life. Echo chambers eliminate all that is not fundamental; they are fundamentalism stripped from any possibility of looking at the other side. An alienation of "the other". A study by the Pew Research Center found that 20% of social media users say they have changed their views on a social or political issue due to social media, while 59% say their social media feeds are mostly comprised of people who share their views. More of the same is the equation to a successfully implemented media strategy. It builds a continuous feed of content that is enough to engage a community on the same idea, repeatedly.

Polarization in Online Discourse has increased over time. In the virtual world, identity is fluid and a fantasy-driven personalized-world reality leads the way. My world, my rules.

If social media platforms have been the incubator for a network-scale evolution of echo chambers, the metaverse is the accelerator. As the RAND Corporation study points out, political polarization is more severe on social media than in face-to-face interactions, with individuals being more likely to express extreme political views online.

Users are exposed to only a limited range of information that aligns with their existing beliefs and opinions. Filter Bubbles lead to the reinforcement of beliefs and the exclusion of alternative perspectives.

The age of the neutral media is over. In fact, it never actually existed.

# Apolitical content is impossible.

**A study by the American Press Institute found that 60% of Americans believe that they regularly see news on social media that is biased, while a study by the Knight Foundation found that 49% of Americans believe that social media platforms are dividing the country.**

Playing on the binary nature of tribal interaction, virtual harassment and cyberbullying become valuable content. They take the headlines, motivate reaction, and are mostly used as extra evidence to mobilize communities and deepen beliefs within eco-chambers.

**According to a study by the Pew Research Center, 41% of American adults have experienced online harassment, and 66% have witnessed online harassment directed toward others. Political and ideological differences are cited as one of the main reasons for online harassment.**

Tribalism in online communities manifested through forums, chat rooms, and social media groups, and fueled by the "algorithm" is the basis of digital tribalism. A haven for the formation of tight-knit communities that can reinforce their group identity and exclude everyone and everything else.

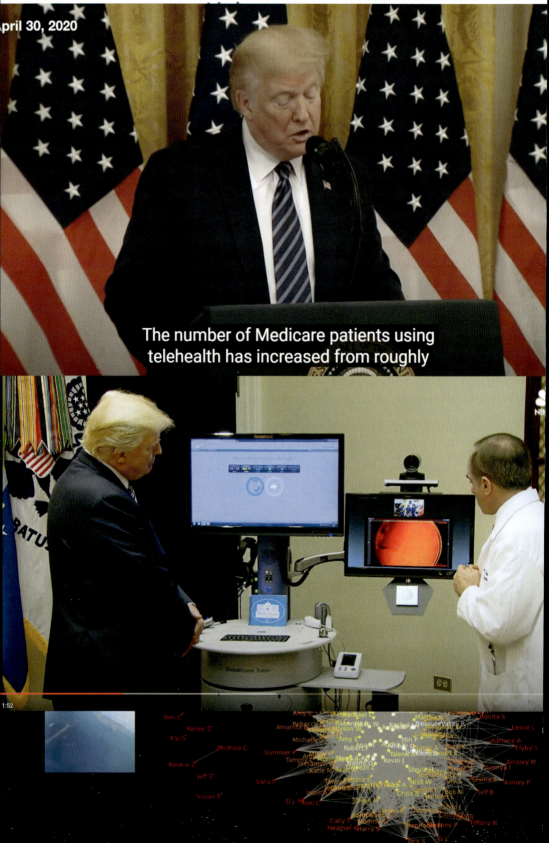

April 30, 2020

The number of Medicare patients using
telehealth has increased from roughly

# TELEMEDICINE

The Napoleonic semaphore was the world's first telegraph network, carrying messages across 19th-century France faster than ever before. In 1810, the telegraph system was extended to Venice and Amsterdam, and in 1813 to Mainz. In 1811, the telegraph was used to announce the birth of Napoleon's son.

The late 1800s show traces of communication between doctors and patients, Before the 1920s came in with radio technology utilized for medical consultations and education, allowing for remote access to medical expertise, the late 1800s show traces of communication between doctors and patients.

Post WWII, telephone-based consultations gained traction, and experiments on video conferencing for medical consultations took place around the 1960s, paving the way for visual communication in telemedicine.

The USSR conducted some of the earliest telemedicine experiments in the 1950s and 1960s, focusing on remote medical consultations and telephonic transmission of electrocardiogram (ECG) data.

With the space age coming to life, telemedicine technologies were used to monitor astronauts' vital signs, transmit medical data, and provide remote medical consultations during space missions, contributing to the advancement of space medicine. The 1970s witnessed both NASA and the Soviets pioneering telemedicine for remote health monitoring of astronauts in space, which led to the development of telemedicine technologies for remote patient care on Earth.

Russian researchers and institutions have made significant contributions to areas such as telecardiology, tele-oncology, teledermatology, and telepsychiatry.

HTTPS://WWW.YOUTUBE.COM/WATCH?V=X-STQ1QPNQAO

With the emergence of communication technologies and networks, the 1990s offered the right environment, as telemedicine gained momentum with the aid of the internet and digital technologies that enable real-time video consultations, remote diagnosis, and telemonitoring of patients.

The 2000s come in at no surprise, telemedicine continues to evolve with the integration of mobile technologies, allowing for telehealth consultations on smartphones and other mobile devices.

A decade later, telemedicine became increasingly mainstream, with the widespread adoption of telehealth services for remote consultations, remote patient monitoring, and virtual healthcare delivery. In 2010, the Russian government approved the "Telemedicine" state program, aimed at promoting telemedicine technologies and services across the country.

A decade ahead, the political response to the COVID-19 pandemic accelerates the adoption of telemedicine globally, it becomes an essential tool for delivering remote healthcare services and managing patient care during the pandemic. From Zoom calls to immersive consultations, the pandemic is an inflection point in the evolution of telemedicine. A new BC. is coined, Before COVID-19, and a new age of telemedicine in the metaverse is on its way.

Users engage with virtual health practitioners for remote consultations. Through avatars or virtual representations, users could interact with healthcare professionals, discuss their health concerns, and receive advice or recommendations for treatment.

Virtual health consultations in the metaverse are convenient and accessible, particularly for users who may have limited physical access to healthcare facilities in the physical world.

Wearables will link real metrics to virtual avatars and identity profiles. Virtual Health Screenings get users their virtual avatars assessed for various health parameters such as blood pressure, heart rate, and body mass index (BMI). They also provide users with insights into their health status and potential risk factors and prompt them to take appropriate actions for preventive care or further medical evaluation.

Virtual health monitoring is the new social obsession. Users opt for virtual health monitoring to get personalized treatment and recommendations. Their virtual avatars communicate with sensors or wearables to track various health parameters in real-time. This could include monitoring vitals, activity levels, sleep patterns, and other relevant health data.

The next market in telemedicine is virtual rehabilitation and therapy. Users engage in virtual rehabilitation or therapy sessions for physical or mental health conditions. Virtual reality (VR) and augmented reality (AR) technologies in immersive environments for rehabilitation or therapy allow users to participate in virtual exercises, simulations, or interventions to improve their health and well-being.

N94-11809

Final Project Report

# U.S.-U.S.S.R.
# Telemedicine Consultation
# Spacebridge to Armenia and Ufa

Presented at the

Third U.S.-U.S.S.R. Joint Working Group
on Space Biology and Medicine

December 1-9, 1989

Moscow and Kislovodsk, U.S.S.R.

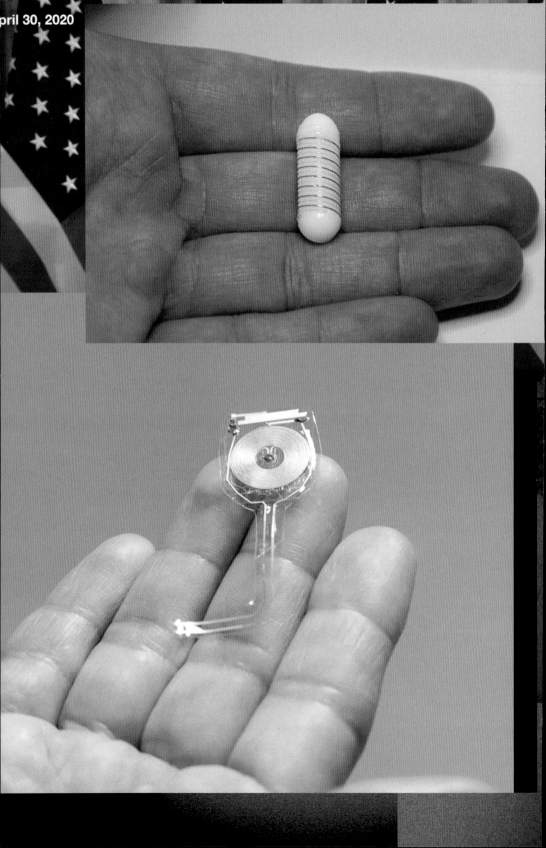

# ELECTROCEU-TICALS

## Chemistry to Electrobiophysics

The promise to democratize medicine, with the IoT-Open Source dream of the mass adoption of personal digital fabrication machines, offering people the freedom to produce locally, has not hit the mark. 3D printing medical pills at home, with P2P consent and a 2-step authentication, was a design idea that did not see light.

Pharmaceuticals have owned the scene. A natural monopoly that runs planetary health. The drug-based industry is now being challenged.

Propelled by cutting-edge advancements in neurotechnology and bioelectronics, a disruptive field is poised to reshape the landscape of medical interventions with its electrifying potential.

Electroceuticals, also known as bioelectronic medicine, have sparked a revolutionary reimagining of traditional pharmaceuticals in the realm of healthcare. Harnessing the power of electrical signals to modulate neural pathways, electroceuticals are ushering in a new era of personalized, targeted, and invasive - and non-invasive - therapies that hold immense promise for treating diverse diseases and conditions with unparalleled precision and efficacy.

The era of electroceuticals represents a seismic shift in our approach to medical interventions, charting a bold path toward the future of medicine.

Implantables, wearables, or external devices that deliver electrical or electromagnetic signals to specific nerves or regions of the body are all electroceuticals.

They are devices that are programmed and controlled to deliver precise and targeted electrical stimulation to modulate neural activity in a specific manner, depending on the intended therapeutic effect. They can also block neural pathways or neural networks in the body.

Aided by the potential of web 3.0 telemedicine, the interaction, monitoring, and control side of the development of the research involved within the electroceuticals industry will flourish.

Augmented senses are now automatic, as signals can be sent from the virtual space to the physical world. Virtual health assistants will automatically modulate the currents for improved breathing. Permanent monitoring is real.

Users are monitored on a continuous basis, while computational models learn and personalize the solutions per user.

# Electroceuticals are the pharmaceuticals of the next century.

**Here is a brief timeline**

→ **Early 19th century** - The concept of using electrical currents for medical purposes is introduced, with early experiments in electrotherapy for pain relief and muscle stimulation.

→ **Late 19th to early 20th century** - Early electroceutical devices, such as electroconvulsive therapy (ECT) machines, were developed and used for psychiatric treatment.

→ **1950s** - The discovery of electrical activity in the human body, including the development of the first cardiac pacemaker, opens up new possibilities for using electrical stimulation as a therapeutic approach.

→ **1960s-1970s** - Advancements in miniaturization and implantable device technology led to the development of neurostimulation devices, such as deep brain stimulators (DBS) for treating Parkinson's disease and other neurological conditions.

→ **1980s-1990s** - Electroceutical devices continue to evolve with the development of implantable neuro-stimulation devices for various applications, including spinal cord stimulation for chronic pain management and cochlear implants for hearing loss.

→ **2000s** - The field of electroceuticals expands with the development of non-invasive electrical stimulation techniques, such as transcutaneous electrical nerve stimulation (TENS) for pain relief and transcranial magnetic stimulation (TMS) for psychiatric and neurological disorders.

→ **2010s** - Electroceuticals gain increasing attention and investment as a promising field for treating various medical conditions, including chronic pain, epilepsy, depression, and other neurological and neuropsychiatric disorders.

→ **2020s** - Advances in neurostimulation, bioelectronic medicine, and wearable electroceutical devices continue to drive innovation in the field, with ongoing research and development focused on improving the safety, efficacy, and accessibility of electroceutical therapies.

ecology == economy.
ecology == economy.
ecology == economy.

# ADDRESS ECOLOGIES

When all is reduced to address, a new archetype of ecology emerges— the address ecology, one that lives on servers, ledgers, blockchains, and interaction. In this situation, economy and ecology do not only complement each other but merge into one. This is a context where ecology is economy.

Address ecologies are the complex and homogenous ecosystems of heterogeneous physical, digital, and hybrid objects flattened to addresses that make up the environments we live in. Addressing and being addressed, as well as finding, sharing, and manipulating addresses, are crucial activities in our everyday lives, and they are changing rapidly in the digital age.

New ecologies of addressing mechanisms and addresses are pivotal while handling complex and evolving relationships between digital technologies, spatial data, and socio-economic processes.

Addresses are physical and virtual addressing systems that are used to identify and locate entities within the digital ecosystem. Address Ecologies encompass various locational identifiers, such as IP addresses, domain names, URLs (Uniform Resource Locators), and other forms of addressing used within the spatial internet.

Address ecologies are political. They shape the ways in which digital technologies are organized, governed, and experienced. Address Ecologies become the environment, taking over the spatial, social, and geopolitical dimensions of the digital world.

Address Ecologies enable the functioning of the digital infrastructure, which enables communication, information flow, and networked interactions. In parallel, address ecologies are limiting, as they empower a mesh of surveillance, control, and inequality. For more context, addressing systems can be used to monitor and regulate access to digital resources, shape power relations, and influence the distribution of information and services.

Address ecologies are the most fundamental element within the spatial internet's infrastructural fabric.

The spatial internet will mutually thrive with advanced address ecologies applied across domains: digital, spatial, and social. Digital addressing handling IP addresses or URLs locate virtual spaces, objects, or avatars.

Virtual spaces, virtual overlays, and extended reality content will have their own spatial addresses or coordinates used to represent their location within the experience. Spatial addresses are the enablers of navigation, teleportation, or communication within the metaverse.

Social addressing collapses both communal and personal information. Social address ecologies host social networks and communities as they acquire unique addresses or identifiers that represent their virtual presence and interactions. It is safe to consider them a precondition to connecting with or joining groups or communities, and forming virtual relationships within the metaverse.

Avatar address ecologies are host Avatars' own addresses or identifiers that designate and differentiate them from other avatars. Communication, identification, and interaction with other avatars or virtual entities will drive this ecology within the spatial internet.

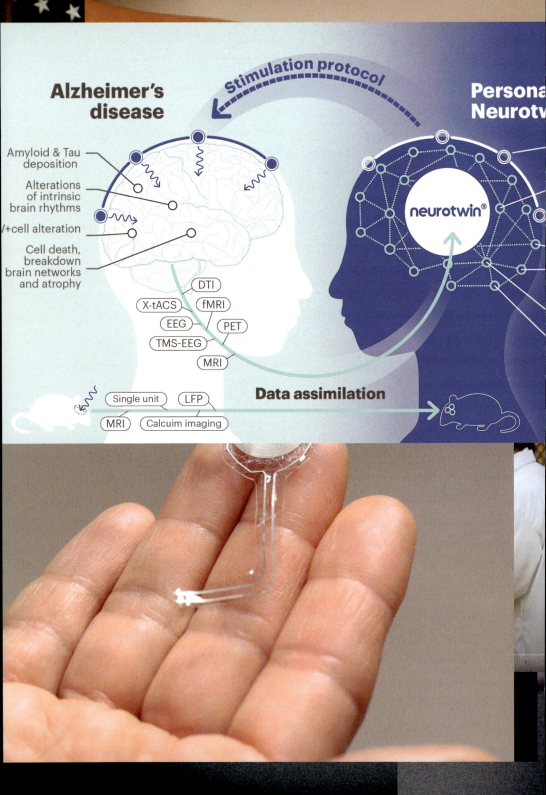

# NEURO-TWINS

## Neuro-Metric IDs

I was introduced to the NeuroTwin project by two scientists I met at the NeuroTechX Global Hackathon 22 I was organizing in Barcelona. An ambitious project by Starlab, dwelling on the premise that "personalized brain models can capture novel neuroscience insights, reduce uncertainty in diagnosis, and provide the foundation for therapeutic breakthroughs."

Thereafter, personalized brain models are custom-designed, and embed individual biophysical and physiological characteristics.

By 2024 the project promises to "develop advanced brain models that characterize individual pathology and predict the physiological effects of transcranial electromagnetic stimulation, and use them to design optimal brain stimulation protocols in Alzheimer's disease.

HTTPS://WWW.UPF.EDU/EN/WEB/
FOCUS/ENGINYERIES-I-TIC/-/ASSET_
PUBLISHER/HPTUZEWT2UC7/CONTENT/
ID/243467700/MAXIMIZED

Personalized brain models, or Neurotwins are the brain's share of telemedicine and electroceuticals. Brains are internalized through digitization and monitored using digital techniques.

As neuropsychiatric disorders are a significant global burden, personalized hybrid brain models, - neurotwins or NeTs- combining the physics of electromagnetism with physiology, will play a pivotal role in advancing our understanding and optimiza- tion of non-invasive brain stimulation for individual patients.

Neurotwins: A hyper-personalized and targeted solution through computational frameworks that integrate data from various scales and levels of detail, encompassing the mechanisms of interaction between electric fields and brain networks, as well as neuroimaging data assimilation.

It is across the personalized spaces of the spatial internet, health rooms, and private spaces with neurotwins monitored continuously. Daily health reports and notifications will line up at the front of the health booth waiting to be read.

NeuroTwins are brain avatars.
They are neuroscience for the age of the spatial internet.

https://cordis.europa.eu/project/id/101017716
https://www.neurotwin.eu/

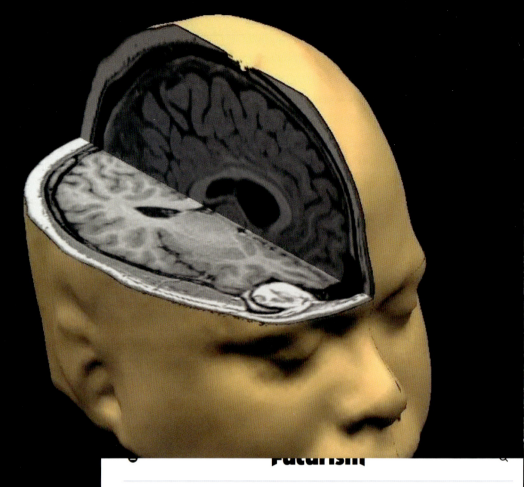

FUTURISM | 4.25.16, 4.26 PM EDT by JUNE JAVELOSA

# Scientists Can Now Identify Individuals Based on Brain Waves— And It's 100% Accurate

Brainprints could one day replace fingerprints.

Hard Science / Binghamton University / Brainprints / EEG

# BRAIN PRINTS

## Neuro-prints are the new fingerprints.

Personalized brain maps or profiles of an individual's brain structure, function, or activity patterns.

Neuroprints are unique to each individual and can provide valuable information about the individual's brain health, cognitive abilities, and potential risk for neurological disorders.

Users have their neuroprint integrated into their virtual avatar, representing their digital presence. Avatars can then interact with other avatars or virtual objects within the metaverse based on the user's real-time brain activity or other neuroprint data.

Neuroprints are used to personalize virtual experiences or interventions, such as virtual neurorehabilitation programs or cognitive training exercises within the metaverse.

They are the basis of data-driven decision-making or personalized content creation. Virtual environments within the metaverse are dynamically generated or adapted based on an individual's neuroprint data and feed on preferences, cognitive abilities, or emotional states.

This is a hyper-personalized immersive virtual experience that is tailored to the individual's unique neurocognitive profile.

University of Wa

# NEURO-IN-HABITAT·ION

The act of control through the nervous system precedes neurotechnology as a measuring discipline. The end of the 1800s kick-started a century of neurotechnology from humble beginnings, poking frog limbs and dead cats' still-alive neurons.

Measuring the brain has become mainstream, but writing to the brain has not, yet. Writing back to the brain, or neuromodulation, is executed at best using invasive devices, targeting bundles of neurons for inhibition or activation.

Controlling external stimuli, through brain commands, through brain-computer interfaces evolves to become bidirectional. Rats can play Doom, and monkeys control robotic arms as machinic limbs to pick up and eat bananas. Neurogaming becomes gaming itself, all games have BCI SDKs. The spatial internet is interfaced with through interfaces that listen to data from the brain.

Neurogames feed back to the brain. Sensations will be communicated through technology, and perceived naturally. Data dimensions collapse.

Living the metaverse "neurally" is its full capacity. The physical and the virtual fuse, and the last frontier of exploration join the party. Brains are no longer sacred. Everything is hackable.

Neuro-inhabitation in the spatial is what undermines the premise of "living in the metaverse". It makes cyber-space literal. The spatial and the neural are in direct communication.

HTTPS://WWW.HACKSTER.IO/NEWS/
THIS-TETRIS-LIKE-GAME-IS-PLAYED-TELE-
PATHICALLY-BY-THREE-PEOPLE-SIMULTA-
NEOUSLY-72368E546A81

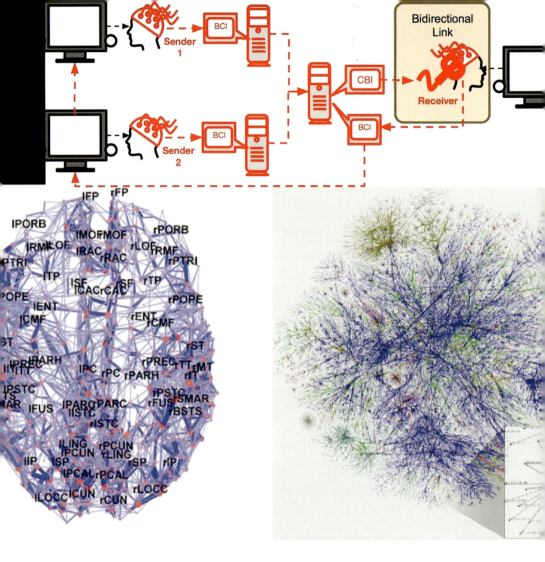

Human cerebral cortical network

Routing paths through a portion of the In

IoT becomes IoN.

# ION - INTERNET OF NEURONS

From Arpanet to the Internet of Things, accompanied by advancements in brain-computer interfaces, biocomputation, and artificial intelligence, the Internet of Neurons - IoN- (Sempreboni, D et al 2021) seems to be the next chapter on the Internet timeline. Hence, a seamless bidirectional communication between our brains and the internet opened a new era of interaction with the physical and digital worlds.

The second Copernican turn has not sufficiently changed the design discourse yet. Thus a new raison d'être is to be operated upon, a pressing need for a design agenda grounded in a projective entanglement with the present elephants-in-the-room[to be]. Specifically, bio-computation, artificial [designable] intelligence, data at scale, and eventually IoN.

We stand upon unprecedented access to designing the neural [both mineral and biological]. Complementary to the material component -and operating at the electrical layer- interactions with neural ecologies, or other sub-ecologies, are rather read-write mechanisms. They are mechanisms that allow not only data mining from electrically active neural environments but also writing back, by changing physical features such as the spatial layout or wiring. Hence, it is an approach that performs on the spatial distributions of material assemblages to construct intelligence.

In parallel, the capacity to bidirectionally communicate between our brains and the web opens doors to a radical shift in design, at the core, moving from a discourse that serves the user; i.e. from **designing for the user, to a "designing the user" directly.**

As nervous systems are connected to the Internet, the planetary scale mesh of connected devices expands, evolving from the Internet of Things to the Internet of Neurons.

The internet of neurons is the spatial internet's paradigmatic shift, where users are connected bidirectionally. Neurological, technological, and social changes are yet to unlock milestones enabling such a shift.

The internet of neurons is yet to come.

Neurons, biological or synthetic, are interconnected using advanced iterations of technologies such as brain-computer interfaces (BCIs), neuroprosthetics, or neural implants. These interconnected neurons exchange information, process data, and collaborate to perform complex tasks or solve problems collectively.

IoN proposes a new idea of creating a collective intelligence by linking neurons together, enabling them to communicate and share information, much like how devices are interconnected in the Internet of Things (IoT).

IoN will revolutionize both AI and cognitive computing. It feeds into new ways of understanding brain function, enhancing cognitive abilities, and developing novel brain-computer interfaces for medical or technological applications.

Ultimately, it unlocks the highway to brain-to-brain communication. Individuals across the panel can exchange information directly from their brains, or enable neural networks to communicate and collaborate across different brain regions or even across different individuals.

A conceptual framework for the spatial internet to come.

# THE PLANETARY-SCALE NERVOUS SYSTEM

A planetary-scale mesh reconstructs a generative process where Geology is a precondition for Biology, and Biology is a precondition for intelligence. Intelligence, in turn, then consumes all the above to create new geologies, biologies, and intelligence simultaneously. Examined at the electrical layer, the electrical is conceived as an advanced state of the charged, and the neural as an advanced state of the electrical.

## NERVOUS SYSTEMS
**The analogy is due to its relevance.**

The Nervous System is a complex network of cells and tissues that coordinates and regulates the functions of an organism. It is divided into the central nervous system (CNS) and the peripheral nervous system (PNS), and is responsible for essential functions such as sensory perception, motor control, cognition, and regulation of bodily processes. Neurons, which transmit electrical and chemical signals, and glial cells that provide support and protection to neurons, are the main types of cells in the nervous system. The nervous system allows organisms to perceive and respond to their environment, adapt to changes, and carry out complex behaviors and cognitive processes.

Essentially, the nervous system serves as the communication and control center of the body, enabling it to receive, process, and respond to information from both internal and external environments.

## PLANETARY-SCALE NERVOUS SYSTEM

Similarly, it is a multi-layered, bottom-up, multi-scalar, heterogeneous, and electrical system at the scale of the planet.

The argument is for conceptualizing a planetary-scale nervous system through the device of Electrical Ecologies. The Electrical in this context is a manner of functionally and operationally flattening all electrical objects [ from charged matter to human brains] to define a new design agenda aligned with an understanding of intelligence as a neural effect of material assemblages.

## AT THE ARCHITECTURE AND URBAN SCALE

Grounded in disciplinary questions and the present-future technosphere, the research is interested in designing neural ecologies - mineral and biological, organic and non-organic assemblages [from silicon assemblages to organoids]. Accordingly, shifts in the material medium in architecture affect the discourse, and thus, the research explores micro ecologies of a near future where brains become grounds for design at the electrical layer specifically.
Along these lines, the manner in which the mentioned assets are recruited is pivotal to producing a viable framework for developing urbanscapes, architecture, and environments. By that, producing ones that surpass the current format of, at best, direct automation, to a more subtle and complex interaction scheme that requires a new kind of agency.

While architecture can be understood as a medium that affects, or is perceived as an experience and therefore changes the user, a shift towards directly manipulating brain circuitry to produce interiority as architecture is of interest here. Intelligent spatial behavior based on the unconscious is an example of how brain-computer interfaces can change how we design.

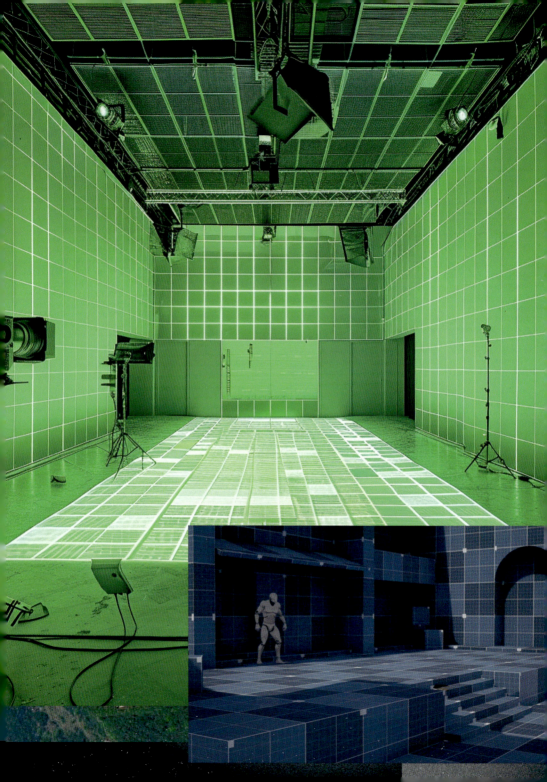

# GREEN-SCREEN ARCHITECTURE

**Let's draw a clear identifying axis when it comes to architecture, one that is bound by the Abstract to Phenomenological. The abstract is concerned with architectural ideas, concepts, formal strategies, spatial structure, etc. The phenomenological is motivated by liveliness, experience, and spirit. In simple terms, the first is concerned with the spatial structure, or the logic, and the second with how the space feels or is experienced.**

Throughout Architecture history, team abstract cared less about buildings, as their asset is in the ideas and drawings; buildings were yet another medium. Architecture can be mediated through texts, models, etc. On the other side, team phenomena had the building as their all, as it's the basis for the experience. No building, no experience.

With the evolution of technologies such as VR and AR, or XR, with milestone context detection and anchoring precision, the physical aspect of the spaces we inhabit becomes increasingly less important. The dissolution of the screen as we know it, moving to a more immersive one, requires and is adopted as graphics. The virtual and the physical live across blurry borders and they function as one.

Just like a simple green screen can host any movie background, and a QR code can be an anchor to any AR simulation, the physical elements of space will be reduced to its bare-minimum functions. It will also be open to host an open-ended library of downloadable filters and effects for users to experience.

One can argue that the space for abstraction in architecture has been on the decline, and limited mostly to research, computational workflow building, and writing. With architects and designers operating within the realm of the virtual, we will see the emergence of a prominent event-based on-demand design.

Metaverse environments are places where the filter logic is widely applicable based on a certain interaction. A cube can become anything. The geometry is an anchor for a customized extra layer of visual and graphical representations.

Physical architecture becomes a bland and blank essential for a more flamboyant, almost disposable graphical content.

At the virtual layer, architecture becomes an inevitable crust to a more important content of how an address ecology thrives. It is an economy where architecture is reduced in its effects and attention attraction metrics, and its resolution and interface capacity as a medium of exchange.

Without it, there is no economy; but it takes no place in the exchange. It is a decisive factor that still has no financial value, just like the air we breathe. It is a precondition for life, but who has ever bought air?

That could be architecture in the metaverse.

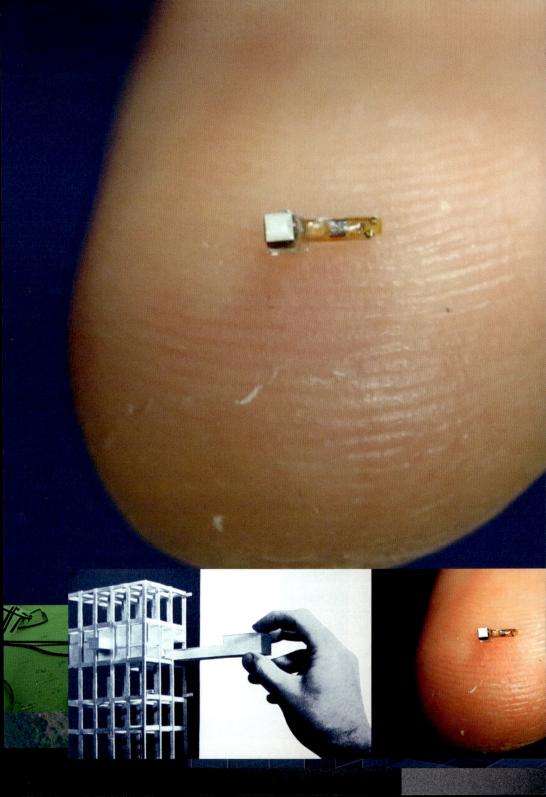

# THE ARCHITEC-TURAL IMPLANT

## Neural Exaptation

The concept put forward by paleontologists Elisabeth Vrba and Stephen Gould in 1982, "Exaptation" (Gould, S et al, 1982) is described by them as "a counterpart to the more familiar concept of adaptation." Exaptation is the process by which features acquire functions for which they were not originally adapted or selected.

A function that was not originally set implies an expected outcome of several functions that haven't been exactly met. Evolutionary systems acquire functionality at a later stage of development, the sequence is gene - structure - function, which implies that function is what the process concludes to. So what is really meant here is a shift in the function or trait during evolution within the two specified circumstances. The first is when things are co-opted for a new use after being evolved to a particular function [an adaptation ], or the second case applies to characters whose evolutionary origin can not be specified and is thus co-opted for a new use.

Neural Exaptation within EE requires a reappropriation or overtaking of objects at any entry scale to arrive at a neural object. Neural exaptation is the neuroticization of electric objects. In this situation, Neural exaptation is the process in which the environment, as referred to in the affordance section, is enriched by increasing all system layers' capacity.

## Neural Affordance

Coined by psychologist James J. Gibson, affordance in this context is "what the environment offers the individual". Being part of his 1966 book: The Senses Considered as Perceptual Systems, the term is resurrected in his 1979 book, The Ecological Approach to Visual Perception: "The verb to afford is found in the dictionary, the noun affordance is not. I have made it up. I mean by it something that refers to both the environment and the animal in a way that no existing term does. It implies the complementarity of the animal and the environment." (Gibson, 1979, p. 127)

Two aspects of the terms are of interest to EE. The first is the complementarity of animals and environment, and by that forming a closed circle. The second is the potentiality within any environment, as it is not merely what it gives or offers, but all the other possibilities that could emerge in some other cases. The likelihood of probable phenomena becomes a more decisive aspect, which would be suggestive but not definitive. The environment is not nature. The environment is everything else, i.e. the environment is relative to each thing in such a way that every other thing becomes the environment. Environments offer stimuli that are selectively sucked in and processed to make sense of. Affordance is a flexible and dynamic term that so far seems necessary for our brains to form and function.

Neural or Electrical affordance, then, is what becomes the environment within the electrical layer. The more objects involved, the bigger the environment, as all that is not the object becomes the environment of that object.

### Neural Interiority
Intelligences, as mentioned before, is a plural term that reflects the ontological variability of various forms of intelligence; biological and mineral. Transitioning from the larger scale to the scale of the urban or the architectural, the agency of mineral intelligence is expanding the discourse, and informing design questions is vital. While it is trivial to ask if AI algorithms can produce 3-dimensional objects, a more subtle question to pose would be whether creative AI algorithms are capable of producing interiority: the condition created by enclosures, contrasted by the perception of the subject.

## "ALL ARE ARCHITECTS. EVERYTHING IS ARCHITECTURE."

1968, HOLLEIN H.

In an attempt to test that, spatial ecologies and spatial intelligence surface as a possibility of creating spatial assemblages - using machine intelligence- that are capable of expressing a complexity of assemblage at the level of intelligence.

Spatial AI Ecologies is an attempt to create an ecology of ai-generated objects, such as the enclosure, the population, spatial sound, and digital material. These spatial ecologies are emergent of machine intelligence and thrive in the same environment.

### Common grounds - New grounds
Our brains have been thought of as a common ground or a middle one between what is "out there" and our conscious experiences. This idea stems from an understanding of the brain as a reality machine. A system that allows us to experience what is out there, as is, through sensory input, that is then decoded by the brain to produce experience.

The following is to confute this idea and put forward the brain as a new ground, based on the current scientific conception of what a human brain is, what it does, and how we actually experience the world.

## "There is a change as to the importance of "meaning" and "effect". Architecture affects."

1968, HOLLEIN H.

### Does our perceptual system favor reality?
Whatever an objective reality is, are our brains wired to comprehend that reality as close as possible to what it is? How can we evaluate that? And if not, what is the way then?

Our realities are perceptions. All perceptions are self-constructed.

Brains host the process, the "black box" between information and affect; the processing layer of where things happen.

If perception happens in the brain, alternative perceptions are possible through new information inputs.

Humanists have designed spaces to influence perception by manipulating what is being sensed. Neurotechnology enables the engineering of such information. This is the inverse design of stimulus.

The task is no longer designing an object of architecture for a user, but designing the object of architecture and the user simultaneously.

**Designing the user.**

# THE BRAIN IS ARCHITECTURE'S NEXT FRONTIER.

### Space in the brain
Spatiality, or interiority is a complex phenomenon that emerges as holistic, as it involves several stimuli, sound, light, balance, etc. The science of all the elements is well-evolved, but the space is probably the least spread out.

Spatiality breaks down neurologically into a set of objects, "place" is perhaps one of the most crucial and obvious. From 1971 - the year of discovery- onward, we have been dealing with what O'Keefe and Jonathon Dostrovsky discovered experimenting with rats; "Place Cells". The other interesting discovery is "Grid Cells", achieved by researchers and scientists at the Centre for the Biology of Memory (CBM) in Norway in 2005.

Place cells are the celebration of various parameters regarding spatial perception, specifically

happening in the hippocampus, which is capable of creating spatial maps. In other and more precise words, place fields get information from the occipital, parietal, and temporal lobes network where the perception of features such as depth and motion happens.

These place fields are non-anthropocentric, as Harry Mallgrave states in "Hapticity" that these fields seem to be strictly related to spatial geometry. Moreover, building on a 2004 study carried out on virtual spaces, mainly museums, the" brain automatically distinguishes between objects at navigationally relevant and irrelevant locations". It was found that it happens independently of the participants' attention to the objects.

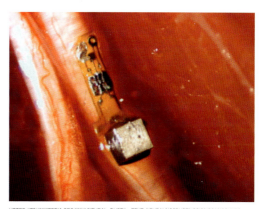

"Place cells fire whenever an animal occupies a specific location in its environment, with each place cell firing at a different spot. Grid cells generate virtual maps of the surroundings that resemble grids of repeating triangles."

"A grid cell is a type of neuron within the entorhinal cortex that fires at regular intervals as an animal navigates an open area, allowing it to understand its position in space by storing and integrating information about location, distance, and direction."

## The Architectural Evolution
Architecture's evolution is destined to step away from the physical as an essential part of architecture.

## Architecture as buildings - Architecture for wood and stone
Wood and stone are shaped by hammers and geometry sets that make up the projects. Architects were builders, immediately communicating with the physicality of structures.

## Architecture as drawings of buildings - Architecture for Paper
Drawings changed architecture, they encoded design intentions and building systems. Architecture, still, in its fundamental phase will change nature with the emergence of indexical systems.

Indexical systems enlarged the space between the logics and the building. They freed the architects from the constraints of the physical. Architecture surpassed the drawing. Drawings of buildings are obsolete, systems take over.

## Architecture as computation - Architecture for Computers
The indexical system in architecture is perhaps the immediate precursor to the emergence of computation in architecture - before actual computers

At its apex, code and modeling softwares allowed for a new way of doing architecture. Structure became spatial, and form became content.

## Architecture for screens - Architecture for screens
BIM systems and game engines started gaining traction, as associative design software was at its peak. Graphical user interfaces layered on top of programming architecture made it accessible and became the state of the art.

## Architecture as Media - Architecture for wearables
Wearables and immersive interfaces changed the screen; and almost internalized it. Content is now immediately experienced.

The shift coincides with evolving AI models for creative application, changing the scene for design as a prompt-based endeavor.

Human-machine interactions and machine protocols came in as binding agents, enabling a new form of architecture. Responsive and immediate.

## Architecture as brain activity - Architecture for the brain
The natural evolution of architecture is from basic human-machine interfaces to brain-computer interfaces, HMI to BCI. Moving one step away from the building, architecture finally becomes the building again, it becomes space itself.

"A house is a machine for living"

1923 - CORBUSIER

**DESIGNING FOR THE USER IS PAST.
DESIGNING THE USER IS THE PRESENT STATE OF
ARCHITECTURE.**

**Our brains can absorb computers, but computers cannot absorb our brains yet.**

The next design medium for architecture is the brain implant. It is the designing and structuring of the system of electrical activity that generates perception, by manipulating the input or by becoming the immediate input.

Designing for the brain, or in other terms, redesigning the brain, given the state of the art, requires an optimal state. It requires a state of interacting with the brain directly, without passing along the bridge of the senses.

Technology becomes the interface, rather than the senses. That claim then puts into question the way design is brought into the world. How is design produced, when housed by brain chips? Our nervous system is electric in the way it receives and transmits inputs and outputs respectively, and hence it requires a compatible other to interact with.

Ludwig lab of

"The building is not the machine.
Space is the machine."

NICK DALTON / BILL HILLIER 1994

Do they teach hand gestures in Italian language classes?

# DIGITAL BODY LANGUAGE

From hieroglyphics to emoticons, an image is worth probably a couple of words. Emoticons art of Avatars' aura, combinations of characters representing facial expressions and emotions in digital communication, serve as a form of extended digital body language. Different emoticons convey varying levels of emotional intensity, and their usage patterns reflect an individual's emotional state, personality, and communication style.

Beyond body language, the spatial internet is a space of embodiment. Avatars, digital representations of individuals in the virtual or augmented space, serve as the body's extension into the digital body language. The customization of avatars, including appearance, clothing, and accessories, reflects an individual's personal identity, self-expression, and social status.

The poses, gestures, and movements of avatars also convey non-verbal cues, such as confidence, assertiveness, or playfulness, influencing how others perceive and interact with the individual in the metaverse.

The spatial internet's digital body language goes beyond Erica Dhawan's interpretation of the term, as an emerging skill to comprehend beyond verbal communication. Her book "Digital Body Language: How to Build Trust and Connection No Matter the Distance." , explores the nuances of non-verbal cues and communication in the digital age while confined to the internet as we knew it, devoid of embodied interaction between virtual representations.

Right topic, not so right context.

Multimedia Integration expands the scene for the integration of various multimedia elements, such as images, videos, and audio, to enhance communication and self-expression. To list a few examples, sharing memes, GIFs, or multimedia-rich posts conveys humor, sarcasm, or creativity.

The use of voice chat or virtual voice assistants adds vocal cues, tone, and inflection to digital communication. Multimedia becomes a natural periphery of an intrinsically media-based existence.

Coordinated gestures or movements among avatars during virtual events or group activities enhance social cohesion, shared experiences, and emotional connection. A new theory of body language for the spatial internet is the interaction synchronization theory: the synchronization of interactions between individuals, avatars, and virtual objects. Virtual objects, such as gifts, emojis, or virtual actions are also used to synchronize interactions and convey social cues such as gratitude, empathy, or playfulness.

Submerged within a network of interconnected addresses, the environment and the avatar become complementary entities, slightly opportunistic in their presence dynamic.

Contextual Adaptation is key. Digital body language adapts and evolves based on the environment, internet cultural norms, and individual preferences, led by their wildest dream.

Different virtual platforms, communities, or social contexts have distinct norms and expectations for digital body language, influencing how individuals express themselves and interpret others.

Influencers develop their own digital body language styles, incorporating their personality, communication habits, and social goals in the metaverse. A self-fulfilling cycle of trendy digital language gimmicks, and a new age of social signaling.

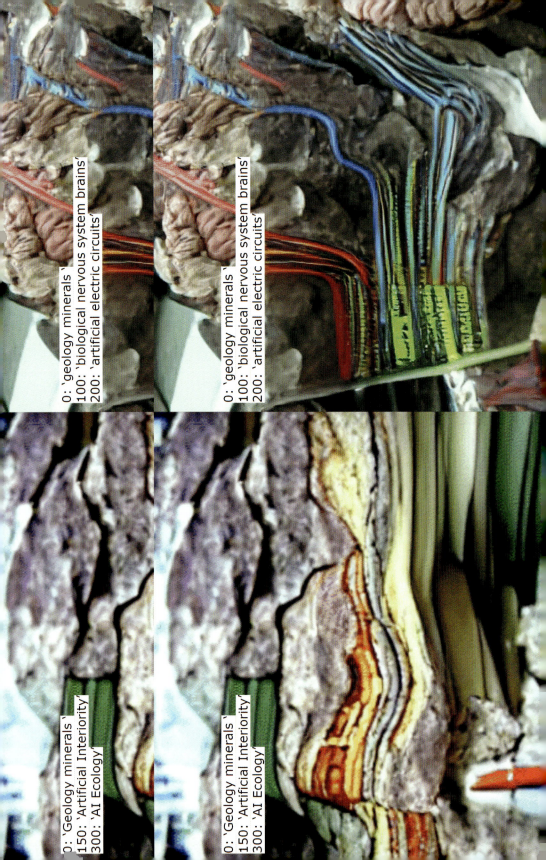

0: 'geology minerals '
100: 'biological nervous system brains'
200: 'artificial electric circuits'

0: 'geology minerals '
100: 'biological nervous system brains'
200: 'artificial electric circuits'

0: 'Geology minerals '
150: 'Artificial Interiority'
300: 'AI Ecology'

0: 'Geology minerals '
150: 'Artificial Interiority'
300: 'AI Ecology'

# MINERAL INTELLIGENCE

## Geology is ground zero. When assembled in certain ways, intelligence emerges.

Artificial intelligence is a misleading concept that dwells on imprecise terminology. Artificial is a vague concept that creates a distance between the core idea of the term and its usage. The word itself carries negative connotations and associations.

Artificial is the opposite of genuine or real.

Artificiality is meaningless.

Mineral intelligence challenges the conventional understanding of artificial intelligence (AI) as of its very etymology. Intelligence is an emergent property of material assemblages, in this case, mainly composed of minerals, holding a potential for cognitive capacities and exhibiting complex behaviors and functionalities.

Mineral Intelligence emphasizes the physicality and materiality of the technology that enables AI, and the critical raw materials required for it to happen. Intelligence is classified as biological and synthetic, organic and non-organic, biological and mineral.

Material assemblages yield cognition, specifically mineralogical cognition capacities such as perception, memory, and decision-making. Synthetic intelligent systems process and interpret information from their environment, adapt their behaviors based on feedback and exhibit emergent properties that resemble cognitive processes.

Self-assembly and emergent behavior: Mineral intelligence could leverage the self-assembly properties of minerals, where they spontaneously organize into complex structures or patterns based on their inherent properties and interactions. This could lead to emergent behaviors and functionalities, where collective behavior arises from the interactions of individual minerals, resulting in complex and adaptive systems.

Computation, as we refer to it, is generally mineral-based computation. It utilizes the intrinsic properties of minerals such as their phase transitions to perform computation and information processing. Computing agents evolve into adaptive mineral networks, as minerals communicate and exchange information to collectively adapt to changing environments.

Mineral intelligence is integrated in a pan-disciplinary fashion, spanning materials science, AI, complex systems theory, and cognitive science.

The wording of synthetic intelligence changes inherently the attitude on ecology, technology, and the emergence of augmented intelligence in all its forms. Through advancements in mineralogical cognition, self-assembly and emergent behavior, mineral-based computation, adaptive mineral networks, and pan-disciplinary integration, synthetic intelligence establishes advanced leaps.

As mineral intelligence continues to advance, it reshapes the landscape of technology, ecology, and intelligence, ushering in a new era of augmented intelligence that transcends traditional boundaries.

Breakthroughs in synthetic intelligence catalyze the development of augmented intelligence, where biological and synthetic intelligence are integrated. This convergence results in the design of hybrid systems that combine the strengths of both biological and synthetic intelligence to achieve a new level of problem-solving and adaptability.

# Intelligence is an emergent property of material assemblages

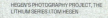

HEGEN'S PHOTOGRAPHY PROJECT, THE LITHIUM SERIES I.TOM HEGEN

# GEO LOGICS

## Geography
## Information
## Architec

**VICENTE GUA**

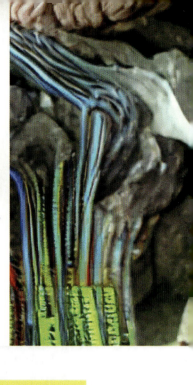

# Bio
# LOGICS

## Minerals
## Biology
## Intelligence

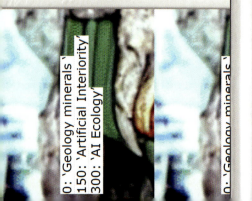

0: 'Geology minerals `
150: 'Artificial Interiority'
300: 'AI Ecology'

0: 'Geology minerals `

# BIO-LOGICS

It was while preparing my slides for a talk that I made a GIF that encapsulated a profound and necessary evolution in discourse, from Geo-logics to Bio-logics. Geo-logics refers to the logics of the planet; Architecture and urbanism for the information society. It encompasses the extraction of ecological and geographical notions, techniques, aesthetics, and logics, and brings them to urbanism and architecture.

While Geo-Logics focuses on Geography, Information, and Architecture, Bio-Logics is its manner of operating within the next turn in the internet and technology, focused on Intelligence, Biocomputation, and Ecology.

Urbanists and architects have been able to project at a global scale for the first time. Networks are at the epicenter of urbanism and architecture while trying to maintain an internal discourse, internalized techniques, and aesthetics of the age. The 2000s have been a time of obsession with low-fi, fold-adoring, geography-adopting techniques, and photoshop-ecology.

To approach architecture and urbanism as part of the 'natural' process requires the homogenization of the operation space. Architecture is nature. Urbanism is nature. Nature with capital N is dead.

Biologics are the next phase of Geologics. Geology evolves into biology.

It is a continuum that makes up Ecology. Ecology == Ecologies, a plural notion of coexisting sub-ecologies. A shift from geography to geology and from architecture to intelligence is understood as an emergent property of spatially-organized material assemblages.

Geography takes a new stance, akin to a new tectonic plate that supports a new ecology of rapid transformation. Geography is real.

Intelligence is an emergent property of matter. Cities are too.

Biologics reduces architecture back to its fundamentals. It perceives all as ecology and operates with intelligence as a goal. This calls for a new ecological consciousness, one that admits all is one.

**No backyards, no hierarchy.**

Within the bounds of the next shift of the internet, and society consequently, the very notion of ecologies and spatial intelligence becomes fragile. Thus, there is a vital need to redefine a new framework for comprehension and action.

Electrical ecologies allow intricate maneuvering within the technology and information-dense space, mobilizing a transformation force at the electrical layer from the cerebral to the planetary.

All space is advertisement space.

# THE ATTENTION ECONOMY

The attention economy is competitive, frenetic, and captivating while distracting. It is an attention-grabbing, alluring, demanding, exploitative, fragmented, and insatiable phenomenon that governs the internet world we live in.

Attention is a scarce commodity. Agents, whether humans or bots, can provide a certain amount of it. Attention is always assigned value through a loophole, it always engages a third party.

Its allocation is influenced by factors such as information overload, digital distractions, and the constant influx of stimuli in the modern digital era. The attention economy is characterized by a rapid energetic pace, with attention-grabbing techniques and strategies employed to capture and maintain users' focus in a highly competitive landscape. Users are continuously bombarded with content.

Media platforms, advertisers, and content creators compete for individuals' attention in order to capture and hold their focus for as long as possible.

Every second matters.

Environmental psychology influences a new placemaking theory of the sensory architecture to come.

Iconic billboards, digital displays, and neon lights continuously swamp spectators with a constant stream of advertisements, entertainment, and information. An overwhelming sensory experience of Times Square is curated to capture and maintain people's attention, creating a hyper-stimulating environment where brands and messages vie for attention simultaneously.

The dazzling lights, elaborate facades, and immersive experiences of the casinos, hotels, and entertainment venues capture and hold attention, creating a sensory overload that is aimed at maximizing engagement and consumption.

The emergence of the shopping mall as a new universal typology, as Koolhaas presents in "Mutations", is the commodification of everything.

## All space is advertisement space.

The attention economy is a density indicator. It is a marker on the intensity map of possible available attention. The massive digital billboards, neon signs, and bright lights that constantly race for attention at the Shibuya Crossing in Tokyo, one of the busiest pedestrian intersections in the world, make the case.

Metaverse environments, just like websites, are full of pop-ups, ads, animation, and interactive elements. The spatial dimension magnifies the immersiveness of the experience. The shallowness of the content does not allow for close reading.

Fast content is disposable content.

The attention economy is a swarm of filtered content designed for fast consumption. It is rendered to impress. The wow factor is everything. In fragments, it tries to keep a high threshold, ever-increasing the attention baseline for focus.

**Extraction Facts**

Serving Size 1 Phone

Amount Per Serving

Weight **164g**

Carbon **64kg CO2e**

| | |
|---|---|
| Minerals | 30% |
| Labour | 10% |
| Manufacturing | 60% |
| Production | 40% |
| Assembly | 20% |
| Supply Chain | 10% |

Note that this is not a major contributor to planetary-scale carbon footprint. iPhones are dedicated for a green planet.

iPhone

**Ingredients:** Copper, Tellurium, Lithium, Cobalt, Manganese, Tungsten, Aluminium, Iron, Gold, Chlorine, Silver, Palladium, Zinc, Lead, Platinum, Sulfer, Nickel, Silicon, Gallium, Bromine, Indium, Antimony, Barium, Titanium, Niobium, Tantalum, Boron, Manganese, Rythenium, and other *extracted matter*

**Traceability is Curation is Political.**

As you take a selfie with your plant-based egg, hyper-organic eco-conscious avocado and inclusive ethical coffee + hemp milk foam

Terms

# MEDIA
# GEOLOGY

"A geologic approach to media, one that recognizes and integrates both the physical substrate and the cultural practices that are embedded in and emerge from it, could lead to a new kind of urban media studies, one that encourages us to dig deep, physically and conceptually, to uncover the history and geography of our urban media ecologies."

(P. 2) - MATTERN, S. (2017). CODE AND CLAY, DATA AND DIRT: FIVE THOUSAND YEARS OF
URBAN MEDIA. THE UNIVERSITY OF MINNESOTA PRESS.

Media geology is the reminder that the virtual is physical. The digital is essentially physical. Both the digital and the virtual demonstrate the effects of material systems. It is traceability, reconstructing the evolution of matter into media. It is simultaneously the material politics, resource extraction, and technological processes involved in creating media.

Archaeology applied to media and media geology are not the same. However, the motivations of people like Ernst and Parikka intersect.

"Media archaeology emphasizes the non-linear dynamics of cultural memory and technological development, and seeks to discover cultural evidence of the past in the present moment by excavating the historical strata of media culture." (p. 1) - Ernst, W. (2012). Digital memory and the archive. The University of Minnesota Press.

Despite Parikka's work being on media geology, rather than archeology, it still has been at the core of the conversation regarding the intersection of geological processes, resources, and media.

"A geology of media describes media technologies as geological formations, embedded in and developed through the earth's material strata." (p. 2) - Parikka, J. (2015). A geology of media. The University of Minnesota Press.

iPhones have no list of ingredients, unlike paper-wrapped, gluten-free, vitamin-enhanced, vegan nutrition bars. Copper, tellurium, lithium, cobalt, manganese, tungsten, aluminum, iron, gold, chlorine, silver, palladium, zinc, lead, platinum, sulfur, nickel, silicon, gallium, bromine, indium, antimony, barium, titanium, niobium, tantalum, boron, manganese, ruthenium, and other minerals make up the smartphone.

Extraction facts are the new nutrition facts.

The tokenization of extraction sites enhances transparency and traceability. Created digital tokens, representing ownership or rights to a specific mine or mining asset, are recorded on the blockchain or distributed ledger technology, and connected throughout the mining supply chain.

Tokens increase liquidity and access to capital. New fractional ownership and trade of tokens representing ownership or rights to mines increase access to capital for mining companies, as tokens can be traded on digital marketplaces, providing a new avenue for fundraising or investment. The consumer base joins the game. Tokenization enables smaller investors to participate in the mining industry, democratizing access to mining assets and diversifying sources of capital for the industry.

Critical Raw Materials are at the foundations of the digital economy, from artificial intelligence and computing breakthroughs to batteries and renewable energy.

Surplus is the root cause of wars. An inflated CRM economy creates a shaky scaffold for the internet in its current state.

**···es Online Spatial Data**: Interactive maps and
···a for regional and global Geology,
···ophysics, and Mineral Resources.

···es

···ources (MRDS)
···ast or present producer
···ct or occurrence
···sing plant
···n
···names

···al deposits of the world

···ium
···inc
···arths
···nd

···names
···rals
···ony
···um

···e
···h
···nium
···te

···h
···nese
···m and Tantalum
···m-Group Elements
···arth Elements
···m

···m
···ium
···um and Hafnium
···e critical minerals

···names

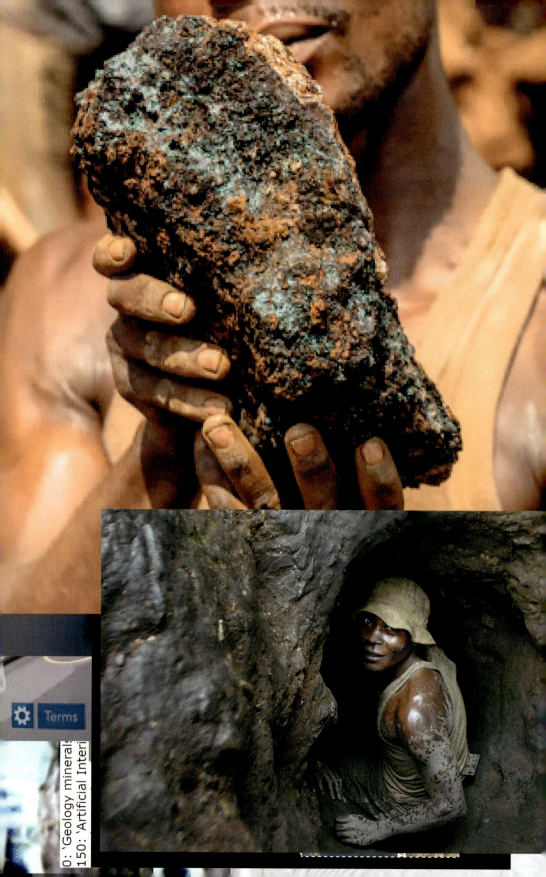
0: 'Geology minerals
150: 'Artificial Interi

# VIRTUAL WHO?

## A Materialist's take on the world

Media geology proves the physicality of the digital and the virtual. The internet is not the WWW. The internet is the network of connected computers. It is the very hard-wired physical hyper-object inhabiting the planet. The WWW is what happens through it: pages, emails, cat photos, and TikTok feed.

The spatial internet, with its enormous computation requirements from graphics to the blockchain, will incentivize the storage and processing economies, making it more physical than ever before.

It is impossible to understand the virtual without examining its blueprint. We need to understand the emerging effect, from its root essence. All are material or material effects.

The exploration of the materiality of digital media and how it impacts our physical world is the discourse. It is crucial to comprehend the virtual and the digital as effects of physical and material assemblages. This is the way to understand their significance and implications.

# ESCAPISM

The Incas' masks used in rituals to represent different personalities or characters are early examples of how people can demonstrate various identities through a signifying object.

This ancient form of art, broadly examined, can be connected to most social situations, interactions, and the public sphere.

If you stand naked on the front porch and the neighbors can't see you, it's rural.

If you stand naked on the front porch and the neighbors call the cops, it's suburban.

If you stand naked on the front porch and the neighbors ignore you, it's urban.

Urban environments, with their density and diversity, lift the burden of being recognized. The appearing no-mask reality is sometimes a constipated masked act of politeness. More people are unmasked on the internet. The societal contract is by definition a mask. A filter between internal intentions and external behavior.

The spatial internet protects a sense of anonymity and freedom to explore and express oneself beyond social pressures or constraints. It is a recovery space for the marginalized or excluded in traditional social settings, allowing them to connect with individuals and form new communities.

Escapism is approached as the psychological mechanism of seeking refuge from the tedious or unpleasant aspects of everyday life by engaging in imaginative or entertaining activities. Humans turn to escapism to distance themselves from persistent feelings of detachment, fear, sadness, or depression. They seek solace in alternative realities that offer a temporary escape from confronting the unpleasant.

The destination can be both physical and virtual.

The spatial internet is a place to create and customize their own avatars, allowing users to express themselves in ways that may not be possible in the physical world. It is Liberating, especially for those who may feel constrained by their real-world identities.

The spatial internet is a place that enables engagement in activities that may not be feasible in the physical world today. It is thrilling and exhilarating, providing an escape from the monotony and mundanity of everyday life. The mundane is all that is static.

As an ecology of experiences, the spatial internet is essentially worlds within worlds. Users can create their own virtual environments, complete with their own rules and physics, and then link those worlds together to create a larger, more expansive universe.

Nested worlds are used to create communities and networks within the metaverse, reinforcing subcultures and subcommunities. This creates a sense of belonging and identity further enhancing the sense of escapism and immersion. Asylum seekers can truly thrive.

Escapism is multi-faceted. It is explored within historical, psychological, and sociological perspectives, demonstrating its complexity and diverse manifestations.

Escapism is symbolic. It happens through signifying objects that highlight the symbolic nature of escapism, where individuals utilize tangible items to convey alternate personas or roles.

Escapism is social. It is always examined in relation to social situations, interactions, and the public sphere, emphasizing its connection to broader social dynamics and behaviors.

Escapism is psychological. In the physical or the virtual, escapism is an attitude.

Escapism is anonymizing. It allows self-exploration beyond social pressures or constraints, providing a sense of liberation and detachment from the Dos and Don'ts of the real world.

Escapism is customizable. It represents the quest for unique self-expression with easy-to-personalize content. It is a landscape of self-defined filter-controlled bubbles.

Escapism is immersive. Individuals are mentally functional in a parallel dimension. A struggle between the psychological and physical immersiveness shapes the scene.

Escapism begs to belong: The creation of nested worlds and communities within the spatial internet reinforces subcultures and subcommunities, fostering a sense of belonging and identity, which further enhances the escapism experience.

Escapism is dynamic: From one world into the other, the abundance of spatial experiences, and the nature of escapism overlap to strive towards an evolving and ever-changing phenomenon that evolves with the user's engagement and customization.

During the Beginnings of the Internet, the physical world was an escape from the Internet.

Today, more and more, the screen is becoming the escape from the physical world.

The phygital takes away this luxury, offers an equally contaminated virtual and physical, both merge, escapism is a default.

The destination can be both physical and virtual.

No City is an Island - Strelk

The city is an ontologically open entity.

# THE INFINITE STACK

MICHEAL LEVIN AND
DANIEL DENNETT

## "Cognition all the way down"

Technology enables access to new information, which in turn unlocks new dimensions for humans. The more senses we engage, the broader our umwelt becomes. Information can only be perceived if the right sensing and processing mechanisms are in place to receive it.

New processing mechanisms, logics, or sensing capacities lead to the perception of new phenomena. The climate is a good example. Without climate monitoring technologies at scale, crossed with the right computational capacity, the phenomena of global warming would have never existed ( as a diagnosed phenomenon known to us ).

What makes our world?

Thinking across the spectrum, from the very physical to the digital and virtual, an infinite amount of discrete layers is possible. Benjamin Bratton's stack breaks down the world into 6 layers, put together to form The Stack. The stack is a stack of stacks, each in itself holds infinite placeholders for new layers to be unlocked.

Similarly, in cities, we are increasingly able to uncover new layers. With the deployment of what makes the Internet of Things, a huge amount of new information can be mapped to urban environments. Space Syntax and spatial computing get richer and richer.

- THE INTERFACE EFFECT BY
ALEXANDER R. GALLOWAY.

## "What I hope this produces is a perspective on how cultural production and the socio-historical situation take form as they are interfaced together."

New interfaces with the world expand our capacity to access further insights. Knowledge is constructed, it's never retrieved.

# INTERFACE THEORY

## Interfaces are always political.

In the worlds of cognitive neuroscience and perception, the interface theory reimagines the world analogous to a computer. The world is the computer, our perception is the screen, and the objects we perceive are icons on a screen. Icons are only representations of the more complex hardware and software formations. Similarly, our perception is merely a representation of things, not the things themselves. A My Computer icon dragged to a recycle bin will never actually make a PC disappear.

What gives us access to new information are interfaces such as senses and technologies that can interface with new forms of data.

Interfaces transcend their mere existence as objects or tools into dynamic environments that influence our cognition, behavior, and communication. As new gateways, interfaces are the conduits through which we access and interact with complex digital systems, shaping our perceptions, actions, and relationships within these spaces.

Interfaces are not passive vessels, but agents actively molding the boundaries and possibilities of our experiences. Interfaces cannot be transparent, for the density of ideologies, values, and available technologies lies within.

Interfaces are local. They are situated within particular technological, social, and historical contexts, intertwined with the societies and technosphere in which they are embedded.

Interfaces are not stagnant entities. They constantly evolve or devolve, adapting to changing technologies and practices. They are not limited to matters of mere usability.

Interfaces are not confined to technical realms alone, but encompass cultural, social, and political dimensions, shaping our intricate relationships with technology, society, and each other.

Our embodied engagement with mediated information through interfaces, devices, and networks shapes our perceptions, behaviors, and relationships with technology.

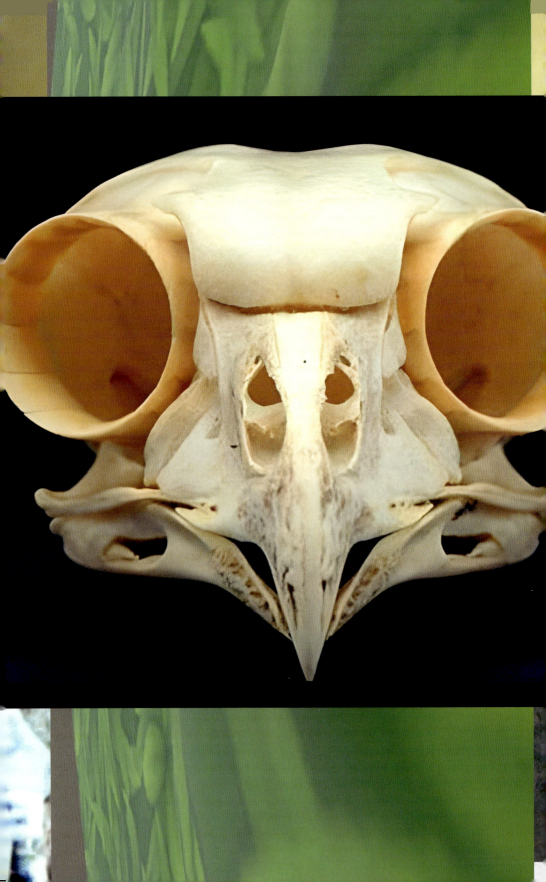

# UTILITY

## Utility is the metaverse's way to attention.

Within the spatial internet, utility holds paramount importance, as it encapsulates the practical functionality, economic value, and societal impact of the emerging virtual realms.

In a world where the boundaries are shifted. The physical-virtual split is obsolete. The notion of utility becomes a critical lens through which we can understand and evaluate the effectiveness, viability, and potential of the new phygital.

At the heart of the spatial internet is the concept of utility, which encompasses not only the functional aspects of metaverse environments but also their broader societal and economic implications. Utility in the metaverse refers to how effectively virtual spaces fulfill their intended purposes, be it for communication, commerce, education, entertainment, or other activities.

Ease of use, accessibility, scalability, versatility, and effectiveness shall be prioritized, enabling users to achieve their goals. What draws attention becomes utilizable. Attention is the currency, utility is all possible ways to retrieve or generate it.

Utility entails the economic value and impact of the environment. Virtual currencies, digital assets, and virtual economies emerge as significant drivers of economic activity within the metaverse, with the potential to create new economic opportunities, foster innovation, and reshape existing economic systems.

Utility within the spatial internet goes beyond purely functional and economic considerations. The Function of Utility is imbued with political, social, and cultural implications that shape our perceptions, behaviors, and relationships with technology and each other.

The market is the litmus test. Utility is function at work, or successful attempts to get attention. The new market attention is extravagant, possible through all spatial parameters, beyond the simple interactive user interfaces of the WWW as we know it.

# Supply chains shape the workplace.

# THE WORKPLACE

A kid racing to secure a chunk of cobalt at the cobalt mines in Congo.

A sewer cleaner in India's hyper-dense urban environments.

A CEO closing a deal from a cabin in a private Airbus A380.

A Harvard fresh graduate at a consultancy firm in London.

A prostitute in the red light district.

A toy-testing girl next to her 2000 colleagues in a factory in China.

An old man, with a wet cloth covering his face, slowly carrying a block of sulfur while inhaling its toxic gas.

A hipster, picking plums in the south of France for summer.

An immigrant black woman, herding cows in the Swiss Alps, producing milk, and making cheese.

A group of 1000 women rolling cigarettes faster than machines in their blue uniforms in a warehouse in Indonesia.

A family wanders the garbage mountains to make a living.

These are 11 different workplaces, with probably nothing that brings them together other than a market.

None of the mentioned above actually defines the workplace. There is no generic workplace. The term itself has been morphed to describe an aircondi-tioned office in a glass tower in a capital city, with badge-wearing, time-trad-ing, smart-casually dressed educated personnel that produce value.

The workplace is not a hyperconnect-ed, collaborative, agile, data-driven, intelligent, adaptive, virtualized, sustainable, integrated, and hu-man-centric environment, where pro-fessionals come together to produce value, by definition. An illusionary image of buzzwords shapes the image of the workplace of yesterday, today, and tomorrow.

The workplace is not an office. Mechanization is political.

"The End of Work" is an incomplete sentence.

Future workplaces vary as well. New demand creates new supply. AI experts flood the scene.

The internet itself has become the new workplace. The spatial internet accelerates a new type of space, and specifically, a new type of office. Geography is eliminated, and teams work collaboratively through the virtual space.

All urbanism is contextual, all cities have context.

# PROTO-META-URBANISM

We are at a milestone in the timeline of urbanism where new urbanism is at stake. From the proto-urbanism of the fifth millennium BC. to Bjarke Ingels, we are on the verge of a new era, a new cycle where a new proto-urbanism is occurring.

While no didactic precedents are available, upon the question of what metaverse urbanism is yet to be, one can consciously only render proto-meta-urbanism. It is an urbanism that feeds from present urban discourse, the current technosphere, and an emerging cosmos of synthetic living.

**"Architecture stands with one leg in a world that's 3,000 years old and another leg in the 21st century...This almost ballet-like stretch makes our profession surprisingly deep... Initially, I thought we were actually misplaced to deal with the present, but what we offer the present is memory."**

-REM KOOLHAAS

When contexts are not there, architects have invented them with a number of different motivations.

An extra mile is how virtual representations of precursor traces can be the base for strata to come. For his Cannergio, Peter Eisenman "invented" a site by instrumentalizing Le Corbusier's unbuilt hospital in Venice as the point of departure, and used the grid of the hospital as a generative system in his project.

Peter Eisenman during an interview with Iman Ansari, Eisenman's Evolution: Architecture, Syntax, and New Subjectivity (2013) affirms: "I needed something in the site, in the context of the Derridean notion of absence and presence. .... And so Corbu offered one layer of that cultural history."

This is to illustrate the spectrum of possibilities, and the " ballet-like stretch"; not only between past and present/future, but also between the virtual and the physical.

The term proto-meta-urbanism came as a logical intention to assemble an etymologically valid concept: proto for being an early mode, meta for metaverse, and urbanism for urbanism.

Digging into references, I discovered that the term has been most probably coined by Peter Trummer in **"Proto-Meta-Urbanism: The Rise of the Urban Machines"** ,which was published in the academic journal Architectural Design in 2013.

"Proto-meta-urbanism is an attempt to develop a new paradigm for the design of the contemporary city, one that takes into account the transformative effects of new technologies and the shifting social, economic, and political landscape. This paradigm recognizes that the city is no longer a static entity, but a dynamic system that is constantly evolving and adapting to changing conditions."

He approaches the concept as "a specific condition of the urban that has emerged in the transition from an industrial society to an information society."

The term, in my approach, is intended for the emergence of new urban forms and spaces that are a product of the contemporary technological landscape. The meta refers to the metaverse, the new spatial internet that will change how we perceive, use, and design cities.

Game environments, alongside a very small amount of architecture and urbanism, were projects from pioneers who envisioned a new urbanism.

Proto is for the lack of direct relevant discourse, and the awareness of the experimental aspect of the endeavor. Doing is a way of creating the discourse. Doing as thinking. A vision requires a position. The framework molded through the process is a take on what a metaverse urbanism could be. It is a seed to be explored further, as a blueprint for the new urbanism emerging.

# INSTANCING

PIER VITTORIO AURELI

## "Less is Enough"

Instancing underscores the socio-political dimensions of content creation and dissemination. Bound to the infrastructural limitations, less becomes enough, as it's used infinitely as a unique event. A scaffold for a new effect is generated continuously.

Instancing is a new commodification where content is reduced to replicable units and value is attributed to its scalability and marketability.

The copy is at stake. Digital reproduction performs copying as creation. Instancing is the creation of multiple, separate, and parallel virtual spaces or instances within a larger virtual world or environment. These instances are generated dynamically based on various factors such as user demand, geographical location, or specific criteria defined by the virtual world's creators.

A space can be explored by a million people, with each using it as a unique space. It is assigned to be unique to every visitor, IP address geography, or any other contextual parameter.

Scalable and distributed virtual experiences call for instancing. The demand for more has its supply in identical unique iterations of the same object. Multiple users or groups occupy separate instances of the same virtual space simultaneously without interfering with each other's activities.

Each instance can have its own rules, characteristics, and interactions, feeding into an economy of mass personalized and immersive experiences.

Instancing is common practice in virtual worlds, online games, and other metaverse environments to manage large populations of users, optimize server resources, and maintain a smooth and seamless user experience. It is the way to accommodate a large number of users while maintaining performance, customization, and privacy, as each instance hosts its own unique content, activities, and interactions.

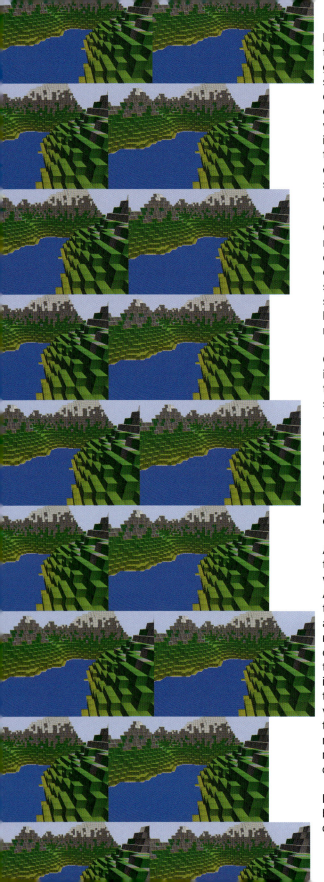

From full worlds and experiences to the objects themselves within scenes, game developers use instancing as a survival mechanism in low-resource environments. In game development or world-building, it is the technique where a single 3D model or object is created once in memory or on the GPU, and then replicated or duplicated multiple times within a scene without creating additional copies of the original object.

Optimizing performance and reducing memory usage is the key objective. As all the instances of the object share the same resources such as textures, animations, and shaders instead of each instance having its own separate set of resources.

Common practice often utilizes instancing for objects or entities that are repeated frequently in a scene such as trees, rocks, or NPCs - Non-Player Characters - in a game environment. It ensures efficient rendering of large numbers of similar objects as it reduces the overhead of creating and managing individual objects, and improves the overall performance of the game or virtual environment.

Aggregation is a revived computational design discourse. It is the way to go for optimal performance. Aggregation, in all its forms, allows the instancing technique to move away from being monopolized for marginal objects and become a core method of creating architecture and urbanism for the spatial internet. It banks on well-established techniques to create complex and visually rich scenes while minimizing the computational and memory resources required. This results in more efficient and optimized games or virtual experiences.

Instancing is a simple pipeline initiated by the creation of a base or source object, a single 3D model or object.

The base or source for the instances. It can be a mesh or any other type of graphical representation.

Following that, the critical milestone of defining the instance data and its attributes will be used to customize or transform the base object for each instance.

Placeholders for maximizing its utility.

Position, rotation, scale, color, texture, or other parameters. Instances vary in their data.

Once in place, buffers and data structures to store the instance data are created, such as vertex buffers or texture arrays, which hold the per-instance data for each object.

Now ready, the instance data is bound to the appropriate shader or rendering pipeline so that it can be used to customize the appearance and properties of the base object during rendering.

Eventually, the rendering of the instances takes place. It occurs as the base object is drawn multiple times using the instance data to transform and customize each instance according to its unique set of parameters. This can be done efficiently in a single draw call, considering that the instance data is shared among all instances and does not need to be duplicated.

Finally, instances can be updated by updating the instance data. As instances need to be updated dynamically during runtime, such as for animations or physics simulations, the instance data can be updated in the buffers or data structures, and the changes will be reflected in the next frame.

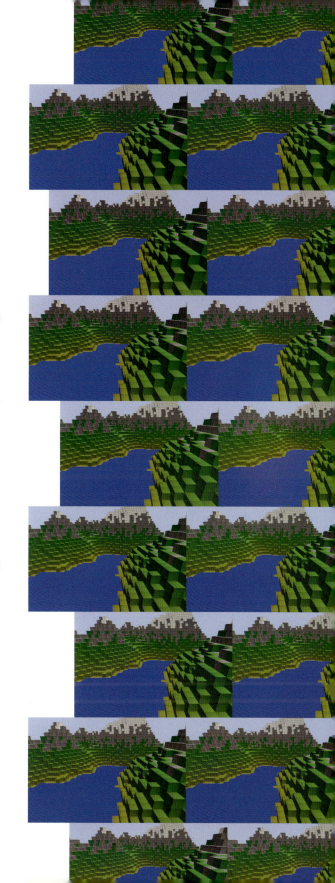

How to build a city from scratch: the handy step-by-step DIY guide | Cities | The Guardian

Visit ›

## ...ina's Private Cities

...lex Tabarrok *January 26, 2022 at 7:25 am in* Current Affairs, Economics, Political Science

...ising private city operators in contemporary China, Jiao and Yu report that China's private cities are growing.

...the last decade has witnessed a large growth in private city operators (PCOs) who plan, finance, build, operate and manage the infrastructure and public amenities of a n... a whole. Different from previous PPPs, PCOs are a big breakthrough...they manage urban planning, industry development, investment attraction, and public goods and se... other words, the traditional core functions of municipal governments are contracted out, and consequently, a significant neoliberal urban governance structure has becom... prominent in China.

In the new business model, the China Fortune Land Development Co., Ltd. (CFLD) was undoubtedly the earliest and most successful. It manages 125 new cities or towns w... area of over 4000 km². Founded in 1998, the enterprise group has grown into a business giant with an annual income of CNY 83.8 billion in 2018. The company's financial statements demonstrate that the annual return rate of net assets has grown as much as 30% annually from 2011 to 2018, which is the highest among the Chinese Fortune companies.

...ajagopalan and I argued in Lessons from Gurgaon, India's Private ...the key development has been to scale large enough so that the ...ate operator internalizes the externalities. Quoting Jiao and Yu ...n:

The key to solving this problem is to internalize positive externality so that costs and benefits mainly affect the parties who choose to incur them. The solution of the new model is to outsource Gu'An New

# CHARTER-POLIS

Charter cities will emerge within the geopolitics of today and slide as a new typology of sovereignty in the urbanism scene of today.

Charter cities are micro-specimens of a network state in the making. They're a node that begs a snowball effect. They embody an abandoning of the social contract towards new and private communities.

It is a step within countries' border paths to the obsolete. Startup nations mirror the social aspiration of all things personalized and community formation on a pragmatic basis. No culture is imposed, and no norms are predefined. All are at the service of the promise of financial growth.

Startup nations are the evolved communities of the spatial internet. It encompasses everything from avant-garde models of new urbanism and state development to black-hole-like echo chambers of a perpetual ideology bouncing endlessly as it gains numerical momentum.

Charter cities are usually of critical land size. Medium size is a burden. Successful countries live at the ends of the bell curve, tiny or gigantic; either a mosquito or a whale. No other form survives.

Charter cities will be cities as nations, and vice versa, as analogous to the metaverse city world. Worlds as cities, and cities as worlds.

Within this context, and while each city can be an enclosure on its own, an interesting dynamic emerges in which various metaverses can coexist in a charter-city manner.

The market leads the way and new cities become new financial networks of exchange. Nested cities, like nested ecologies, form a more complex multiscalar ecosystem.

The charter polis is an emerging emblem of the new market, towards a new privatized commons, governed in a decentralized manner with an aligned vision and mission. New cities adopt the new internet infrastructure. Cities with a virtualized environment, decentralized economy, and a DAO-governed community mediate between the physical and the real. They are hybrid entities.

Architects and urbanists become essential to a branded city, design is relevant, and a brand is unthinkable. Zaha Hadid Architects Roatan is a preliminary experiment on what could be next.

**Startup cities, like startup nations, are for architecture and urbanists to create.**

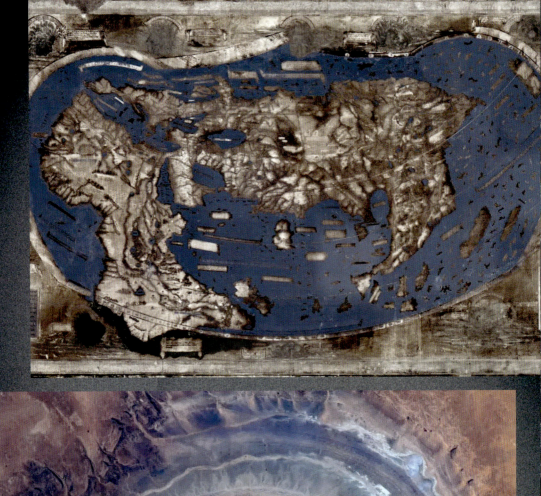

# PSEUDO GEOGRAPHIES

System architectures become new geographies. Visual boundaries, locations, distances, heights, and all metrics are false. No geography is relevant other than the architecture of the system at the foundations of a metaverse world.

Geography of the physical world, locations of IPs, and servers prevail.

Geographies of the spatial internet are of a different element. They are digital landscapes. The concept of distance is out of bounds. Users can teleport between virtual spaces without the constraints of physical geography.

Within an open metaverse world, deploying real-world physics and geography will still be relevant, and it will shape economic and financial decisions, land value, and user concurrency. Everyone wants to own the parcel adjacent to Snoop Dog's parcel.

These worlds mimic real-world geographies but are not bound by physical constraints. These pseudo-geographies take various forms, virtual replicas of real-world cities, landscapes, or landmarks. They can also be entirely designed virtual spaces that resemble real-world locations or unique ones.

While the geography of worlds might be relevant within their domain, a universe of invisible geographies shapes how things work.

Geography entails the relationship within the population too, one that is influenced by place. An internet of places yields a new geography. It is a Pseudo-geography to be defined.

# Tell the Truth or at Least Don't Lie

Song by Akira the Don and Jordan B. Peterson

8:09

YouTube • Jordan B Peterson Clips

Tell the Truth, or at Least Don't Lie (12 Rules for Life)

← Post

 Kevin O'Leary aka Mr. Wonderful ✓     Subscribe   ...
@kevinolearytv

Calling a bottom on any #Stock is always risky but that is exactly what I'm doing on $FB I think the toilet has stopped flushing on #MetaPlatforms Here is my #Investment thesis. Time will tell if I'm right or wrong!

0:01 / 5:13

8:40 PM · Feb 9, 2022

💬 58     🔁 34     ♡ 223     🔖 10     ⬆️

Don't Lie | Shortform Books

# The metaverse is the sum total of all metaverses

 Facebook • Dr Jordan B Peterson

# DOMAIN-SPECIFIC ONTOLOGIES

Knowledge representation frameworks that are designed and used within specific domains or fields of knowledge take center stage. Generally tailored to capture the unique concepts, relationships, and rules that are relevant to a particular domain, DO may allow for more precise and specific modeling of knowledge within that domain.

As DO evolves to capture the specific semantics and structures of knowledge within specific domains, a rise in relativity thinking makes DSOs valid in their own right. No authority is needed to legitimize. They are generally intended to draw a formal representation of domain-specific knowledge that can be shared, reused, and reasoned about within that specific domain.

### "Tell the truth or at least don't lie."

JORDAN PETERSON, 12 RULES FOR LIFE BOOK

These two sides to the statements are radically different. Partial truths, when studying and operating within complex systems, can be easily false. Within system thinking, context is crucial.

Domain-specific ontologies can prove in-compatible definitions and representations of terms, resulting in an impossibility of merging within larger systems.

The lack of a common upper ontology further compounds the issue, making ontology design a politically playful arena.

The discrepancies in domain ontologies arise from varying languages, intended usage, and perceptions of the domain influenced by ideology.

The concept of an upper ontology-foundation ontology- offers a top-down validation to a bottom-up process. It provides a model of shared relations and objects that can be universally applied across different domain ontologies.

The spatial internet differs from the previous iteration, as it holds the potential to be built in a bottom manner. From computer science to mass-adopted media culture, domain-specific thinking, acting, and perceiving is shaping more and more of the world. Clusters of self-righteousness form the social sphere.

Contextualizing ontologies and spaces developed from different perspectives, methods, and ideologies is the act of social cohesion.

'During Feudalism,
no one was employed.'

# THE CLOUDALISTS

YANIS VAROUFAKIS **"Capital is everywhere, yet capitalism is on the wane. In an era when the owners of a new form of "command capital" have gained exorbitant power over everyone else, including traditional capitalists, this is no contradiction."**

A new form of capital is forming. One where the top of the hierarchy is paid by the global population as a form of renting the new commons. It is a new cloud-based elite, as put by Varoufakis who coined the term.

## The mass commercialization of nostalgia is the new object.

Designing the desires of the population is a game to be mastered.

"First, cloudalists can extract huge rents from manufacturers whose stuff they persuade us to buy because the same command capital that makes us want that stuff is the foundation of platforms (Amazon.com, for example) where those purchases take place. It is as if Sterling Cooper were to take over the markets where the wares it advertises are sold. The cloudalists are turning conventional capitalists into a new vassal class that must pay tribute to them for the chance to sell to us.

Second, the same algorithms that guide our purchases also have the capacity surreptitiously to command us directly to produce new command capital for the cloudalists. We do this every time we post photos on Instagram, write tweets, offer reviews on Amazon books, or simply move around town so that our phones contribute congestion data to Google Maps."

- Yanis Varoufakis

Centralized power-house entities or platforms will control and influence the virtual space at its very foundations, using significant command capital and wield power in terms of setting the rules, policies, and economic structures within platforms.

A decentralized economy in the metaverse promises otherwise utilizing blockchain or other distributed technologies to create a peer-to-peer economic system where users have more autonomy, ownership, and control over their digital assets, transactions, and interactions.

The coexistence of cloudalists and a decentralized economy in the metaverse is a paradoxical reality that is optimally enabled through 4 main features of the spatial internet.

Interoperability is where decentralized platforms and virtual worlds can be built across platforms, allowing users to move their digital assets and identities across platforms.

User empowerment happens through ownership and control over digital assets, identities, and transactions for increased agency and autonomy.

Collaborative governance is mediated through collaborative and inclusive governance models that involve users and stakeholders in decision-making processes. Rules, policies, and economic structures are more transparent and accountable to the community, mitigating concerns of concentrated power.

Hence hybrid models will emerge, and both centralized and decentralized elements coexist in the new internet.

# The mass commercialization of nostalgia is the new object.

Microsoft Outlook

Your machine isn't set up for Information Rights Management (IRM). To set up IRM, sign in to Office, open an existing IRM protected message or document, or contact your help desk.

OK

# MACHINE RENDERED REGIMES

The next chapter of the history of intelligence will be co-played by human and artificial intelligence together. As more and more aspects of quantification, classification, pattern recognition, and surveillance are held by machines and machine intelligence, new regimes will emerge. Regimes are produced based on machinic convenience to solve complex problems at a multitude of scales.

Governance, rules, or policies are determined and enforced by automated systems or algorithms. Machines, artificial intelligence, or decentralized autonomous organizations (DAOs) play a significant role in shaping and governing various aspects of society, tinkering with accountability, transparency, and the balance between human agency and automated control.

HTTPS://WWW.NBCNEWS.COM/TECH/
TECH-NEWS/AMAZON-S-LARGEST-WARE-
HOUSE-HUB-HAS-CORONAVIRUS-CASE-WORK-
ERS-SAY-N1169946

HTTPS://WWW.NEWSCIENTIST.COM/ARTICLE/
MG23130932-900-UBER-AND-GOOGLE-
RACE-AGAINST-CAR-FIRMS-TO-MAP-THE-
WORLDS-CITIES/

HTTPS://WWW.WAREDOCK.COM/MAGAZINE/
WHAT-IS-AMAZON-ROBOTIC-FULFILL-
MENT-CENTER/

HTTPS://LEARN.MICROSOFT.COM/EN-US/
ANSWERS/QUESTIONS/1064893/WHEN-US-
ERS-SELECTED-THE-SENSITIVITY-LA-
BEL-FACING-I

Algorithmic law enforcement and policing become heavily reliant on algorithms to predict crimes. Predictive policing algorithms digitally patrol neighborhoods and make arrests based on statistical probabilities, while a team of researchers investigates civil liberties and data-set biases.

# URBAN DAOS

Tokenized engagement takes over a new mode of urban belonging and organized social urban interaction through a new form of governance.

Democratizing decision-making.
Urban DAOs shall democratize urban governance.

Citizens, residents, and AI entities shall participate in decision-making processes via blockchain-based voting systems. Zoning changes, public expenditure allocations, and policy adjustments will be subject to direct, transparent, and consensus-driven decision-making. By that, urban planning becomes truly inclusive. Urban DAOs boost the creation of socially hyper-connected metropolises.

Fancy words work in low-income spaces too.
Let's walk through FavelaDAO, a digital Town Hall where residents can propose and vote on initiatives to improve their neighborhood. Using blockchain-based voting, residents can collectively decide on projects such as upgrading sanitation systems, installing community lighting, or enhancing security measures.

Residents earn tokens by actively participating in community projects or reporting issues. These tokens represent voting power and a share in the potential benefits generated by the DAO.

The DAO allocates resources based on community priorities. Through smart contracts, the FavelaDAO ensures universal access to basic services such as healthcare, education, and clean water.

Residents have secure digital identities recorded on the blockchain, which they use to access services and participate in community decisions. A reputation system promotes responsible citizenship and determines access to specific benefits.

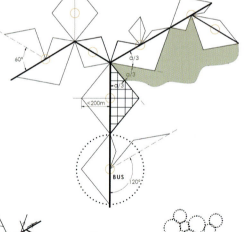

**1.** City is developed by branches

**2.** In every joint l/3 is open for the nature

**3.** Everyone is no further than 200 meters away from a bus stop

**4.** Everyone is closer than 200 meters from the forest stop

**5.** Grid is always perpendicular to the street

# RULE-BASED URBANISM

Generative urban design is based on algorithms to create adaptive geometrical structures that can govern a first-degree layout for urban life. It is a geometrical system that frames social order at the very basic level.

Geometry has led city planning since ancient times, from medieval fantasies to our modern times. The spatial layout as an interface has been repurposed. Walled cities had clear segregation and a single hierarchical structure that concentrically governed order.

Urban structures have been more and more complex as urban planning becomes more dense, encapsulating a large number of parameters.

Cerda's grid is an all-in-one solution for a multifaceted problem, from urban hygiene to coach-oriented mobility. The rectangular (Octagonal ) grid is scalable, adaptive, and geometrical.

Rule-based urbanism is the machine language of spatial urban structures. Its DNA encodes the bedrock for navigation and mobility, land use distribution, property division, infrastructure planning, major economic zoning, social interaction at the macro scale, and urban aesthetics from a spatial perspective.

Metaverse urbanism is data-rich with a capacity that allows the stratification of urban structures that densify the urban stack.

Rules are quantitative, machine-comprehensive, and interoperable within an address-based ecosystem. Rule-based urban structures allow the co-existence of several systems within nested hierarchies. Both are scalable due to their generative and numerical nature.

While the geometrical system is laid out, organic and generative sub-systems emerge, with the capacity for self-assembly and grouping, aggregations, agglomerations, splitting and branching, or any other form of geometrical emergent phenomena.

This is an urban form finding and making that can bridge the physical and the digital, an application to future virtual city planning that is computable, geometrically valid, and mathematically approached.

# TERRITORIAL PLANNING

In the epoch of the Anthropocene, a defining era characterized by humanity's profound influence on the Earth's crust, we find ourselves at a juncture in history where our actions have unintentionally redesigned the planet's landscape within a wide spectrum of human impact.

This reshaping of the Earth's surface goes beyond designing walled cities, to span across vast territories, encompassing megalopolises, entire regions, countries, continents, and beyond, reaching space.

From spatial computing and remote sensing to sophisticated modeling tools, we have a toolkit at our disposal that equips us with a comprehensive understanding of our territories, whether at a local or global scale.

7000 years of urban settlement and city planning have stretched cities from 1000-2000 inhabitants to urban environments with great populations, 30 million inhabitants in the case of Tokyo. This is 15000 fold in growth at an average of doubling every year.

We are at a unique moment in time where it has become possible to design territories beyond any previous time in history. Mega-projects in the Middle East, China, America, and soon other places gain momentum.

## Territorial planning is what technology, the market, and power systems allow.

# NEW CUISINE

## Bioengineers are the new farmers.

Future Cuisine is personalized yet communicates a blueprint for global advancements; efficiency, profitability, and abundance are the main drivers while animating a market that creates more and more ideology-driven demand. New cuisines change as fast as social media trends.

Scientists have restored grains that are extinct; de-extinction has become real and is used within various industries.

The "Extinct Butcher Lab" is a new online meat vendor selling meat cuts of extinct animals like Quagga, Irish Elk, Mammoth, Camelops, Ancient Bison, and more.

New Cuisine is monitored, tracked, and optimized, creating a network around the act of acquisition, consumption, and digestion. Traceability is expanded to encompass post-consumption regimes. It is not limited to where things come from, but where things go to.

Food becomes polluted.

Food is not necessary.

Food is a luxury.

Food to secure nutrition is a chapter of the past, nutrients are ingested as tabs, pills, liquids or several drops within a cup of tea.

The most important ingredient in a croissant is air.
Texture is the new flavor.

HTTPS://REPORTERGOURMET.COM/EN/
NEWS/5794-AIR-CROISSANT-THE-BREAKFAST-
DELIGHT-MADE-OF-AI
R-ALBERT-ADRIA-S-INGENIOUS-RECIPE

Story is the new value.

ÜÜÖ

**OnlyFake: nueva amenaza de fraude cibernético con identificaciones falsas**

MÜTÜÖ

**Data is a new asset class and Ocean Protocol unlocks its value. (Weforum.org, 2021)**

# SELF-SOVEREIGN BRAINS

**Will identity rights be separate from Neuro-rights?**

Moving from a centralized identity politics to a decentralized one through user-centric protocols, Self-sovereign identity promotes individuals having full control and ownership of their digital identity, without relying on central authorities or intermediaries.

People must have sovereignty over their own cognitive functions or digital rep-resentations of their intelligence. To the expression of self, agency, and identity.

**How can we secure that, in an age where machines have unlocked our emotional code?**

Fast forward to a future capacity for neuroscience and neurotechnology, in light of new modes of knowledge-sharing and health, privacy is the keystone.

It once used to be pay-per-view, and now it's pay-per-gaze.

Pay-per-view is control over what users watch.

Pay-per-gaze is optical surveillance that gets reworked to neuromodulation.

**"The better we can provide information, even without you asking for it, the better we can provide commercial information people are excited to be promoting to you" - Larry Page ex CEO of Google.**

The question for big tech companies is never ethical, it is always about dosage and timing. If it's the right dose at the right time for a society in a given moment. All doses are bearable, if they come at the right time. We might all be boiling frogs.

Neurorights are designed to secure mental privacy, personal identity, and free will, and to protect from algorithmic bias, digital surveillance, or any further biosensing that can be used by a third party.

Regulations are forming, such as the EU's 2016 General Data Protection Regulation (GDPR), and the EU Citizen ID Wallet that can be used by its holders for online and offline endeavors. In parallel projects such as Ocean Protocol, an open-source smart contract software that allows users to tokenize, gain sovereignty, and monetize their new digital asset class.

**Data is a new asset class and Ocean Protocol unlocks its value. World Economic Forum**

**Will we form Neurorights DAOs?**

The topic of neuro rights, self-sovereign brains, and digital barriers are simmering, they will soon become more mainstream.

DAOs are forming and various methods to generate algorithms, or data within a decentralized system or through nodes in a peer-to-peer network are appearing. They can be interesting proposals to the current state of a-legal situation. A-legal refers to a situation before its regulation, things are not legal nor illegal.

Self-sovereign Identity, Self-sovereign Brains, Self-sovereign self.

Identity and its sovereignty becomes increasingly relevant as embodiment is a central part of the spatial internet.

Self-sovereign self is the spatial internet protocol for identity.

# METAVEARTH

The next generation of the internet will continue to grow in infrastructure, from data servers, mining farms, and cables that cross the oceans to all mobile phones, wearables, and computers. It will grow to finally consume the planet. Earth becomes more digital, the internet becomes more physical, the Metaverse becomes MetavEarth.

Metavearth is also an acknowledgment of the physicality of the internet itself as an enabling infrastructure at the scale of the planet. Metavearth is the internet of places; while hybridization happens, the planet is uploaded to the internet.

HTTPS://FORTUNE.COM/2017/06/15/GART-NER-CLOUD-RANKINGS/

# IKER'S

# TO

# RSE

# ANISM

Metaverse

Metaverse changes the way we engage with each other—learning, growing, working, and playing together in a shared virtual reality. This is a completely new way of traveling.

# A BRIEF
# HISTORY
# OF CITY
# ADJECTIVES

Since the conception of the Internet, new forms of communication, public spaces, information dissemination interfaces, supply chains, social interactions, and platforms have all become rooted in communication and information technologies.

The explosion in "city adjectives" reflects the trends and explorations of territories within the urban discourse in very different directions. The emergence of new technologies is at the heart of that, as these adjectives come to describe a response to how urbanism changes in the shadow of such technologies and their applications.

Through the same lens, Metaverse Urbanism emerges as a new possibility, triggered by a technological foundation that enables its realization. In parallel, it resonates with previous reflections and ideas that came in over a decade ago. While it's important to lay out the precedents and extract the relevant speculations, it's equally as important to highlight how much of these ideas have been realized today and can be further implemented in the future to shape a new Urbanism.

*If you know, you know.*

Perhaps a new adjective is placed before the term city, polis, or urbanism at every new project presented at an urbanism course or whenever a new urban theory or book comes out ( including this one ). We have almost taken away all value from the terms themselves, celebrating a new way of looking at things.

Network, Data, Meta, Digital, Embodied, Sensorial, Augmented, Slow, Virtual, Interface, sentient, responsive, tactical, bio, sensible, Ecological, New, Tactical, and the list can go on forever.

One thing has been common in all urban visions during the last 15 years. Everyone is preoccupied with technology — from tech evangelists to conservatives, and LEED-certified green corporate CEOs to ecological thinkers, technology is inescapable.

Emerging technologies and their use impact the main driving forces behind most urban 'theories'

Here is a list from my notes, bringing together some of the work on the topic

→   The "Spatial City" by Yona Friedman (1958)

→   The "Plug-in City" by Archigram (1960s)

→   The "Computer City" by Archigram (1964)

→   The "No-stop City" by Archigram (1970)

→   The "Right to the City" concept by Henri Lefebvre (1996)

→   The "Splintering Urbanism" by Stephen Graham (2001)

→   The "Embodied Interaction" by Paul Dourish and Genevieve Bell (2001)

→   The "Virtual Urbanism" by William J. Mitchell (2001)

→   The "Network City" by Kazys Varnelis (2008)

→   The "Sentient City" - "Toward the Sentient City" (2009) and "Sentient City: Ubiquitous Computing, Architecture, and the Future of Urban Space" (2011) edited by Mark Shepard

→   The "Augmented City" by Bruce Sterling (2010)

→   The "Sensorial City" by Mirko Zardini (2014)

→   The "Responsive City" by Stephen Goldsmith and Susan Crawford - "The Responsive City: Engaging Communities Through Data-Smart Governance" (2014)

→   Tactical Urbanism and DIY Urbanism (2014)

→   The "Smart Citizens" project by the Barcelona City Council (2015)

→   The "Digital Urbanism" by Jani Vuolteenaho, Koen Leurs, and Johanna Sumiala (2015)

→   The "Data City" by Rob Kitchin (2016)

→   The "Senseable City" by Carlo Rati (2016)

→   The "Ecological Urbanism" by Salvador Rueda (2016)

→   The "Post-Urbanism" concept by Nigel Thrift (2018)

→   The New Urbanism movement and Smart Cities (2018)

→   The "Platform Urbanism" by Sarah Barns (2020)

→   The "Hybrid City" by Nina Rappaport (2022)

With all the new technologies that emerged post WWII, Architecture became an interesting field. Now, it is unconstrained with the physicality of the building. Robotics and physical computing came in alongside utopian visions to outlive the war. Architecture grew as a form of critical cultural production of worlds through various media, from film to robotics, writing, drawing, and more.

With the second wave of industrialization and the promises new technologies held, a new society was imagined. Archigram, a group of architects in the 1960s, envisioned the "plug-in" city. They envisioned an organism that could be constantly reconfigured and adapted to changing needs and desires. One could consider it an early version of the virtual city.

Cedric Price, an architect, proposed the "non-plan" which first appeared in an article entitled "Non-plan: an experiment in freedom" in 'New Society' (Banham, et. al., 1969; 1974). Price's contributions go beyond, but this highlights the then-new approach to city design, which emphasized flexibility and adaptability, and saw the city as a constantly evolving system with a social dimension.

**The 70s and the 80s were transitional phases/periods, building up to the Internet age. They are foundational in the experiments in architectural computation, indexical systems, and technologies.**

## Liquid Architectures in Cyberspace ( 1991 )

Digital Life and the power of computer interfaces were at a point to become consolidated. Nicholas Negroponte, who worked closely with other AI pioneers, highlights in his book "Being Digital," ideas for a new life. A life that is founded on the interaction of bits and atoms, a crucial interface layer, and a new form of spatial cognition.

Negroponte's Being Digital encapsulates a variety of constructs that are important in the lineage of arriving at the spatial internet. For example, the book discusses cybernetic subjectivity, a concept that is foundational to understanding digital embodiment within this new paradigm.

**Within the same frame, Ray Ascott's Cyberception, Neil Spiller' Nanotopia, and Marcos Novac's Transmitting Architecture shaped the zeitgeist**

A decade after Being digital, the term Spime was coined by Bruce Sterling in his book "Shaping Things".

"...these future-manufactured objects with informational support so extensive and rich that they are regarded as material instantiations of an immaterial system."

Spime -derived from the terms space and time- was a term that most importantly referred to objects, archetypes, or user instances whose information was stored on the cloud. Consequently, Spimes thrived upon six main facets.

# Calculus changed architecture forever.

- → "Small, inexpensive means of remotely and uniquely identifying objects over short ranges, for example, radio-frequency identification.
- → A mechanism to precisely locate something on Earth, such as a global positioning system.
- → A way to mine large amounts of data for things that match some given criteria, like internet search engines.
- → Tools to virtually construct nearly any kind of object; computer-aided design.
- → Ways to rapidly prototype virtual objects into real ones. Sophisticated, automated fabrication of a specification for an object through "three-dimensional printers."
- → "Cradle-to-cradle" life spans for objects. Cheap, effective recycling." - Wikipedia Page ( Spime )

Paul Virilio's work comes at a stage of relative relevance to radical thought that conceptualized concepts important to extracting a new vision of the emergence of a new type of city, primarily shaped by telecommunications technologies.

- VIRILIO "The concept of trajectory has replaced the notion of geography" and takes a position, making the statement, "In cyberspace we are performing, not living and experiencing."

The real-time revolution transforms physical space into temporal reality within the trinity of teletopia, atopia, and utopia. Telepresence and optoelectronics facilitate distant meetings, while urbanization in real-time moves activities to interfaces.

Paradoxes of acceleration distance us from the immediate, and tele-technologies invest in augmented layers that threaten to reduce our notions of reality, identity, physicality, and presence to insignificance.

The new dromosphere gradually densifies the world's dimensions through digital tools. Real-time images shift from explicit to implicit information. Video replaces classic photography, and the screen acts as a window or frame, shaping videoscopic information.

The dominance of technological culture expands, while the interface of instantaneous transmission affects subject vitality.

From passive to active optics, virtual reality stimulates adaptive optics.

Distance gives way to electromagnetic proximity, challenging a representation of tangible reality through digital means.

For Virilio, communication is permeated by technological reductionism. The transmission revolution, influenced by electromagnetic processes, unveils the "law of proximity" in space, time, and light. Electromagnetic proximity surpasses mechanical proximity. It questions the nature of virtual representation.

https://rebeccawoodallphotography.wordpress.com/2015/03/15/paul-virilio- open-sky/

The concept of the "cyberflâneur" by Michel de Certeau explores the possibility of navigating virtual cities in a similar way to the traditional practice of urban flânerie.

https://www.theatlantic.com/technology/archive/2012/02/the-life-of-the-cyberfl-neur/252687/

Telepresence has the potential to create virtual meetings and shared workspaces across geographic distances.

The "urbanism of screens", or the city as an interface, proposed by Martijn de Waal, examines the impact of screen-based technologies on urban environments and the ways in which they shape our experiences of the city.

https://www.degruyter.com/document/doi/10.7312/will17892-006/html?lang=en
https://www.degruyter.com/document/doi/10.1515/9789048517954-005/html?lang=de

The "virtual placemaking" approach seeks to create virtual public spaces that offer similar benefits to physical public spaces.

The concept of "digital placemaking" by Kim Dovey, explores how digital technologies can be used to create new forms of public space and civic engagement.

https://discovery.ucl.ac.uk/id/eprint/10130788/1/Maldonado,Psarra_PlaceMakingInTheDigitalMediaEra[11].pdf

# 1. THE DENSIFICATION OF THE URBAN STACK

**The virtual layer of cities has experienced significant densification due to advancements in technology and its implementations, adding layers upon layers of information to expand our sensory perception and umwelt.**

**Over the past two decades, city design has become increasingly reliant on technologies for simulation, measurement, modeling, and visualization. Urbanism has evolved into a predominantly digital (and virtual) practice, with the entire process streamlined through computation and software.**

Think about a stack of a million layers, from the more "Physical" to the more "Digital" or "Virtual. Just like any continuum, between every two layers, we can always fit a layer. Then add one more between the newly formed layers. We can make a stack of infinite layers. The Urbansphere is made of a ground, the very physical layer, the buildings, electrical infrastructure, and things like telecommunications, and wifi, radio waves, etc are its foundations. Now take the CO2 layer, the data of carbon concentrations in the air within the city. If that is a layer, it is one that we owe its unlocking to sensing and processing technologies.

Every time we expand our sensing capacity, we expand our umwelt–our sensorial world–and by that, we expand the urban stack. The urban stack is in fact a connectome where layers intertwine with each other.

The virtual layer of cities has experienced significant densification due to advancements in technology and its implementa-

tions, adding layers upon layers of information to expand our sensory perception and umwelt.

Over the past two decades, city design has become increasingly reliant on technologies for simulation, measurement, modeling, and visualization. Urbanism has evolved into a predominantly digital practice, with the entire process streamlined through computation and software. This is not to overlook the importance of Urban life, but to take a closer look at how we practice urbanism.

INDICATIVE GEOTHEMATIC LAYERS

RADONIO

GRAVITY MEASUREMENTS BOUGUER

TECHNICAL GEOLOGY

GEOLOGY

DEM

TOPOGRAPHY

HIGH RESOLUTION SATELLITE DATA

NATIONAL BESTSELLER

# being digital

## NICHOLAS NEGROPONTE

"Succinct and readable.... If you suffer from digital anxiety, that creeping sense that technology is racing along much faster than you can follow, here is a book that lays it all out for you.... We need visionaries like Negroponte."
— *Newsday*

State or condition of existing or functioning in a digital or electronic form

NATIONAL BESTSELLER

# digital

## being

"Succinct and readable.... If you suffer from digital anxiety, that creeping sense that technology is racing along much faster than you can follow, here is a book that lays it all out for you.... We need visionaries like Negroponte."
— *Newsday*

Essence or nature of something as being fundamentally digital, being through digital means

# 2. VIRTUAL WORLD-BUILDING, VIRTUAL-WORLD BUILDING

Amongst these multifaceted endeavors, it is the domain of world-building applications that is an indicative vector worthy of careful study.

The practice of world-building within virtual environments has become the standard approach, empowered by the aforementioned technologies.

Virtual-world building is the design and modeling of virtual or phygital worlds, obviously using computational tools.

What began as a niche within gaming has now become an integral part of urban development, manifesting as an online virtual or augmented layer superimposed on our physical world.

Resting on technological pillars, the current technologies are key limitations to what is possible, from low-fi to high-fi graphic systems, open and closed platforms, etc.

*Let's eat, Grandma, or Let's eat Grandma.*
**Punctuation matters.**

The Metaverse rests upon an array of foundational breakthroughs, encompassing numerous projects and incremental changes in the development of gaming, the internet, and technological advancements.

The lineage of constructing virtual worlds - digitally- can be traced back to the emergence of interaction interfaces with computers, notably the teleprinter. In the 1960s, the technological bedrock allowed the rise of text-based strategy video games such as "The Sumerian Game" and "Hamurabi," which capitalized on the management of land and resources, providing narratives that were inherently urban.

The 1980s were home to the first ever 3D graphics video game BattleZone. It was a basic tank game that marked a milestone in the timeline of game development. SimCity was released at the end of the 1980s with 2D graphics, but interestingly, it included collecting taxes, building infrastructure, etc. From there onwards, with more ubiquitous computers, and advancements in computer graphics, hardware, and software, more elaborate games emerged.

Now, we have the capacity for visual representations that are much more complex.

The evolution of world-building games was intertwined with the evolution of computer interfaces, from the teleprinter to arcade machines, personal computers, consoles, mobile devices – and ultimately, virtual reality. As computers became more widespread and compact, interfaces transitioned from simple text-based interactions to more sophisticated button-based arcade experiences, visually captivating PC gaming with more advanced graphics, and the portability of consoles and mobile platforms. Finally, virtual reality emerged, imbuing the experience with immersive spatial dimensions.

Virtual World-building, just like the internet, evolved from a text-based to a more immersive endeavor as technology allowed.

But what exactly do world-building games offer?

It seems to me that the key element is rapid expression.

Life as we live it is not only about 'hard utility'.

Culture and expression probably drive the planet.

As highly emotional and social beings, we engage with the world through desires, identities, cultures, and expressions. In this context, virtual world-building, as a practice of cultural expression, assumes a pivotal role as a foundational element within the spatial internet.

World-building is an open process that can be infinitely complex. Yet within digital environments and gamified processes, it is shredded down to seemingly simple commands with immediate feedback.

In the virtual, design and realization are synonymous.

World-building is set for a trans- formative decade, driven by the development of AI integration, financial layers, widespread adoption by "non-gamers," advanced graphic engines, advanced digital identity and embodiment, and emerging network communities and technologies.

Game engines, software, and frameworks used for game creation and play are rapidly evolving to offer versatile solutions. They now integrate physics, simulations, scripting, asset management, and other features, while also achieving unprecedented levels of realism through hyperrealistic real-time rendering.

Contrasting with the hi-fi heavyweight integrated solutions like Unity and Unreal, Web-Based Platforms leverage web-based frameworks, such as WebGL, A-Frame, and Babylon.js. These technologies empower developers to craft interactive 3D experiences accessible directly through web browsers. They are the answer to hard utility. We don't necessarily play games because they have great graphics, are fun, offer financial incentives, and other things of the like. Think about Snake.

Simultaneously, the democratization of 3D modeling and asset generation is underway. Open-source tools like Blender and no-code creator platforms enable anyone to construct and personalize their own virtual worlds. While examples are plenty here, Bezel is worth a mention. To put it simply, it is an online, real-time multiplayer Blender.

In parallel, advancements in AI are shaping everything. This definitely and naturally includes world-building and virtual environments. Generative models are now integrated within builders, making creators just a click away from generating full worlds. Language models, on the other hand, serve a different purpose and are probably the most powerful tool for interfacing. And the newest edition, Co-pilots, are AI-driven assistants that aid creators throughout the process.

Other new techniques and tech-nologies are being integrated too; procedural and algorithmic pipelines speed up development. Photo-grammetry and other real-world object-capturing technologies are integrated to internalize physical environments and objects, and they manipulate or interact with them as virtual environments.

World-building is at a pivotal point in its history.

## List of Sim Grid

## List of World Building Video Games

# 3. METAVERSE URBANISM

'METAVERSE URBANISM IS THE URBANISM OF THE 4TH INDUSTRIAL REVOLUTION'

Discourses on Metaverse and Urbanism intersect heavily in the form of practice and technologies used. More importantly, the aspects intertwine as the virtual layer becomes more and more useful.

Urbanism engages with the physical, social, economic, environmental, and cultural dimensions of life. It is an evolving discipline that integrates diverse fields of knowledge, ranging from architecture and sociology to ecology and governance, in pursuit of thriving urban futures.

There is no way to go down this lane without heavily engaging with an increasingly important virtual layer.

To establish the distinction between both, clear definitions must be laid out.

If: Urbanism is the multifaceted study and practice of understanding, designing, and managing the complex spatial interplay of human societies, built environments, natural systems, and cultural expressions within urban areas.

Then: Metaverse Urbanism is the expansion of urbanism through engaging with emerging virtual layers, the convergence of both the virtual layer and the physical layer of urban life, and form.It is a new urbanism where a bidirectional mutation is constant, as the virtual becomes integral to cities as we live them.

# Navigating the next industrial revolution

| Revolution | | Year | Information |
|---|---|---|---|
| | 1 | 1784 | Steam, water, mechanical production equipment |
| | 2 | 1870 | Division of labour, electricity, mass production |
| | 3 | 1969 | Electronics, IT, automated production |
| | 4 | **?** | Cyber-physical systems |

The mechanization of production came around with a steam-powered industrial shift during the last quarter of the 1700s. Around a century later, mass production and the disruption of electrical power, caused a major shift in the workforce and the concept of labor.

Following our trip to the moon, the 1970s witnessed a third shift. With an explosion in the development of the usage of electronics, it was a new world of information technology and a major shift towards automated production.

The third revolution sits on the shifts in paradigms of energy, communication, and economy, all enabled through technological breakthroughs and applications at scale.

During the last several decades, with a trend towards reducing greenhouse gas emissions, the transition to renewable energy sources, such as solar, nuclear, and wind to replace fossil fuels, formed a central pillar of the third revolution. One that focuses on decentralizing energy production and enabling individuals and communities to generate their own clean energy.

With the evolution of the Internet of Things, an extra pillar was realized through the widespread integration of digital technology and sensors into everyday objects. The emergence of IoT as a new technological phase enables a highly interconnected network of devices, facilitating connection, control, communication, and real-time data sharing, and improving efficiency in various sectors.

The development of advanced communication technologies, including high-speed internet and wireless connectivity, ensures seamless data transmission and facilitates collaboration across geographical boundaries. This creates a reliable and accessible communication infrastructure of communication technologies.

A decentralized and Collaborative Economy is an extra layer to the foundation of the third revolution. A shift towards decentralized and collaborative business models is enabled by the sharing economy and peer-to-peer platforms. By that, collaboration, open innovation, and resource sharing are fostered, leading to a more sustainable and equitable economy.

Finally, a major transformation in transportation systems took place through the adoption of electric vehicles, smart grids, and shared mobility solutions. This came as a response to the proposed need to reduce carbon emissions from the transportation sector and promote more efficient and sustainable modes of transportation.

The city of the third industrial revolution is, at best, a technological beast. In an urbanism of technology giants, the market is saturated with technologies to save the world.

The new shift in urbanism is a technology-based shift that integrates cyber with physical, and bio with tech.

Biocomputation, synthetic biology, decentralized economies, finances, applied artificial intelligence, robotics, the Internet of Things, autonomous vehicles, advanced 3-D printing, nanotechnology, biotechnology, materials science, energy storage, and quantum computing are the main drivers of the next decades.

Rabbit is the new beef, indeed. But rabbit has a new texture. It is lab-grown from stem cells.

The cosmological is abandoned, and the cosmetic is all that we have.

# 4. THE CONTEXT IS NOT BLANK

Context is one of the foundational aspects of design, at any scale. All physical locations have an obvious physical context. While they also have clear socio-economic, political, and other contexts, the physical one is always the most obvious. Navigating Urban design in the virtual world can indicate the absence of context, a black screen on a computer.

The context is not blank, and it brings to the surface the "The non-visual strata of financial, computational, and technological context".

The context that seems nonexistent is one where the advancements in technology, state-of-the-art urbanism, and the speculative market surrounding blockchain investments and financial space imply the introduction of certain concepts into the workflow.

Bringing these driving concepts forward is an attempt to create a comprehensive conceptual framework of ideas and phenomena that govern that design space, and that we actively navigate arriving at a solid ground to move on with.

To do so, we have developed a list of driving concepts that we either define or invent for the sake of well-positioning the design motivations.

These driving concepts are political, position-driven ideas that we operate upon.

I have been practicing urbanism for years now, completing over 30 design schemes at all scales, from the street, through the block, and to the territory. Each project exists in a specific location on this planet and has a de facto physical, political, ecological, and social context.

These are all obvious bounds upon which the game happens; they're constraints we respond or act upon.

It is trivial in the physical world, but what happens when designing a virtual city?

While it seems that the starting point is a blank screen, a blank digital canvas, it is crucial to acknowledge that things are beyond blank. There are layers of non-visual strata of financial, computational, and technological context that govern the process.

What the chosen hardware and software allow users to achieve is wired within the software, as every program has its limitations, and in some, its own aesthetic, etc.

Other questions arise, such as, what is the financial cycle like in this city? What are the main functions to be used? Which communities does it attract? Which social life is to be framed? And so on and so forth.

It is important to note that we are not discussing several virtual world games and metaverse worlds, which are based on virtual real estate, or open worlds where the actual context exists.

In that virtual world, users have neighbors and the surrounding environment.

This is already in a stage past the initial point of the design of the world initially. We will return to this later, answering the golden question: How much should we design?

Therefore, when designing a metaverse city, it is important to consider the non-visual strata of financial, computational, and technological context. These factors provide a place of departure for the main framework that leads

to how the city is laid out, how it functions, and what kinds of experiences and interactions can be created within it, alongside a long list of other constraints.

The financial context refers to the economic infrastructure of the metaverse city, such as the systems for generating revenue, managing resources, and funding development. This includes the design of virtual currencies, payment systems, and investment models that support the growth of the city.

The computational context relates to the technology and software that underpin the city's design and operation. This includes using artificial intelligence, machine learning, and other advanced technologies to create dynamic, responsive environments that can adapt to the needs and preferences of users.

The technological context encompasses the hardware and infrastructure required to support the metaverse city, such as servers, networks, and data centers. This includes considerations of scalability, security, and performance, as well as the potential environmental impact of these systems.

Taken together, these non-visual strata provide an essential foundation for the design and implementation of a metaverse city. By understanding and accounting for these factors, designers can create immersive, engaging, and sustainable virtual environments that offer unique experiences and opportunities for social interaction, economic growth, and cultural exchange.

# "The non-visual strata of financial, computational, and technological context"

# 5. PLANNING

**Urbanism spans the spectrum of planning from "Strategic" to "tactical".**

**Designing the virtual layer, whether by designing entirely virtual worlds, or designing virtual augmentations to the physical world, begs the question of how much do we design?**

If the first question was about establishing a clear context, the next questions are , how much should we design, how much needs to be fully deployed, how much needs to be framed, and how much needs to be left totally open? It is a play within the top-down bottom-up spectrum, assigning various degrees of freedom at each layer of planning.

Within this spectrum, there are three key positions:
A top-down, bottom-up, and centrist hybrid way of dealing with the topic.

While the first two positions, at both extremes of the spectrum, are clear, there is an infinite amount of possibilities within the third position type, the in-between, where certain degrees of freedom are available.

Let's take a concrete example of a very basic simple urban situation and examine it within a hierarchical layering, from top to bottom.

In this situation, within the fully top-down solution, all of the above are previously assigned. On the other end, all of the above are totally left to users to make decisions collectively. Things get interesting when one or more of these starts to be open.

On the other hand, we can draw a Y-axis for governance, ranging from personal governance to DAO governance, where the designed environment belongs to the community and is governed by a decision-making model.

**Infrastructure**

**Land Use and Urban Functional Layout**

**Urban block plot division types and sizes setbacks**

**Building height regulations**

**Density and Number of inhabitants**

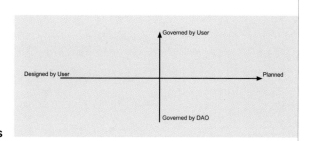

# 6. AUTOMATED URBAN MORPHOLO-GIES

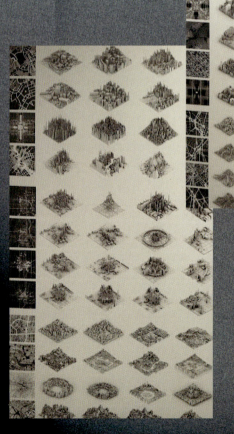

GENERATIVE URBANISM - EMERGING PLANETARISM - THE 13TH ARCHITECTURAL DIGITALFUTURES SHANGHAI SUMMER WORKSHOP ( PHOTO TAKEN FROM THE EXHIBITION AT THE UNIVERSITY IN SHANGHAI, SEPTEMBER 2023 )

## Rule-based data-informed generative algorithms that can produce viable - scalable - morphologies for both the physical and the virtual.

Creating automated urban morphologies refers to the use of algorithms to generate or design the form of a city or urban space. This can involve using data-driven approaches to analyze and model different urban systems, such as mobility networks, land use patterns, and building typologies, to create specific, generic, optimized, and/ or efficient urban layouts.

Automated urban morphology can also involve the use of machine learning techniques and artificial intelligence to generate and optimize urban design solutions. The core intent though is to produce a system rather than a final fixed layout, where the system is based on rules and parameters and can adapt, expand, and scale based on new input, rendering it infinite in that sense. A square grid is a basic example.

From tribal hut community formations to urban grids, and past that, to advanced data-driven spatial urban systems, patterns are present in how the built environment is laid out and how it operates.

We propose code-based urban configurations that are comprehensive, scalable, geometrically driven, and quantifiable. The master planning scheme is, therefore, system-based, and due to its nature, can be worked across all scales.

So far, the morphologies highlighted are all planar configurations, mainly inspired by real-world urbanism, where cities are often developed with a singular ground floor. The metaverse allows for new morphologies that are more complex, and are not limited to a singular floor plane, but rather surpass it to an infinite number of ground floors.

The ground datum disappears, it vanishes in the continuous space that unfolds in three dimensions.

Hong Kong is exemplary of its 3D urbanism, with public space at a number of levels within the urban sphere. By exploding the floor datum into various places within the 3D space, the possibility of 3D urbanism unfolds.

Yona Friedman's spatial configurations highlight an early example of urban space in an almost voxel topology filled up with units.

Automated urban morphologies hold the promise of 3D urbanism, an urbanism that exhausts all empty space. No space is free, no space is public. Algorithmic growth fills up the last void. Urban space is topologized, and every part of it is addressable, accessible, and commodified.

# 7. THE DAO STACK

**Within the Metaverse context, a new definition of stakeholders is possible.**

**An ecosystem of interactors.
( The DAO Stack )**

A significant shift in the governance structure brings together a diverse range of stakeholders to collaborate and create mutual value in a decentralized and participatory manner.

Enabled by the use of smart contracts and blockchain technology, the DAO Stack shall boost innovation and entrepreneurship within the metaverse ecosystem. A sophisticated set of smart contracts and protocols allows for the creation and management of decentralized autonomous organizations (DAOs), which function as self-governed entities.

The power structure is distributed among the various stakeholders, with decision-making power allocated based on a variety of factors, including stakeholder participation, reputation, and contribution to the ecosystem.

At best, value is created within the DAO Stack through the creation of innovative new applications, the development of immersive experiences, and the provision of hosting and other services. Value is produced through the use and consumption of these applications and experiences, as well as through the sales and exchange of virtual assets and currency. In a word, Utility.

Looking at the current metaverse ecosystem, and projecting ahead, eight main nodes determine the players on the table. The DAO stack aims to lay out the hierarchical structure of the emergence of such an ecosystem, and the economics of how it operates.

# METAVERSE LANDSCAPE STAKEHOLDERS

1. **Users:** Individuals who engage with the metaverse, including non-expert content creators, consumers, and participants in various activities and experiences.

2. **Developers:** Software engineers, programmers, and technologists who build and maintain the infrastructure, applications, and smart contracts underlying the metaverse.

3. **Designers:** 3D UX/UI designers, 3D artists, and world creators who contribute to the spatial, visual, and interactive aspects of the metaverse.

4. **Token Holders:** Users, individuals, or entities who hold tokens representing ownership or participation rights within a DAO ecosystem.

5. **Curators:** Community members responsible for curating and organizing content, ensuring quality, relevance, and appropriate moderation within the metaverse.

6. **Validators:** Entities or individuals who validate transactions and ensure the security and integrity of the metaverse's blockchain or consensus mechanism.

7. **Governance Participants:** Community members actively involved in the governance of the DAO, proposing and voting on decisions, protocols, and parameter changes.

8. **Service Providers:** Entities offering specialized services within the metaverse, such as hosting, storage, security, identity verification, or virtual asset management.

9. **Investors:** Individuals, venture capital entities, or institutions providing funding, resources, or financial support to DAO projects and metaverse development.

10. **Researchers:** Scholars, academics, and experts studying and contributing knowledge to advance the understanding and evolution of the metaverse.

11. **Regulators:** Government agencies or regulatory bodies responsible for overseeing and ensuring compliance with relevant laws and regulations.

12. **Partners and Collaborators:** External organizations, businesses, or platforms collaborating with the DAO stack to bring additional capabilities, integrations, or interoperability.

13. **Merchants:** Individuals or businesses offering goods or services for sale within the metaverse, facilitating virtual commerce and economic activity.

14. **Educators:** Trainers, educators, and mentors who provide learning resources, tutorials, and guidance for users and developers within the metaverse.

15. **Community Managers:** Individuals responsible for fostering a vibrant and inclusive community within the metaverse, organizing events, and facilitating communication.

16. **Legal Experts:** Lawyers and legal professionals specializing in blockchain, smart contracts, virtual property rights, and intellectual property within the metaverse.

17. **Media and Influencers:** Journalists, bloggers, YouTubers, and social media influencers who cover and promote the metaverse, its projects, and developments.

18. **Bots and AI agents,** such as software, virtual assistants, and any AI operate on a decision-making basis within the system.

Surely, a single entity can be one or more of the above simultaneously.

# THE METAVERSE CORPORATIONS

**A quick search on Google reveals a diverse array of companies involved in shaping the metaverse. While they are all crucial to a thriving ecosystem, these companies cover a wide range of functions, including enabling-technology development, social media, blockchain, interactive commerce, gaming, and beyond.**

Understanding the key players in this landscape is important as they contribute to shaping the future of digital interaction and immersion. The reality of life itself.

With the rebranding to Meta - from Facebook- the company signaled a new hype and raised the wave for a phenomenon that has been cooking for a while. Aside from what we witnessed in the last years of a rapidly growing hype and a sobering down period punctuated with spikes of technological advancements, the next iteration of the internet is in process. A paradigm shift is happening.

### Meta Platforms, Inc.
Meta has been heavily investing in the development of virtual reality and augmented reality technologies through Oculus. With research on BCIs, advanced HMI, and a legacy of a global social media platform, the combination can be the basis for the next digital life revolution.

### NVIDIA
An elephant in the room.
It moved from being primarily a GPU company to becoming a foundational part of the new global power map when it comes to the digital world, as its units happened to be exceptionally well-suited for AI workloads. Parallel computa-

tions are essential for the deep learning algorithms powering AI applications, and GPUs excel at that, growing NVIDIA's evaluation to over 1.7 Trillion

One of the major developments, besides its chips, is Omniverse. It is a cloud computing platform that will contribute to shaping an array of significant aspects of the next internet, such as real-time collaboration in shared virtual environments, simulations and visualizations, asset management, and sharing. That leads to the two key components of interoperability and AI-aided features, from content creation to ai-avatars that walk around the new extended reality space.

### Alphabet Inc.
Google's investments in technologies like Google Glass and Google Daydream is the tip of the iceberg in its explorations of domains including virtual reality, augmented reality, immersive experiences, and the significant advancements in developing AI and advanced search methods.

### Microsoft
Microsoft has been actively involved in developing VR and AR technologies through products like HoloLens and initiatives like the Microsoft Mesh.

https://www.cnet.com/culture/nba-is-using-microsoft-teams-to-brings-virtual-fans-into-its-real-world-games/

The company's Azure cloud services also play a significant role. Infrastructure, mixed reality services, collaborative tools, content delivery network (CDN) capabilities, and developer resources are essential for the development and deployment of immersive experiences.

**As of 2021, the leading provider of cloud business intelligence is Microsoft Azure, with 69% of the market share. This company is closely followed by Amazon Web Services (55%), Google Cloud (53.5%), and Oracle Cloud (33.5%).**

### Epic Games
With Unreal Engine, Epic Games provides one of the most important tools for building immersive experiences. Its acquisition of companies like Sketchfab and the development of Fortnite demonstrates a commitment to metaverse development. Going beyond gaming into the metaverse.

### Unity Technologies
The other half face of the coin. Unity powers a wide range of interactive experiences, including games and virtual simulations. It offers one of the accessible, cross-platform compatible solutions, fitted for scalability and increased adoption.

### Roblox Corporation
This is arguably the single most interesting platform that allows users to create and share games, experiences, and virtual worlds. It has gained significant traction, particularly among younger audiences, and is often considered a key player in the evolution of the metaverse.

### Tencent Holdings
Tencent, a Chinese multinational conglomerate, has investments in various sectors including gaming and social media. Its stakes in companies like Epic Games and Roblox, along with its own developments in virtual spaces, position it as a significant player in the metaverse landscape.

The list is long, with Apple's Vision Pro, the contribution of Amazon, and other platforms. The main point here is to highlight the diverse landscape of giant entities that are shaping the next digital turn, the next internet, and the next generation of the social arena-- life arena.

# A. THE METAVERSE ENTREPRENEURS AND FOUNDERS

Visionary individuals and teams conceive and create the metaverse's various components, such as virtual worlds, digital assets, games, and applications. They are the main force behind conceptualizing and implementing innovative solutions to address the challenges faced by users in the metaverse at various scales.

Founders add fundamental value to the ecosystem by creating and developing the metaverse's infrastructure and experiences, attracting users, and generating revenue through the sale of virtual goods, advertising, or subscriptions.

Roblox is a popular metaverse platform founded in 2006 by David Baszucki and Erik Cassel. Today, it has over 200 million registered users and a market capitalization of over $40 billion.

The founders/entrepreneurs layer is crucial to the development and launching of various companies, ideas, applications, platforms, and services within the metaverse. They transform and shape the digital space. This includes virtual marketplaces, social networks, gaming platforms, and other innovative technologies.

One of the early champions within the first layer is Philip Rosedale, the creator of Second Life, or the team behind Decentraland, a blockchain-based virtual world.

# B. END USERS

End users are the individuals who ultimately use and consume the products and services offered within the Metaverse ecosystem. They may be individuals seeking entertainment or socialization, businesses looking to establish a presence and engage with potential customers, or even researchers or educators exploring the possibilities of the metaverse for their respective fields. End users are crucial stakeholders as they provide demand for the products and services offered by the other stakeholders, driving the growth of the metaverse ecosystem.

End users are the individuals who use and interact with the various applications, platforms, and services within the metaverse. These can include gamers, social network users, virtual event attendees, and even virtual real estate investors. Examples of metaverse end users include players of virtual reality games like VRChat and Rec Room, users of virtual social networks like Second Life and High Fidelity, and attendees of virtual events like the Virtual Burning Man festival.

End users may generate profits for other stakeholders through various means, such as paying for access to premium features or virtual real estate, purchasing virtual goods and services, or even participating in virtual events and experiences sponsored by businesses. For example, a clothing retailer may hold a virtual fashion show within the metaverse, and end users can attend and purchase virtual versions of the clothing showcased. In this way, the end users generate profits for the retailer while also enjoying a unique and immersive experience within the metaverse.

# C. LAND OWNERS

These are individuals or organizations who own virtual land within the metaverse. Virtual land is a scarce and valuable asset that can be used for various purposes, such as building structures, hosting events, or mining resources. Landowners add value to the ecosystem by providing a physical location for virtual activities, attracting users, and generating revenue by renting or selling virtual land. For example, Decentraland is a virtual world that allows users to own, build, and monetize virtual real estate. In Decentraland, land sales have generated over $50 million in revenue.

Landowners within the metaverse are individuals or organizations that own virtual land. This land can be used for a variety of purposes, including building and hosting virtual events, creating digital art installations, and even launching virtual businesses. Examples of metaverse land owners include the Sandbox, a decentralized virtual gaming platform that allows players to buy and own virtual land, and Somnium Space, a blockchain-based virtual world where users can buy and build on virtual land.

# D. DESIGNERS

These are individuals or organizations who design the user interface and user experience of metaverse platforms and applications as well as the assets, worlds, and experiences within. Value is defined as creating intuitive, immersive, and engaging experiences for users, which increases retention and revenue.

From virtual fashion and furniture to entire virtual cities and landscapes.

# E. REAL ESTATE DEVELOPERS/ OWNERS

These are individuals or organizations who develop and manage virtual properties within the metaverse. They add value by creating and maintaining high-quality virtual properties, attracting users, and generating revenue by renting or selling virtual properties. Sandbox can be taken as an example once again; it allows users to create and sell their virtual games, assets, and experiences. Real estate developers and owners can create and monetize virtual properties within the Sandbox.

Real estate developers and owners are individuals or organizations that specialize in creating and managing virtual real estate properties within the metaverse. These properties can include virtual homes, businesses, and other commercial real estate. Examples of metaverse real estate developers and owners include Anshe Chung Studios, a Japanese company that owns and manages virtual real estate properties within Second Life, and Propy, a blockchain-based real estate platform that enables users to buy and sell virtual real estate.

# F. TENANTS - HOSTING ORGANIZATIONS

These are organizations that rent virtual space within the metaverse from landowners or real estate developers. They add value by providing engaging and immersive virtual experiences for users, attracting users, and generating revenue by selling virtual goods, advertising, or subscriptions. For example, Upland, a blockchain-based metaverse platform, allows users to buy, sell, and trade virtual properties and assets.

# G. OWNER-OCCUPIERS - HOST ORGANIZATIONS

These are organizations that host and manage metaverse platforms, applications, and services. They add value by providing the technical infrastructure and expertise needed for the smooth operation of metaverse services, attracting users, and generating revenue through hosting fees or commissions. For example, Amazon Web Services (AWS) is a popular hosting service used by many metaverse applications and services.

Owner occupiers and tenants are hosting organizations that provide space within the metaverse for others to create and host their own virtual experiences. These organizations can include virtual event spaces, virtual galleries, and virtual stores. An example of owner, occupiers and tenants is the Vastari Virtual Museum, a virtual museum platform that allows museums to create and host their own virtual exhibitions. Another example is Upland, a blockchain-based virtual real estate game where users can buy, sell, and trade virtual properties.

# H. THE INVESTORS - VCS, TOKEN HOLDERS

These are individuals, organizations, or groups that provide funding to metaverse entrepreneurs and projects. Venture capitalists (VCs) invest in metaverse startups and offer expertise, mentorship, and resources to help them grow. Token holders invest in blockchain-based metaverse projects through cryptocurrencies, such as Ethereum or Bitcoin, and receive tokens in return. They add value to the ecosystem by providing the capital needed for innovation, growth, and expansion. Investors make profits through the appreciation of their investment, the sale of their stake, or by receiving dividends from the metaverse project's revenue.

Investors in the metaverse can come in many forms, including venture capitalists (VCs), angel investors, and token holders. These investors provide capital to fund the development of new metaverse technologies, platforms, and applications. Examples of investors in the metaverse include Andreessen Horowitz, a VC firm that has invested in various metaverse-related startups, and Galaxy Digital, a cryptocurrency investment firm that holds a stake in Decentraland.

https://www.youtube.com/watch?v=WvhL-GKHHoqw

# 8. VIRTUAL URBAN ECONOMIES

# THIS IN TURN CREATES A NEW URBAN ECONOMY, AND THEREFORE NEW POLITICS IN THE URBAN SPHERE.

Virtual cloud economies are economic ecosystems within virtual environments, or real economies influenced by the new virtual layer. At best, they run on decentralized hierarchies and are largely driven by user-generated content and activities.

From In-game economies in video games to virtual marketplaces in online social networks. They are often designed to encourage user engagement and activity, with users able to earn virtual currency through activities, such as completing quests, participating in social events, or creating and selling virtual goods.

Virtual cloud economies are driven by the increasing popularity of virtual worlds and online communities, as well as the rise of blockchain technology and non-fungible tokens. These technologies have enabled the creation of more sophisticated and decentralized virtual economies, with users able to own and trade virtual assets with greater ease and security.

Tokenization is the process that breathes digital life into both tangible and intangible assets. From real estate to cultural experiences, the very foundation of the metaverse urban economy is built on the representation of value through blockchain-based tokens.

Think of it as a digital currency treasure hunt – "Follow the money" takes us to the heart of decentralized autonomous organizations and an entirely new value proposition.

Metaverse economies as shareholder economies with platform tokenomics.

They're a fresh take on participatory economy.

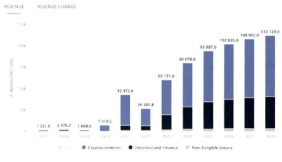

REVENUE    REVENUE CHANGE

1 561.0  2 370.2  1 668.6  7 310.2  26 501.8  42 473.0  60 151.0  80 070.0  93 997.0  102 035.0  108 052.0  112 129.0

● Cryptocurrencies  ● Decentralized Finance  ○ Non-fungible tokens

Notes: Data shown is using current exchange rates and reflects market impacts of the Russia-Ukraine war.

Most recent update: Aug 2023

Source: Statista Market Insights

https://www.statista.com/outlook/fmo/digital-assets/worldwide#revenue

https://www.fortunebusi-
nessinsights.com/
digital-asset-manage-
ment-dam-market-104914

## The global digital asset management market size is projected to grow from $3.97 billion in 2023 to $12.29 billion by 2030, at a CAGR of 17.5% during the forecast period.

Shifting the focus to creators is crucial because everyone becomes a creator.

It's no longer just about the 'what'. The 'who' behind the creation adds a layer of significance. The value proposition is shaped not only by the hard utility of an asset but also by the cultural expression embedded within it.

A Hermès is not a bag.

The next Taylor Swift will most probably produce a song that has no audio. It does not matter; Its value is elsewhere.

In the virtual, all are assets. Lands, objects, files, data, experiences, rents, tickets, you name it.

All assets are tokenizable. Physical and digital. From a coal mine to an online experience.

Utility is king, as cultural expression becomes the star-utility. When value shifts positions, Community reaffirms " Network=Networth"

DAOs suggest a new value proposition.

As websites become webspaces, a virtual real estate market is the new "web development".

Companies will hire experience-builders to build their webspaces. Others will rent.

In the context of the metaverse, lands are not only virtual real estate ( parcels, plots, etc ) Lands can be digital tickets to a network. Lands and what's built on top are disconnected.

The China land 'ownership' model does not allow private ownership of land. Instead, It allows for the use of land for 70 years. You can trade the land, while you have no access to what's on top. Virtual land is a digital asset. Virtual spaces, objects, and lands are sold or rented out, on or off platform - within the world's ecosystem or through a third-party NFT market.

Everybody can have a share, the community, promoters, platforms, and creators. Value distribution is automated, and it follows a market logic.

Just like ads take over cities, architecture, clothing, and websites ads abuse metaverse space, bombarding users with subtle - not always - sticky information.

While the list is endless, I would like to highlight two of the 'hybrid' and crucial new ways virtual cloud economies create value.

Server and cloud computing on the one hand, and royalties on the other.

If there is one thing that will impact cities, it's the virtual layer that is growing exponentially. As mentioned previously, apps like Airbnb, Uber, and other localized apps for food delivery, place recommendations, travel apps, etc. have shaped cities–literally.

Cloud economies will continue shaping the urbansphere. As the distance becomes less important, augmented layers become widely used, computation power and cloud capacity become so high, and the city runs on the cloud.

In parallel, virtual economies change governance and ownership models. The right to the city will be redefined.

Royalties are payments or fees that creators receive for the use, reselling, or reproduction of their intellectual property, whether in the form of sales royalties, usage royalties, licensing royalties, or subscription royalties. They are the incentive and IP guarantee for the new creators' economy.

New urban economies will emerge from an expanding virtual and digital layer, entering the urbansphere from all three levels: Financial ( markets, money, revenue streams), Social ( Identity, Communities, networks ), and Governance ( DAOs, right to the city ).

(SUB)CULTURE

### Someone Spent $450,000 for 'Land' Next to Snoop Dogg's NFT House

Crypto fans are scrambling to buy and monetize metaverse land plots as Snoop Dogg, Adidas, and other brands start building virtual worlds

BY SAMANTHA HISSONG

DECEMBER 7, 2021

Snoop Dogg of hip-hop supergroup Mt. Westmore performs at Rupp Arena on November 20, 2021 in Lexington, Kentucky  STEPHEN J. COHEN/GETTY IMAGES

https://www.rollingstone.com/culture/culture-news/sandbox-decentraland-virtual-land-sales-soar-metaverse-nfts-1267740/

https://medium.com/@chervinska.anastasiia/samsung-galaxy-s23-ad-on-the-cathedral-of-barcelona-a-cool-marketing-stunt-or-an-ethical-concern-15f7870e0bc7

# 9. EXPERIENCE
# - INFORMATION
# - INTERACTION

# EXPERIENCE, INFORMATION, AND INTERACTION AS THE TRILOGY OF THE NEW SHIFT

The metaverse is an experience-driven endeavor.
The other two pillars of the foundation of the metaverse are information and interaction.

The metaverse bets on the electronic limitlessness,
Consensual hallucinations and autonomous realities.

Cyberspace shows up as a new global brain,
its presence is the enabler for the rest to happen.

Moving forward, cyberspace has already leaked to the physical world, contaminating it;
changing it slowly, consuming it from the outside in.

It has conquered capitalism, globalization, human imagination, and overall, perception and the concept of reality itself.

We are addicted to more. No static knowledge survives.
Objects become events. The fourth dimension of time is introduced and distance is crossed out.

The notion of events has changed. Before phones, broadcasting, and telecommunication, things happened once. Events were non-recordable; if you did not see a World Cup final's last-minute goal, you missed it, forever.

Today hardly anyone at the stadium watches the game, people mostly record it.

Experience encompasses the immersive qualities of the environment, including sensory inputs such as visuals, sounds, and even tactile sensations. Experience is about perception, and in perception, filters are the norm. What constitutes "real" barely matters, the experience is all that counts.

Being Spatial is the Metaverse's way to answer the need for more. From being text-based, to becoming more visual and graphic rich, and to becoming more dynamic. Finally, the internet becomes spatial. Being Spatial is this decades' "Being digital".

Spatial is what feels more natural, no effort is needed.
Spatial is seamless, it brings both the virtual and the physical to one arena. Spatial is the basis for an experience-driven economy and ecology.

# Photo shows fans at the game watching LeBron James break the NBA scoring record on their phones instead of watching him

https://www.businessinsider.com/fans-watched-lebron-james-break-nba-record-on-their-phones-2023-2

Alan Dawson  Feb 8, 2023, 7:48 PM GMT+1    Share    Save

LeBron James breaks NBA scoring record.  Photo by Getty Images

Information is the critical raw matter that makes this possible, think data, content, and knowledge, in an explosion of stimulating environments. Information requires space; It exhausts 'the spatial' to its benefit. All spatial interfaces, surfaces, and elements are information, they are attention traps.

Information abundance is what we live in today. Information everything is what the next internet could look like.

Interaction is enabled by spatiality and information. No interaction, no experience. User-to-world and user-to-user (s), include communication, collaboration, and the manipulation of virtual objects or environments. Interactivity is foundational.

In the physical, interactions are intuitive and evident. We interact with things and people around us naturally. And while we might attempt kicking a pebble, we don't usually attempt kicking a large rock expecting it to roll ahead. We know rocks are heavy. In the Metaverse, rocks can be weightless and will move only if they were designed to. A pebble also won't move unless it was designed to. Interactions in the metaverse are largely experimental too. I've seen people clicking on everything, jumping everywhere, falling off buildings, and more. Exploration is the first layer of interaction.

Interaction goes beyond exploration and experimentation to objectives, such as customization, manipulation, communication, control, etc.

The internet has evolved from a 'read-only' interface to a 'read-write' interface.

https://www.youtube.com/
watch?v=YJg02ivYzSs

https://holograktor.com/

DATA, DATA,
DATA, DATA,
DATA, DATA, DA
STARTUPS FROM
~~TOMORROW~~
TODAY, DATA,
DATA, DATA, DATA
ATA, DATA, DATA
DATA, DATA
DATA, DATA

# AS THE DIGITAL BECOMES A UNIVERSAL SOLVENT, DATA GAINS PROMINENCE. DATA IS THE NEW OIL.

**The total installed global data storage capacity base is projected to grow steadily through 2024. The total installed base will increase from 6.8 zettabytes (2020) to approximately 13.2 zettabytes (2024). The total amount of data in utilized storage is expected to reach 8.9 zettabytes by 2024.**

**The digital becomes a universal solvent, data gains prominence. Data is the new oil.**

While we have always been building up human skills, know-how, and expertise, the last century has been probably the most important in terms of creating the technologies. For the last 50 years, we have created all the machinery that enables the digital era we inhabit, and with this, data has been clinical– in quantity, and in quality. When it comes to data, quantity has a quality of its own.

**The trilogy: Data - Skill - Computing Power.**

AI is no longer a technological issue, it has already become political, an issue of national security for the world's largest powers, China and the USA. Looking at the matter strategically, a simple graph with three main indicators is made. Skill, Computation power, and Data are the magic ingredients to the next big thing.

**While skill and computing power can reach a plateau, the data graph can be the decisive factor.**

Data in the metaverse is a goldmine to be unlocked. In the metaverse, mining will be focused on data, as it is the most valuable and useful asset.

We probably need a couple more books like this one to cover the vastness of the topic, walking through the extraction, processing, and utilization of data, and how it has become central to innovation, economic growth, and societal progress.

Instead, I thought I would invent a list of applications, bridging future ideas and speculations in seemingly realistic scenarios, making it more digestible, and bringing it closer to the "every day".

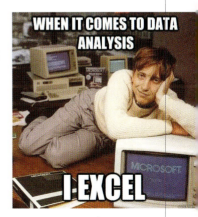

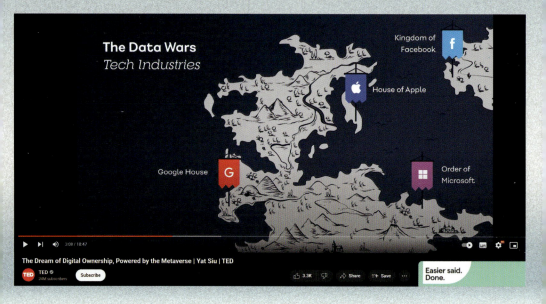

The Data Wars
*Tech Industries*

Kingdom of Facebook

House of Apple

Google House

Order of Microsoft

3:08 / 10:47

The Dream of Digital Ownership, Powered by the Metaverse | Yat Siu | TED

TED ✓
24M subscribers

Subscribe

3.3K

Share

Save

Easier said.
Done.

## Intelligencer

Mar-a-Lago, Donald Trump once again encouraged the world to just forget about the very strong possibility that Russian hackers meddled with the presidential election, saying, "I think we ought to get on with our lives." The Obama administration is reportedly close to announcing retaliatory measures for the alleged hacking, while Republican senators Lindsey Graham and John McCain on Wednesday called for the incoming administration and congress to impose "much tougher" sanctions on Russia. Noting that Graham "ran against me" in the GOP primary, Trump said that he hadn't discussed sanctions with the senators, though he added that he "certainly [would] over a period of time."

Trump — who, for extra flair, spoke with an American- and Israeli-flag-wielding Don King at his side — blamed the whole controversy on the confusing nature of "computers." "I think that computers have complicated lives very greatly. The whole age of the computer has made it where nobody knows exactly what's going on," he said. "We have speed, we have a lot of other things, but I'm not sure we have the kind of security we need."

Eric Geller · Dec 29, 2016
@ericgeller · Follow
.@realDonaldTrump just took a few questions at Mar-a-Lago and said this about @LindseyGrahamSC et al.'s

# THE FOLLOWING ARE LETTERS FROM THE FUTURE, A SPECULATIVE FUTURE THAT IS NOT HERE YET BUT HAS ALL ITS INGREDIENTS AVAILABLE. I NEED TO REITERATE THE POSITION-BASED PROJECTIVE NATURE OF THIS WORK.

# NVIDIA, THE EUROPEAN CRITICAL RAW MATERIALS ACT, AND BLACKROCK EXIST, BUT THEY ARE SELECTIVELY USED, AMONG OTHER NAMES, IDEAS, AND EVENTS TO PAINT A PICTURE OF POSSIBLE FUTURES, USING TODAY'S LANGUAGE. THE STYLE IS INTENDED TO ADD REALISM AND FAMILIARITY TO WHAT CAN SEEM DISTANT AND ABSTRACT.

# MOST OF THE NEXT PART IS FAKE NEWS, YET FUNCTIONAL.

wielding Don King at his side — blamed the whole controversy on the confusing nature of "computers." "I think that computers have complicated lives very greatly. The whole age of the computer has made it where nobody knows exactly what's going on," he said. "We have speed, we have a lot of

"We are in a cyber world, this is now a cyber world "

- Donald Trump in Redding, CA

# STARTUPS FROM ~~TOMORROW~~ TODAY

## HoloTrace

As a phygital experience-enabling startup, HoloTrace is revolutionizing the way we interact with the world around us. With its cutting-edge technology, HoloTrace is leading the way in the next generation of immersive experiences.

HoloTrace collects data from virtual objects and their interactions with the physical world.

The company is held by a consortium of game-engine development companies, including Epic Games, the leading company behind Unreal Engine, one of the world's most advanced game engines.

## Cybersphere

Cybersphere is a technology company offering a unique and innovative solution for the analysis of data on the behavior and interactions of virtual entities within the metaverse.

The company celebrates its unique solution that deals with data on the behavior and interactions of virtual entities within the metaverse.

It has been recently acquired by NVIDIA and operates within its ecosystem.

## GDAE - Global Database for the Attention Economy

The largest global stock exchange platform, where the trading of stocks is based on attention indices.

NaDAE has rapidly become unavoidable after acquiring the SETAE - stock exchange tower for the attention economy- in the Kaban neighborhood of Gamium.

The company's webspace offers over 2 Million stock options of attention collected through various streams. It utilizes techniques and technologies, such as tracking user interactions with virtual objects, analyzing the time spent in virtual spaces, and monitoring user engagement with virtual advertisements and branded content.

The attention data is also collected through the use of biosensing and eye-tracking technologies, which measure where a user's gaze is directed within the virtual environment.

# NeuroScape

Initially, a data company that brings neurotechnology and brain research to the metaverse, it has attracted brain-computer-interface specialists globally and acquired hardware and software companies such as Blackrock Neurotech, Emotiv, and OpenBCI.

As a spinoff from the University of California, San Francisco, NeuroScape leverages research-backed methods to create immersive environments that help individuals enhance their cognitive abilities, manage stress, and improve overall mental health.

With their innovative technology, NeuroScape provides a new level of insight into human brain function and empowers users to understand the impact of experiences on their emotional states and mental health.

The company has recently launched a new social point system, tokenizing the learning capacity and student attention at a school in Shanghai.

# MetaMinerals

The company has emerged in response to the European Critical Raw Materials Act, to create a new data industry, centered on the relationship between the spatial internet and geographies of information. It holds the promise of mass-traceability, a new data mission to use blockchain technology as a verification method for all minerals extraction, supply chain, and manufacturing in what is connected to the internet.

MetaMinerals builds on tokenization, media geology, and consumer awareness as three main pillars of the future of resource extraction and digital awareness.

# QuantumNet

With a focus on quantum entanglement and teleportation, QuantumNet is revolutionizing data communication within the metaverse.

The next-gen company is leading the global market in next-generation data transfer technology. An advanced network infrastructure enables lightning-fast, secure, and seamless communication between virtual entities, paving the way for a new era of interconnectedness within the metaverse.

The project was initiated by DARPA, as a national interdisciplinary security project in collaboration with MIT, Stanford, and the Metaverse campus of Harvard China - the new Harvard branch, regulated by the Chinese authority.

# TransDimension

Founded in 2020, this is a rapidly growing company that specializes in collecting, processing, and analyzing data on the relationship between physical and virtual spaces in the metaverse.

As an emerging unicorn, TransDimension is quickly becoming the main player in the data market, with a particular focus on understanding how physical and virtual spaces interact and overlap. By leveraging advanced technologies and avant-garde analytics tools, TransDimension is helping shape the future of the metaverse at its finest-- a seamless world of virtual and physical conversion.

# SynthiVerse

Elon Musk's new venture into metaverse data companies, this time with data on the creation and manipulation of synthetic biology and genetic material within the metaverse. It is the first Metaverse company to adopt the third variation of CRISPR, with labs for testing and simulation across various Metaverse environments.

The company has put out its roadmap and vision, dedicating its resources for the next decade to reach its 2 main objectives:

→ Risk-free child feature design lab, a virtual lab with an immersive user interface to design offspring features. The goal is set at 50% accuracy.
→ A personalized aging solution, by reverse-engineering features through a gamified AI-powered age simulator. It works by projecting future scenarios on digital twin avatars.

# MetaPulse

A virtual bio-sensing startup that leads the way on biometric data collected from avatars and their interactions within the metaverse. MetaPulse enables the measuring and analysis of a wide range of physiological responses, from heart rate and skin conductance to facial expressions and eye movements.
The data acquisition is possible through its neck wearable technology that internalizes human users' data to their avatars and visualizes it on the MetaPulse personalized hub - the next-generation MetaPulse App.

With a record-breaking performance, the company leads the way in providing businesses and developers with valuable insights into user behavior, enabling them to create more immersive and engaging experiences within the metaverse.

# Urbanitarian++

Founded in 2022, the world's largest platform for urban data resources has acquired several startups to lead the scene regarding urban data in the spatial internet era.

Establishing partnerships with industry giants, Urbanitarian++ processes a hybrid data type of urban environments across the spectrum, simultaneously processing the virtual and the physical.

As the company's white paper suggests: "The cities of tomorrow are hybrid urban environments of the virtual and physical element. Similarly, the urban data of tomorrow is a highly complex multidimensional inquiry into understanding planning, flows, and urban metrics generally."

The company collects an extensively wide array of data, such as:

→   MPSM - Mass personalization spatial metrics, a novel patented metric that illustrates the patterns of personalization within the phygital experience of people in the city.
→   MindScapes, one of the first additions to the company's archive, is a metric that demonstrates the emotional mapping of spaces.
→   ARCI - Aerial robotics communication index, a novel index acquired through a centralized receiver platform. The index monitors the health of aerial robotic communication.
→   UIA - The urban index of attention, the new standard index for the level of attention the environment draws. Like all Urbanitarian++ data, the index monitors the amount of attention invested in virtual content, visualized as an overlap on the physical environment, content consumed in the physical city, and on virtual platforms.
→   AVEI - Autonomous Vehicles Efficiency index, the evolutionary metric that indicates the margin of efficiency within the overall network of autonomous vehicles.

# 3urbiData

This recent spinoff from Urbanitarian++ is the world's largest archive of 4D assets of urban environments.

The company has been recently gaining visibility as it became the exclusive provider of 4D urban assets for content creation, the film industry, marketing, advertising, and urban design education. The 3urbiData archive is a tokenized bottom-up archive created through a platform that enables all contributors to add value and monetize it.

3urbiData has been in the news, reportedly negotiating access to the world's largest data center at the South Pole.

# DigEco

An emerging startup that operates on providing consultancy based on their bank of data on the virtual ecosystems within the metaverse and their impact on the physical world.

It is an award-winning company that aims to help clients understand and optimize their operations in the metaverse while minimizing their environmental impact. DigEco's services include data analysis, impact assessment, and sustainable solutions for virtual operations.

The company's ultimate goal is to bridge the gap between the virtual and physical worlds while promoting ecological thinking.

# OmniFlow

OmniFlow is a startup that specializes in data related to the movement and flow of people, goods, and information between physical and virtual realms.

The company is part of the growing ecosystem of startups in the metaverse that focus on collecting and analyzing data on the interaction between the real and virtual worlds.

By tracking and analyzing the flow of data and people across these different realms, OmniFlow aims to provide insights that can help companies optimize their operations, improve customer experiences, and stay ahead of the curve in the rapidly evolving metaverse landscape.

OmniFlow has been partially acquired by Amazon.

# HyperSpace

The world's bank of data on the navigation and exploration of virtual space within the metaverse. As a startup that specializes in collecting, processing, and storing data on the navigation and exploration of virtual space within the metaverse, the HyperSpace platform provides users with a seamless experience in exploring the vast virtual universe by analyzing the behavior patterns of avatars and tracking their movements.

The company offers executive consultancy services for businesses looking to optimize their virtual operations and improve their user experience. HyperSpace is at the forefront of the growing metaverse industry, which is expected to revolutionize the way we interact with digital content, each other, and our new sense of self.

Collaborating with other metaverse embodiment companies, HyperSpace has been able to revitalize ancient civilizations through groundbreaking AI implementations.

# MetaMorph

MetaMorph is a unicorn that specializes in recording the changes, evolution, and transformation of virtual entities within the metaverse, building a data bank on the history of metaverse assets.

The company's key expertise is in dealing with data on the changes of virtual entities over time, and in offering valuable insights into how these changes can affect the ecosystem of the metaverse.

During the last market cycle, the company's pattern recognition team was awarded the prestigious prize of data innovation, granted by a portal that engages 70% of the creators within the ecosystem on a 1 token 1 vote system.

# ChronoVerse

An innovation-based solution, the company leading the way with the data on the manipulation and management of time within the metaverse.

The company deploys advanced data-driven solutions to help in the collection, processing, and visualization of data related to the temporal aspects of virtual environments. Its ground-breaking brain implant has been compared to "a controlled time manipulation technology, almost like being on LSD" by Forbes.

ChronoVerse is currently developing its SDK for builders to integrate its software as part of their solution. Consequently, empowering the community through insights into how time can be used as a tool in virtual worlds, and how it can be managed to improve user experience and achieve various objectives.

It is important to highlight that the company has changed its name after being accused of high-level perceptual crimes, and other illegal engagements.

# QuantumScape

QuantumScape is a publicly traded metaverse data company that specializes in regulating the global ownership of data on quantum mechanics and phenomena within the metaverse.

Recruiting the front-line of experts, and advanced technology and expertise in the field, the company provides valuable insights into the behavior of virtual entities within the metaverse. QuantumScape offers solutions such as the simulation of quantum systems, the use of quantum computing for metaverse-related applications, and the exploration of quantum-inspired phenomena in virtual environments among others.

As a trusted and established company, QuantumScape provides the most reliable and secure data on the complex interactions and patterns that emerge within the metaverse.

# TerraSynth

TerraSynth is a metaverse company that archives all data on the creation and manipulation of virtual landscapes and terrains. The world's go-to platform offers a wide range of tools and resources that enable users to create immersive and visually stunning terrains for their virtual worlds.

TerraSynth is the next-generation enterprise of entities dealing with planetary-scale topography data. It was founded by ex-NASA, the European Space Agency, the United States Geological Survey, and the National Oceanic and Atmospheric Administration executives.

Through satellite-facilitated workflows and AI-empowered systems, the company has been able to seamlessly comprehend both the physical terrain of the planet and all integrated features and terrains from the metaverse.

# DigEdu

The state-of-the-art solution for data on the education and learning experiences within the metaverse. With a focus on leveraging the latest technologies and data analytics, DigEdu is leading the way in transforming the future of education in the metaverse.

DigEdu has broken records on the number of patents in education-related innovation and revolutionized the learning system through data-driven tokenization, curriculum building, and learner analytics.

It is a rapidly growing multi-unit company that collects and analyzes data on how people learn and interact in virtual environments. Based on that, the company provides valuable insights for educators, learners, and organizations.

# AvoSphere

An emerging company that enables the metaverse agro-gaming industry. It deals with data on the creation and cultivation of virtual avocados and other produce.

AvoSphere enables virtual agriculture and food production with minimal environmental impact. It also provides insights into the potential for tokenized food production in the real world.

# MetaMarket

The global platform with data on the virtual economy and market-places within the metaverse

The company provides a comprehensive bank of data on virtual economic systems, including virtual currencies, virtual goods, and the exchanges of value within the metaverse. By offering insights into the behaviors and trends within these virtual economies, MetaMarket helps the community, businesses, and investors make informed decisions regarding virtual investments and transactions.

MetaMarket has an edge through its involvement in economics, not only financials.

The consulting unit advises governments and network states.

# MetaMuse

The Metaverse's go-to platform for data on the creation and curation of virtual art, music, and culture within the Metaverse.

It offers a vast array of information on art content that is being created and consumed by users within the Metaverse. MetaMuse's data can be used by artists, musicians, designers, and cultural analysts to stay updated on the latest trends, styles, and techniques, and to better understand the tastes and preferences of the Metaverse's diverse communities.

# MetaMind

MetaMind is a spinoff company from DeepMind, leading the charge on data related to the development and evolution of artificial intelligence and machine learning within the metaverse.

The company collects and analyzes huge amounts of data to provide insights into how AI is shaping the virtual world and transforming the way we interact with it.

In its founding policy, MetaMind's board includes avatars of the great minds within DeepMind, a joint venture with Starlab on the development of decision-making neuro-twins.

# MetaSport

The new unit within the global health organization leads the work on global sports and athletic metrics. Building a database of sports, players, and avatar interaction, with a mission to engage a maximum number of people in metaverse sports to improve people's well-being.

The MetaSport database is open to all Network State governments and can be used by established game companies and sports organizations to maximize efficiency and reach.

Sports data on the spatial internet is a new elephant in the room, as companies like MetaSport have started to monopolize the athletic data landscape.

# DigVoyage

DigVoyage is the go-to platform for data on the exploration and discovery of virtual worlds and civilizations within the metaverse.

The company offers a rigorous database of information on the landscapes, cultures, and inhabitants of the metaverse, providing valuable insights for researchers, developers, and explorers alike. With novel technology and innovative data analysis methods, DigVouage pushes the boundaries of virtual exploration.

As the leadership boards have announced, the company has been rising in stock, short after commercial flights have been reduced dramatically. The company expanded its portfolio of voyaging in the metaverse to internalize real locations as augmented digital twins.

DigVoyage uses technologies of time manipulation, immersive storytelling, and civilization archiving at its foundations.

# Partial

The death of death as we know it. Information coupled with rendering technologies can create virtual AI avatars of people, and once they pass away, the avatars can live forever.
These avatars can be overlayed over a physical environment ( a dinner table on Christmas ) or a virtual environment experienced through goggles.

The startup capitalizes on a new form of citizenship, that of the avatars of the dead.

# Uncanny

## Uncanny is an AI startup that thrives on Natural Language Processing - NLP and Large Language Models - LLM to build products that enable natural and seamless interaction with humans.

## UncannyBots

An Uncanny owned unicorn that monopolizes the market of "real avatars". It is an emergent technology that is used for populating the Metaverse - the physical world in AR, and the virtual world in VR - with AI-enabled human-looking bots that use the unique Uncanny NLP technologies for seamless communication.

UncannyBots can be integrated into any metaverse engine or hosting service, where customizable AI-generated Non-Player Characters - NPC bots now autonomously roam the virtual world.

The list can go on forever, it is an attempt at reality through fiction. A fiction that has its roots in the current techno-sphere. While all of the above is imaginary and invented, the means to achieve it is either here or under development.

# SPECULATIVE FOUNDATIONS

# A QUICK RUN THROUGH WHAT ENABLES METAVERSE URBANISM.

**Seamless Integration:** Metaverse urbanism dwells on the fuzzy boundaries between the physical and virtual, seamlessly integrating the two to create a seemingly unique and immersive experience.

**Virtual Architectural Freedom:** Green Screen architecture offers boundless possibilities for architectural expression, enabling buildings and structures that defy the constraints of the physical world. Creator tools enable content creation that is rapid and personalized.

**Augmented Overlays:** Augmented reality overlays merge the virtual and physical worlds, enhancing the urban environment with dynamic information, interactive elements, and virtual objects.

**Social Virtual Spaces:** The new Commons.
At its core, metaverse urbanism is the framing of social life and interaction, the core aspiration of spatial design. Geography is irrelevant. Webspaces are the spatial expression of social media into placemaking. The new social space is phygital.

**Shared Virtual Infrastructure:** Virtual infrastructure is the engineered collective virtual systems used to move, transact, and interact within the metaverse environments.

Metaverse urbanism is ultimately bound to shared virtual infrastructures, pathways, and protocols that enable high-level, multi-user interaction.

**Avatar-based Navigation:** Avatars are digital representations of individuals, allowing them to navigate the metaverse urban landscape and interact with virtual elements and other users. Avatar-based navigation is the shift from digital identity to a digital embodiment.

**Virtual Ecosystems:** Metaverse urbanism fosters the creation of virtual ecosystems, where digital flora and fauna thrive, providing a sense of biodiversity and biophilia.

**Dynamic Weather Systems:** Virtual weather systems can simulate realistic atmospheric conditions within the metaverse, enhancing immersion and adding an element of unpredictability. The control is bidirectional. Real weather can be simulated within the virtual environment, and virtual weather can be translated to the physical environment. Aerial robotics chemically control the climate.

**Digital Currency and Economy:** A digital currency system enables transactions and economic activities within the metaverse, enabling a virtual economy to thrive. The token economy is the current that runs the ecosystem.

**Digital Twin Cities:** Physical cities have their digital twin counterparts in the metaverse, allowing for real-time data analysis, simulations, and urban planning. Digital twin cities are customizable, both in the virtual and the physical world. Twins are used for anchor extraction and animation simulations, among other applications. Moreover, they're providing a testbed for experimentation, evaluation, and iterative design processes.

**Gamification of Urban Life:** Elements of gaming, such as achievements, challenges, and rewards, are integrated into the metaverse urban experience, fostering engagement and exploration. Tokenization for incentivization is key to metaverse urbanism.

**Virtual Education and Learning Spaces:** Through gamified user experiences, the virtual urban space becomes an immersive and interactive learning environment, accessible to learners from anywhere in the world.

**DAO Governance:** Decentralized virtual governance structures enable community participation and decision-making in shaping the metaverse urban environment. DAOs are the way to engage in metaverse city-making.

**Personalized Digital Assistants:** AI-powered digital assistants provide personalized guidance, recommendations, and support to individuals navigating the metaverse urban landscape. Assistant AIs operate on user data, and other users' data, overlapped with data of the place.

**Haptic Feedback and Sensory Immersion:** Advanced haptic technologies allow users to experience realistic touch sensations and sensory immersion within the metaverse. The sensory causations are now cross-media, virtual touch is perceived in the physical world.

**Spatial Audio and Ambiance:** Spatial audio technologies replicate realistic soundscapes, creating immersive sonic environments that enhance the metaverse urban experience.

These concepts form a foundation for a creative and imaginative exploration of metaverse urbanism, providing a glimpse into the potential future of digitally integrated urban environments.

# THROUGH A MORE URBAN-ORIENTED LENS;

**Hyperconnected Urban Nodes:**
Where digital infrastructure converges with physical urban centers, fostering a symbiotic relationship between data-driven networks and human-centric urban design.

**Algorithmic Urban Planning:**
Advanced algorithms analyze vast sets of data, generating real-time simulations and predictions that inform metaverse urban planning decisions, optimizing spatial configurations, and maximizing efficiency.

More and more, the urbansphere becomes quantified.

**XR Placemaking:** Extended reality placemaking techniques reimagine the urban landscape, instantly overlaying dynamic digital elements that respond to user interactions, creating multi-sensory, transformative environments.

**Responsive Landscapes:**
Metaverse urbanism embraces responsive landscapes, where real-time data streams inform the adaptation of urban elements, such as street furniture, lighting, and vegetation, optimizing user experiences and resource allocation.

**Immersive and Multi-sensory Wayfinding:** Integrating dynamic virtual signage, soundscapes, and haptic feedback to guide users seamlessly through the urban fabric.

**Participatory Co-designing:**
Platforms empower communities to actively participate in the design and evolution of metaverse urban spaces, enabling inclusive decision-making processes and fostering a sense of ownership.

**Data Visualization in Urban Contexts:** Metaverse urbanism leverages advanced data visualization techniques, transforming complex urban datasets into visually compelling representations that facilitate informed decision-making and enhance public engagement.

**Adaptive Mixed-Use Environments:** Metaverse urbanism embraces adaptive mixed-use environments, where physical and virtual spaces merge seamlessly, enabling flexible programming and multifunctional integration, responding to dynamic urban needs.

**Gamified Urban Interventions:**
Gamification strategies integrate game-like elements into metaverse urban interventions, incentivizing public engagement, fostering behavioral change, and promoting collective problem-solving for urban challenges.

**Virtual Urban Biophilic Integration:** Virtual biophilic integration infuses metaverse urban spaces with virtual greenery, natural elements, and immersive soundscapes, enhancing user well-being, restoring ecological connections, and promoting sustainable urban living.

**Spatial Data Analytics for Inclusive Design:** Spatial data analytics techniques provide valuable insights into diverse user needs, supporting inclusive design practices within the metaverse urban environment, ensuring equitable access, and enhancing social cohesion.

**Smart Urban Materiality:** Metaverse urbanism explores the realm of smart urban materiality, where intelligent, self-adapting materials respond to environmental cues, modulating their physical properties to optimize energy consumption, thermal comfort, and structural integrity.

**Virtual Urban Cinematography:** Metaverse urbanism employs virtual urban cinematography techniques to craft immersive narrative experiences, using dynamic camera perspectives, lighting, and visual effects to evoke emotions and create compelling urban narratives.

**Immersive Digital Cultural Heritage Preservation:** Metaverse urbanism becomes a catalyst for immersive digital cultural heritage preservation, capturing and recontextualizing the rich history and cultural identity of urban spaces, fostering appreciation and understanding.

**Blockchain-enabled Urban Transactions:** Blockchain technology facilitates transparent and secure urban transactions within the metaverse, supporting decentralized economies, and peer-to-peer exchanges, and fostering trust in urban governance.

**Parametric Urban Commons:** Metaverse urbanism explores the concept of parametric urban commons, where the design and management of shared spaces are informed by algorithmic parameters and community input, ensuring equitable access, resource allocation, and participatory governance.

**Urban Simulations:** Augmented reality simulations enable stakeholders to visualize and interact with proposed urban interventions within the metaverse, facilitating informed decision-making, stakeholder engagement, and iterative design processes.

**Embodied Virtual Urban Experiences:** Metaverse urbanism embraces embodied virtual experiences, where users can physically engage with virtual urban environments through advanced haptic feedback systems, allowing for tactile exploration, sensory immersion, and a deeper sense of presence.

# 12. CIRCLING BACK ON WHAT IS METAVERSE URBANISM

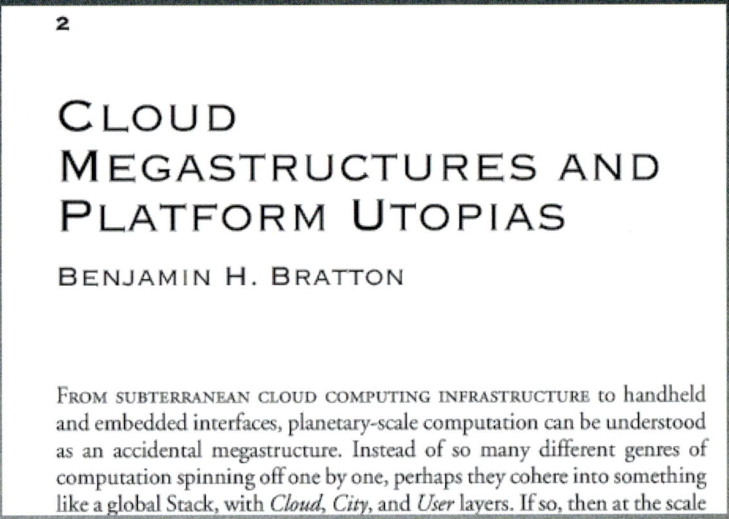

**2**

## CLOUD MEGASTRUCTURES AND PLATFORM UTOPIAS

### BENJAMIN H. BRATTON

FROM SUBTERRANEAN CLOUD COMPUTING INFRASTRUCTURE to handheld and embedded interfaces, planetary-scale computation can be understood as an accidental megastructure. Instead of so many different genres of computation spinning off one by one, perhaps they cohere into something like a global Stack, with *Cloud*, *City*, and *User* layers. If so, then at the scale

"Gravity is a mood"

JEFF KIPNIS

**From an urban design perspective, Metaverse urbanism is the cultural discourse that engages with framing-by-design an urban ecology across the virtual-physical spectrum.**

**So, what is Metaverse urbanism? In Definition, it is in the likes of Beirut-solidere . The implications, we need to take a look at the case of the sidewalk.**

Let's think about Metaverse Urbanism in a practical way to come back to a more holistic understanding. Metaverse Urbanism can be understood in 2 ways:

On the one hand, it is urbanism affected by the Metaverse, or metaverse enabling technologies, or its implications. For example, how would physical public squares change when more people interact in virtual environments?

On the other, it is a new urbanism of the virtual environment that makes up the Metaverse. For example, designing a virtual city as an environment for a metaverse world.

While both ways of understanding the term are inseparable, the following will focus on the second way, creating a new urbanism for a new virtual world.

Urbanism involves understanding how social, economic, cultural, and environmental factors interact in urban settings, and how they affect the quality of life of people - and all other biological and non-biological agents- who live and work in cities.

Nevertheless, urbanism has evolved, as cities have evolved from human-centric settlements to more diverse ecologies where multispecies systems govern the system.

Only 37% of the internet is populated by humans, the rest is bots and machines, running the party. Will only 37% of the urban sphere be populated by humans?

Changes in urban design and planning are strongly tied to the way we live and to the decisive technologies that transformed urban form.

The automobile was a main driver behind our street-saturated and high-way-rich landscapes.

The elevator enables the vertical growth of cities.

Air-conditioning, urban sensors, autonomous urban machines, etc.

https://www.lecfc.fr/new/articles/204-article-7.pdf

"Le concept de dérive est indissolublement lié à la reconnaissance d'effets de nature psychogéographique et à l'affirmation ludique-constructive, ce qui l'oppose en tous points aux notions classiques de voyage et de promenade."

While a lot of the facets of this new urbanism have been discussed, the following two titles are in a way the distillation of foundational aspects of what constitutes Metaverse urbanism, digital assets, ownership, spatiality, and the physical as a new interface. Simplistic, yet delivers the message.

The beginning of the 1990s wasn't only a paradigm shift globally, but locally too, in a country with a population of almost 3 million people.

As the armed combat came to an end, putting an end to the last chapter of the civil war, the country woke up to a broken social and urban fabric, a torn built environment, and a heavily wounded capital.

Right after, Solidere was a precedent that left the local community of private landowners with nothing more than stocks in a company that acquired their estate.

The city center was suddenly owned by a private company, Solidere. The original owners of the real estate, the most physical of all assets, were transformed into stock owners in the new private company.

Property ownership was transformed and exchanged from a material to an immaterial asset class. It became a fluctuating curve in an unstable region.

When things are digitized, everything becomes objectified again, and therefore, it becomes commodified.

**BEIRUT**

**WHO OWNS THE CITY? THE MARKET.**

The death of the sidewalk is the evolution of streets to Programmable and Flexible Spaces.

Future streets adapt to various activities and events, they are the new platform.

Future streets are adaptable, as they address challenges such as personalized programmes, diverse populations, micromobility, etc.

Streets in the future city are data-rich environments, with a strong emphasis on connectivity. High-speed wireless networks, technological and information infrastructure, and data collection sensors enable real-time monitoring, analysis, and optimization of various urban functions, contributing to more efficient and responsive street systems.

Humans, vehicles, and nature occupy the same surface.

No sidewalk is all sidewalk, the next urban is flat.

The physical surfaces become interfaces for activity, and anchors to a new augmented layer. The city is comprehended both by machines and humans, it becomes legible by computers, for computers.

**THE NEW *URBAN* IS ALSO AN INTERFACE.**

# 13. WHY ARCHITECTS AND URBAN DESIGNERS

## & WHY NOW

Architects do not produce
buildings, they produce
drawings of buildings

**As the digital gains prominence, architecture, for example, is freed from its physicality to become heavily focused on the production of interiorities, forms, experiences, and interactions, i.e. its essence beyond its interface medium.**

**In this context, urbanists, architects, and spatial designers are natural candidates for designing metaverse urbanism.**

Architects and urbanists own expertise in creating interiorities, recruiting sophisticated confluence of technical acumen and a nuanced comprehension of spatial dynamics. The metaverse urbanism shift necessitates a reevaluation of the conventional notions of scale, animation, and media in architectural practice. Architects design chairs, dining sets, houses, and cities, **'all are architects, and all is spatial design.'**

HTTPS://WWW.HOLLEIN. COM/GER/SCHRIFTEN/ TEXTE/ALLES-IST-AR- CHITEKTUR

Spatial designers own a distinctive toolkit, uniting technical proficiency with an acute understanding of spatial organization, human behavior, and contextual relevance. Spatial design practitioners leverage the understanding of human behavior, spatial organization, and contextual integration.

At its core, architecture is the production of interiorities, whether through text, drawings, bricks, or storytelling. The virtual or the digital frees architecture from matter, and suddenly, design and realization are merged. In the virtual, architects produce buildings, as the building becomes the drawing itself.

Patrick Schumacher
https://www.youtube.com/ watch?v=93AjRPhTP7E

In parallel, the metaverse is a social space, and therefore, framing it is a spatial design practice, the closest it gets to urbanism. If spatial design does one thing in the context of architecture and urbanism, it frames social interactions by providing an interface to spatial cognition, and therefore, provides experience.

As the next internet, where spatialization takes command, the transition question is set to UX/UI designers. Now a new toolkit is needed, one that includes design-build tools for interactive immersive engagement through efficient world-building. A toolkit native to architects. It is to be tested if the future UX/UI designers will become spatial designers or whether spatial designers become 3D UX/UI designers.

Chasing efficiency, LEED certificates, and other quantitative fetishes, architecture has been stripped from its cultural aspect as a critical discourse that produces new interiorities, be it by type or by nature.

A shift in discourse to an increasingly experience-based craft is taking place, where storytelling, gamification, and narrative are central. Narrative building has moved from being character-centric to world-centric. All heroes in movies are main characters; the next generation will remember environments and worlds that had more impact.

The metaverse is a natural space for architects to operate in. Not only because of the tools, methodologies, design dimensionality, and nature of the discourse but also because of two major aspects that are crucial and shall be addressed.

No space is apolitical.

No futurism is about the future.

Architects, urbanists, and spatial designers in general speculate on the politics of space, a foundational aspect of creating narratives and worlds where life happens. In this capacity, architects are interpreters of the zeitgeist, with the ability to translate the pulse of the present into worlds.

Futurism is a contemporary diagnostic tool and a lens through which we can characterize the present moment. Nobody knows the future. Futurism, as an intellectual and creative device, is inherently concerned with envisioning and shaping the future based on the present.

Within this metaverse milieu, such bandwidth is central. It is essential to extrapolate current features and trends and model situations to anticipate 'imagined' future needs. Moreover, there is a need to decipher the complex interplay of technological advancements, societal shifts, and environmental considerations. There is also a need to operate within the complexity of the phygital at the scale of urban life itself.

## Architecture as such might have died; only the dead, shall be resurrected.

Futurism says more about the present than it does about the past.

Futurism runs on current situation diagnostics, a way to characterize the now.

# 14. STEPS TO DESIGN-BUILD A METAVERSE CITY-WORLD

The next chapter showcases samples of a Metaverse CityWorld that we design-built in 2022.

Here is a simplification of the process followed to achieve what we designed, the cake recipe style.

## LEVEL 1 - THE BIG PICTURE / GROUND ZERO

→ Position and Vision for the city-world, scale, utility features, logics, etc.
→ Establishing the content for a virtual context
→ Narrative-building and world conception
→ Spatial Layout, automated morphologies
→ Formalizing a strategical urban strategy
→ Algorithmic Urban Strategy development and deployment

## LEVEL 2 - SPATIAL LAYOUT

→ Spatial Layout and Hierarchies
→ Production of Lands - producing a comprehensive list of lands with all attributes.

## LEVEL 2.1 - THE NEIGHBORHOODS

→ Neighborhood specifics - audience, functions, aesthetics, etc.
→ Morphology and urban strategy algorithm building
→ Terrain, networks, proximities, clustering, massing, etc.

## LEVEL 2.2 - THE VIRTUAL BUILT ENVIRONMENT

→ Building-design and narrative
→ Scripting the buildings - developing operational workflows to produce the buildings
→ Technical Development to achieve game-ready milestone

## LEVEL 3 - GAME ENGINE IMPLEMENTATION

→ Unity Implementation of the base ground zero / Context
→ Implementation of all design - neighborhoods, etc.
→ Implementation of Interactions and gamification

## LEVEL 4 - DEPLOYMENT AND GOVERNANCE IMPLEMENTATION

→ Deployment of identity, financial, and governance protocols

THE GAM
CITY
–

UM

WORLD

## It is the expansion of the internet to consume the urban, and the expansion of the Urban beyond the physical. It is where physics is optional, yet seductive.

**CREDITS**

PROJECT CORE TEAM
**FIRAS SAFIEDDINE**
**FRANCOIS NOUR**
**ROBERTO VARGAS CALVO**

PROJECT TEAM AND
COLLABORATORS
**MICHEL AZZI**
**YIMENG WEI**
**TEDDY FADOUS**
**CHIEN-HUA HUANG**
**STEFANA ZAPUC**
**PRATIK BORSE**
**ANTON KOSHELEV**
**KRZYSTOFF GALANT**
**ANTONIO LOPES**

UNITY - ENGINE TEAM
**ROBERT BECHARA**
**KARLO RAJIC**

SOUNDSCAPE
**NAJIB SAFIEDDINE**

TIMEFRAME
**THE GAMIUM CITY-WORLD**
**PROJECT WAS INITIATED AND**
**FINALIZED BETWEEN FEBRUARY**
**10, 2022, AND JULY 10, 2022.**

**DAO SPACES CAME IN LATER,**
**AS DEVELOPMENTS WITHIN**
**THE LARGER URBAN CONTEXT (**
**DECEMBER 2022 )**

## Urbanism

Beyond the definitions and domains within the last 200 years of urbanism, Urbanism, urban design, and planning, the current technosphere demands a new definition of what the discourse of urbanism is. Just like every discourse, it changes and grows in different directions to confront new challenges, internal and external.

Within the current challenges, and building on past endeavors, we define urbanism as the multifaceted study and practice of understanding, designing, and managing the complex spatial interplay of human societies, built environments, natural systems, and cultural expressions within urban areas. It is the framing of social life through spatial operations such as spatial hierarchies, forms, etc. It docks on all aspects such as the physical, social, economic, environmental, and cultural dimensions of urban life.

Metaverse urbanism is the realization that the virtual is real. It is the augmented discourse that surrenders to the new umwelt, a stack of infinite layers that we unlock with every sensing technology emerging. It is both the design of virtual urban spheres and the design of physical ones, with an augmented layer. The metaverse is phygital.

World-building is at the core of both architecture and urban design practices. Virtual-world building, on the other hand, is an aspect within discourse that this paper will highlight through the case of the Gamium City-World.

The Gamium City project is a world-creation project that conceives a city as a world and vice versa for the Gamium Metaverse project.

## Introduction

The Gamium City project is a world-creation project that conceives a city as a world, and vice versa for the Gamium Metaverse project.

It is a design for a configurable city-world, made of 10 neighborhoods*, deployed in Unity. The seemingly blank tabula rasa situation brings important decisions to be made on building such cities of the present future while lacking a history of precedents, and constraining context.

### The zero-context is not blank.

The Gamium city-world is made of ten neighborhoods, each made up of island(s) in a lagoon of an area over 100 square kilometers - the size of Moscow[TTK]- surrounded by mountainous terrain. The underlying urban strategy / spatial structure of the project is a fractal branching system that draws zones at nodes as it branches out. After the branching and nodes occur, hence the spatial layout, clustering of the nodes brings forward agglomerations of land as chunks that are then partitioned following directionality and proximity from other nodes and a loop connection that connects all the clusters.

At the center, Genesis - neighborhood zero - sits as the icon of Gamium City.

# THE CITY-WORLD

"The city is like a great house, and the house, in its turn, is a small city."

— LEON BATTISTA ALBERTI

**The scale of cities, to a very large extent, is governed by the slowness of the physical realization of the built environment, in addition to territorial, economic, and population constraints. In the virtual world, the driver is a market-based workflow where quantity is quality; more is more.**

Architecture, or world-building in general, is an endeavor carried out in the frame of another world, always. All worlds belong to some other world that forms the "outside", architecture is about defining the limits.

The city occupies a whole world.
The world becomes the city itself.
City as a world, or world and a city.
The city-world is a city that exhausts its full context and a world that can be reduced to a city.

The scale of operation covering urban planning and design occurs simultaneously to conceive a world that is worked out as a city. Cyberspace as a network of virtual cities becomes the world as a network of worlds, the metaverse is plural, open, and interconnected.

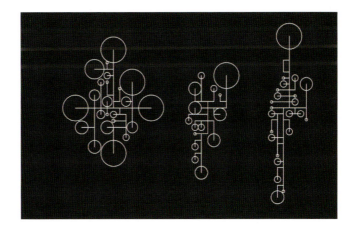

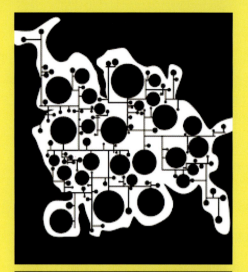

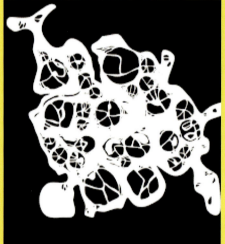

## GROUND ZERO

The context is not blank. It is saturated with non-visual strata of financial, computational, and technological bedrock where things happen. Not having the same language of the design itself, i.e. not being a visual/perceptual spatial context, does not eliminate the presence of one. Hence, creating a spatial context, embedded in machine logics opens up a horizon of possibilities, geometrically structured to produce a ground zero.

**Ground zero** is designing – pre-designing, it is an artificial representation of the need for a context and its necessity even as a made-up.

Most importantly, it is made up along the lines of the politics of the Metaverse cityworld.

## GROUND ZERO RULES

→ Starting from a center point, a random number of branches are drawn with a minimum length, until 10 nodes are reached.

→ At the endpoint of these branches, a node is created, with a radius smaller than the length of the branch.

→ After the circles are drawn, a second cycle of branches is made while maintaining a minimum distance between secondary and primary nodes.

→ At the endpoints of the secondary branches, circles are drawn with a radius smaller than the minimum distance to the closest limitation.

→ Once primary and secondary circles are established, a clustering process is deforming the perfect geometries into organic integrated forms.

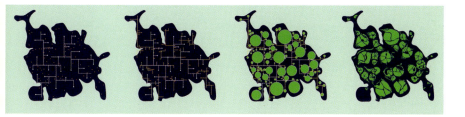

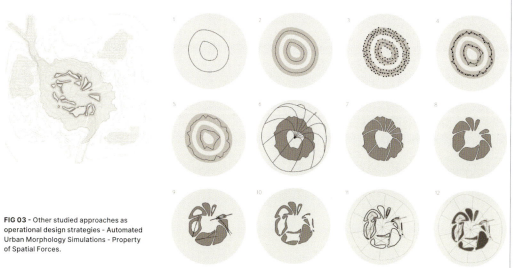

**FIG 03 -** Other studied approaches as operational design strategies - Automated Urban Morphology Simulations - Property of Spatial Forces.

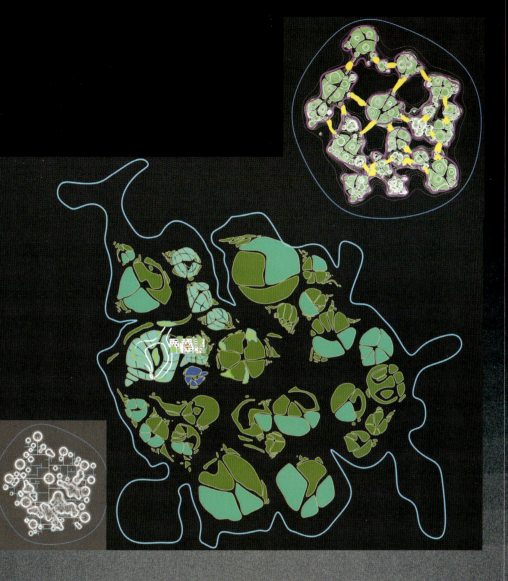

# DESIGN REALIZATION

In the metaverse context, design and realization are synonymous, the physics, politics, and building occur differently. Once the virtual city is built- and gamified- the project is realized, and it is at its last phase. Unlike real cities, designs are only schemes that take years to be realized, alongside politics, wars, social dynamics, and enormous economic and ecological constraints.

World-building offers an immediacy that is crucial to the virtual. Ideas, as invisible scaffolds of form are permanent; ideally, they become the form itself. Design decision-making becomes the last interface, as opposed to the physical built environment. The design has more power and becomes the immediate world itself as we perceive it.

The question of realization is an interesting one in architecture, as it gets flexible to locate specifically where architecture stops or ends. Is it the drawing, the building, or the perception?

Realization of the project includes the agency of various factors, especially in the building and perception. The actors are external. Metaverse worlds are realized environments, they are the end of the production process, maybe. Virtual designs are capable of being amended infinitely. They are reprogrammable, editable, hackable, and most importantly, only accessible through the machine interface. The nature of architecture and its realization is unified, and therefore, architecture becomes possibly infinite.

Back to pragmatic considerations, realization in the metaverse today is bound to technical limitations that impose constraints on the complexity of possible designs. Technological capacity becomes the new budget. It is geometrical and made of data. The mesh police are the new electro-mechanical engineers.

# NEIGHBOR-HOODS

The world, at the level of the urban structure, is configured as a scalable system that can expand infinitely. As a first iteration, the city constitutes a central neighborhood, Neighborhood 0, Genesis, and another 10 neighborhoods.

Each of the neighborhoods has a different identity within the whole, characterized physically by specific urban patterns, ecological morphology, community, and functions.

The Neighborhood is simultaneously a neighborhood, a city, and a world. It travels seamlessly through the hierarchy.

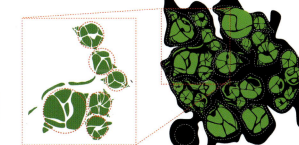

**District**    **Island**    **Neighborhood**    **World**

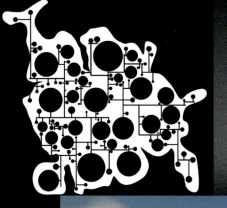

NEIGHB(

RHOODS

# NEIGHBORHOOD
# O. GENESIS

At the center of the Gamium City-World, Genesis, neighborhood zero sits as the quintessential emblem of the Gamium world. It is a present and monumental urban formation that converges and spirals inward to culminate in the iconic 800m Genesis Tower.

The urban form gradually unfolds with a gradual ascent from its periphery towards the nucleus. Characterized by a low footprint,the neighborhood embraces expansive green spaces, interspersed with emblematic landmarks, urban sculptures, and communal recreational and game areas.

On its peripheries, where heights are minimal, the neighborhood hosts designer buildings delineating the interface between Genesis and its surroundings.

## URBAN MORPHOLOGY

The urban layout follows an organic grid driven by a field of vectors - forces that open up towards the circumference and allow hybrid, aerated, and high-quality urban spaces. The Genesis Tower ties together the islands of the neighborhood; it serves as the focal point, linking the neighborhood's islands.

Organized radially, the nucleus is mainly occupied by the tower, connecting to a first ring of public facilities. Expanding outward, secondary radial zones encompass vibrant public squares and open spaces, leading to other major buildings within the neighborhood. Beyond the buildings, nature takes over creating a belt of parks and pocket forests. Genesis is populated with sculptures and specific buildings, arriving at the periphery with light sculptures and vertical assets.

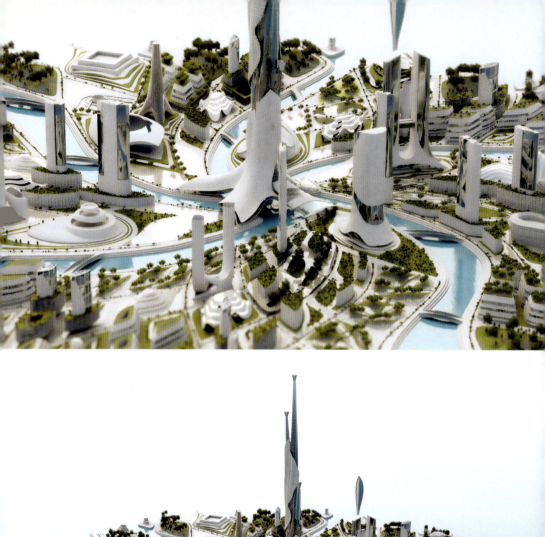

# NEIGHBORHOOD
# 1. SAT

The inaugural neighborhood, SAT, stands as a symbiotic counterpart to Genesis, designed for the broader community as a livable urban entity. Anchored by communal ethos, it integrates public functions, private spaces, and a vast open terrain with lands for sale.

The neighborhood's iconic building is the Museum for Future Human Relationships, a record of the evolution of interpersonal dynamics. The intent is twofold, it preserves antiquated modes of interaction while speculating on emergent paradigms. The first is to indicate

a shift to a new form of human interaction and communication, therefore leaving the antiquated modes way documented and speculated upon, and the second is a clear attempt to theorize for new forms and ways human relationships crystalize in the future.

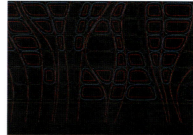

## CENTRAL ICON

All is data. The Museum of Human Relationships makes all human interactions tangible. Relationship typologies, moods, feelings, mental state transfers, and many more avatar interactions are yet to be uncovered. It will host artwork and media as a record of the history of human relationships, but also, speculative work imagining its future.

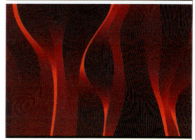

## URBAN MORPHOLOGY

Spanning a rectangular expanse of 600 by 1200 meters, SAT's urban grid, comprising 300-meter square blocks, juxtaposes against the organic contours of its islets. This hybrid grid, a hybrid of rectilinear and curvy elements, harmonizes with the underlying terrain while fostering fluid internal organization. Leveraging 3D mobility, aerial pathways, and multi-level connectivity, the neighborhood evolves into a hyperconnected urban ecosystem.

The rest is land and digital nature with mountain formations and severe topographies. The larger island formation, vastly covered with lands for sale, hosts a central micro island where an icon will sit atop a rocky formation.

The pure geometrical limits of the neighborhood are contextualized by topographies that create a second layer of spatial framing, yielding different zones within the same neighborhood.

SAT is an experiment in hybrid layouts and organizational techniques, with an emphasis on soft clustering, while capitalizing on terrain features and the framing roles they can play.

## ARCHITECTURE

Buildings are clustered into generated form families and dispersed across four principal zones. The Central Valley houses the Museum alongside a skyline bound by an array of towers.

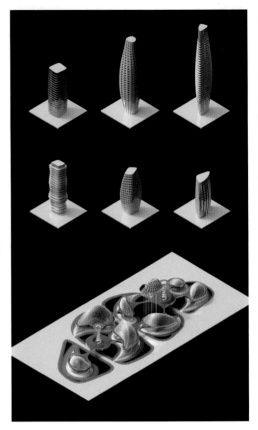

The Elefeet towers are high-rise copper towers that delimit the central axis to the east. With a smooth form inspired by growth, and a broad base that narrows as it ascends punctuated by intricate façade articulations. To the west, adjacent clusters feature organic towers, with basic contours echoing fluidity.

On one side of the valley, three form families dominate—residential units, pod-towers, and vertical slums— each of unique typologies. The latter, vertically stacked, affords flexibility in configuration, size, and orientation. To its border is the Ferris wheel, a recreational icon with panoramic vistas.

Conversely, the opposite sector pulsates with urban density, a number of residential complexes, and simple towers with metallic façades and rooftop greenery. A canopy envelops the ground plane, fostering a parallel active green axis.

At the center of the second large island of SAT there is a cluster with a hill where a cloud-floating museum hangs on light pillars.

## LANDS

Augmented by supplementary islets, the neighborhood hosts an inventory of 15,000 land units, with the primary clusters hosting approximately 9,000 parcels.

A water-lands platform introduces diversity into the real estate offerings, enriching the neighborhood's market.

## SUPER POWER

Boundary Manipulation, Subjective Reality, Virtual Warping, Accelerated Rotation, Additional Limbs, Amalgamation [ Plant Merging, Solid Merging ], Anatomical Liberation, Body Part Substitution, Bone Manipulation, Camouflage, Deflection of [ Energy, light, interaction, etc ], Helicopter Propulsion, Invisibility, Matter Ingestion, Replication, Self-Detonation, Wall crawling, Bubble Generation, Dust Generation, Echolocation, Web Generation, Aquatic Breathing, Enhanced Vision, 360-Degree Vision, Accelerated Vision, Astral Vision, Atomic Vision, Aura Vision, Caustic Vision, Chrono Vision, Dark Vision, Ectoplasmic Vision, Emotion Vision, Freeze Vision, X-Ray Vision.

# NEIGHBORHOOD
# 2. KABAN

Kaban is a finance-oriented neighborhood,
distinguished by skyscrapers and gem-like towers.

Characterized by uniformity in building height, this
neighborhood caters to high-value properties
and is tailored to accommodate thriving business
communities.

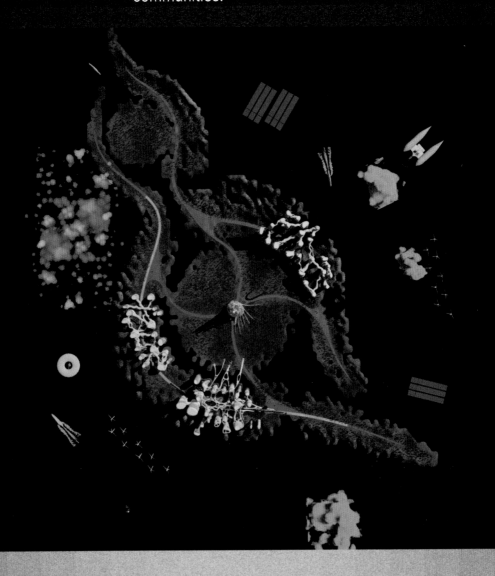

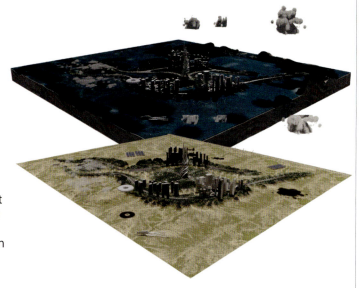

## CENTRAL ICON: THE EXCHANGE-LISTING MONUMENT OF THE ATTENTION ECONOMY

At its center, The exchange-listing Monument of the Attention Economy is a phenomenon that redefines how information and attention intersect in virtual spaces.

The attention economy will become the elephant in the room. This emblematic building of Kaban is one where all data and exchange listings of the attention economy are displayed, dramatized, and visualized. It functions upon data of the whole metaverse, and Kaban specifically Herbert Simon coined the term "Attention Economy":

"What information consumes is the attention of its recipients. Hence a wealth of information creates a poverty of attention"

"Attention economics is an approach to the management of information that treats human attention as a scarce commodity and applies economic theory to solve various information management problems."

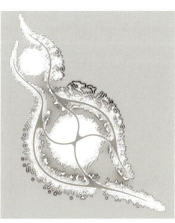

Kaban's iconic tower, the exchange-listing Monument of the Attention Economy, pioneers the metaverse attention-driven architecture, where the building communicates and visualizes attention data streams from the metaverse. Attention drives attention. People look where other people are looking, especially if they're many.

The tower emerges as a bundle of strips that wrap around each other, adorned with functional screens and high-tech displays that showcase information related to the attention economy and the businesses that thrive within the Gamium world.

The building also features interactive elements that allow users to engage with the content on display, such as touchscreens through augmented reality interfaces.

Inside the tower is a range of spaces designed to facilitate the exchange of attention-based goods and services. For example, the space can be a trading floor where companies can buy and sell "attention shares," or units of attention that can be traded like stocks or commodities.

## URBAN MORPHOLOGY

The neighborhood's layout intensifies and facilitates interactions. It amplifies and streamlines reward-based social interactions.

Embracing a linear-city distribution model, the neighborhood spreads within a multi-ground infrastructure as connections at several levels, connecting various parts of various buildings. A skywalk elevated above ground level creates an additional floating platform, expanding the surface area for avatar interactions and enhancing accessibility.

Deployed across three distinct clusters along the island's periphery, Kaban's urban fabric is strategically designed to optimize land utilization and maximize value for landowners. A central island encircled by a water ring hosts the primary land plots, strategically positioned between the central icon and existing urban developments to maintain the highest value for landowners.

02/03

"ATTENTION IS A RESOURCE—A PERSON HAS ONLY SO MUCH OF IT."

# NEIGHBORHOOD
# 3. PANTHERA-
# 4. EGEA

The Panthera-Egea (PE) cluster is the natural fusion of two distinct yet complementary neighborhoods, exclusive and luxurious.

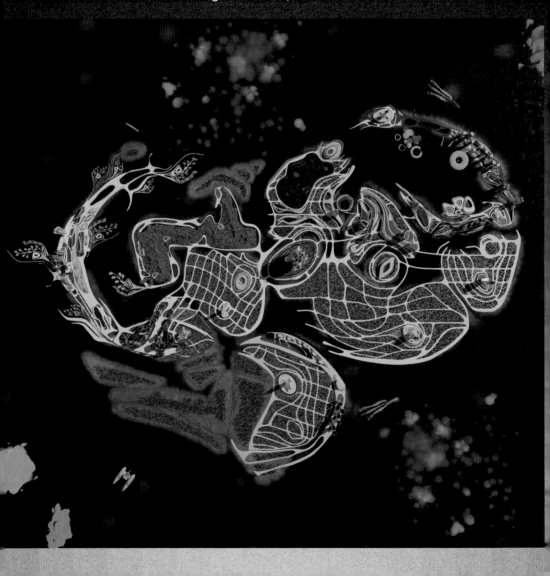

**Panthera** is where the action happens, with floating pavilions, towers, and a social interface for exclusive communities. Designed as a haven for the elite, It is a neighborhood targeted at exclusive communities and superstars, fostering a dynamic social milieu.

**Egea** is a luxury short-stay neighborhood with clusters of floating villas hosting several communities and amenities that can be enjoyed within the neighborhood context. Serving as the perfect counterpart to Panthera, it is where more entertainment, luxury retreats, and leisure happen. Situated adjacent to Genesis and bound by Ilios, EGEA occupies a strategic position within the cluster.

Both neighborhoods cater to the same community and therefore act as one.

## URBAN MORPHOLOGY

The Urban layout is one over both neighborhoods, they follow a singular unifying aesthetic. An organic grid frames the spatial layout, creating a narrow interface around the neighborhood's water area. Another organic grid delineates the spatial layout, framing the water areas with a narrow interface that blurs the boundaries between buildings and the ground.

 In both neighborhoods, the formed lagoons are the vital areas where buildings are distributed or float within. The rest of the terrain is open for further development by the community and its future creators. Specifically, a grid flows over the terrain, homogenizing the strategic vision while keeping the rest open to bottom-up developments. Within that terrain, a series of emblematic buildings are positioned as anchor points to inspire the developments around.

## THE CENTRAL ICON OF PANTHERA: THE BEACON OF LIGHT

## THE CENTRAL ICON OF EGEA: THE RADAR TOWER OF AVATAR WELLBEING

The single most important building of the neighborhood, the Beacon of Light, is home to 3 main functions: leisure, finance, and business, it lights up as a beacon to celebrate the leisure-oriented life of Pantera, and is an important link to Egea.

The beacon of light, Panthera's icon, is a luxurious tower that hosts the community's most important events. Its light is visible from other neighborhoods, signaling status and presence. As this area is concerned with an exclusive community, avatar well-being, and experience are the highest priority. Therefore, a radar that can empower and enhance the avatar experience from a distance, displays analytics and metrics of avatar wellbeing.

Avatars are either autonomous or representative, i.e. they are either being controlled, and therefore, the embodiment of a human user in real-time, or otherwise, an autonomous avatar, i.e. a bot. The well-being of both is crucial but largely differs as the first one requires the understanding of the well-being of the user controlling the avatar.

To achieve that, The Radar Tower of Avatar Wellbeing is the space where data on the emotions of the user will be stored and visualized. It is a domain for, financial, emotional, and performative metrics of users, bots, and their embodiment.

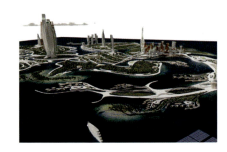

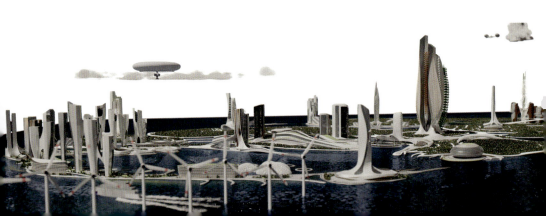

# NEIGHBORHOOD
# 5. ILIOS

Recreational, experience-driven, and human-scale aggregation of units of small to medium scale. The neighborhood hosts a multitude of islands, born from introducing a vector field and a grid layout to the already existing terrain.

Various zones allow the emergence of various moods and effects within the same neighborhood, pumping up the value of each and reaching out to a diversified clientele. There are areas for private villas and other zones for vacation, recreation, urban games, and exclusive experiences.

## URBAN MORPHOLOGY

The ILIOS urban plan is based on a vortex where a dormant volcano is situated. A fluid grid creates the urban floor on a small scale to create an ultra-human-scale urban context. The grids transform the terrain, suggesting a new way of moving from "Ground Zero" to the urban design, one that works in parallel to morph the existing base while introducing organizational systems that overlap.

Plot sizes in Ilios vary largely, in some areas, the urban blocks are minimized to host a villa, while in others, there is a cluster of other structures. In the first ring, a bubbly form of metaballs is designed for exhibitions and themed experiences; artificial flora and fauna. Colors, patterns, and a playful mood dominate the scene.

Data of all experience levels affect the formation and color of the structure. It emulates flora and is populated with homes where visitors can have a solo retreat. The Data forest is enriched as more experiences happen to become a monstrous structure of artificial flora and branches and with a population of retreat seekers.

The data forest sits atop an island as a clyster of bird-house-like spaces, with floating platforms, slides, and a Ferris wheel promoting an exploration mode that enriches the experience. The data forest is one to explore, where each niche is equipped with screens that display data performance, as the structure itself changes. The aggregation model for the data forest is an interactive one, based on the number of users and the amount of data circulating. And avatars teleport between one niche and another, maintaining a never-ending experience.

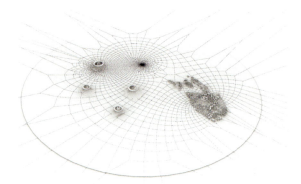

Central icon Height: 300 m
Superpower - Scale play
Central icon: The Data Forest

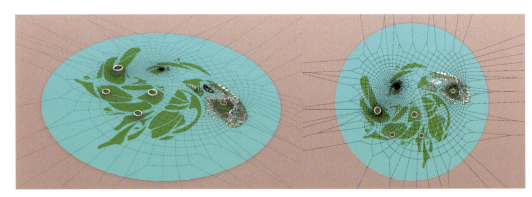

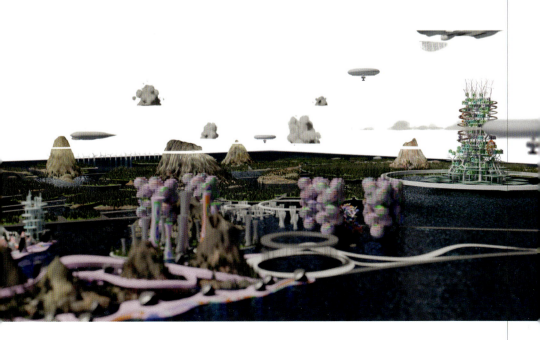

This is a jungle of buildings. It is an urban labyrinth– mundane yet monumental, infused with humanscale juxtaposed against a backdrop of dystopian cyberpunk aesthetics, and accentuated by classical undertones and a virtual drone port runway.

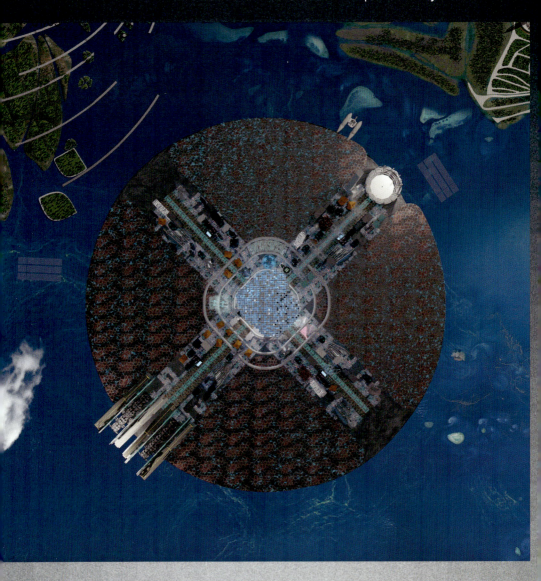

OX is a social jungle, a lab for human illegal activities and in-world games, and an open space for the community to fill and densify the urban fabric. A retro-futuristic roamable fabric that alienates avatars due to its scale and elements, yet offers paths that connect all buildings, all the way to the central cloud cluster. It embodies a Manhattan formal typology with a futuristic Hong Kong-inspired language.

## URBAN MORPHOLOGY

OX adopts a cross-shaped urban layout. The center hosts a large public square area under a floating 'cloud' of vertical and horizontal tectonics, with a translucent material texture and a dusty fog around on top.

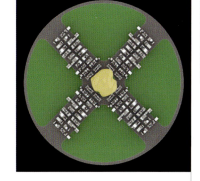

Four linear-urbanism orthogonal branches govern the main organizational spatial framework. While converging at the central point, each linear alley within the branches unfolds into unique spatial experiences, such as OX's arena and airport.

The interstitial spaces between the branches, the negative space, is populated with glowing tree-like lanterns and open for the OX DAO to overtake the area and densify it further to match the constructed urban fabric.

## CENTRAL ICON: THE CLOUD

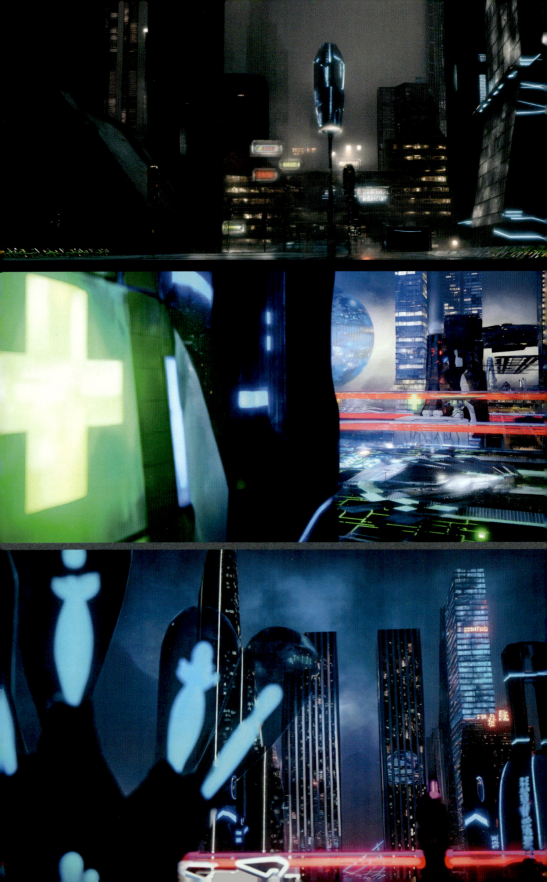

# NEIGHBORHOOD
# 7. KHALA TUA

Khala Tua is a take on ecological parametricism. It is an enclosed archipelago experiment on isolated ecologies, a neighborhood under a dome. This neighborhood is inspired by natural forms and patterns, with an alien feel– low rise yet well-populated with large-scale constructions and ecological towers.

The neighborhood's formation is based on fragmenting the initial island and manipulating the terrain to attain complexity within each of the "island" clusters.

## URBAN MORPHOLOGY

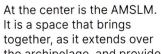

The urban morphology is based on a morphed circle packing as an underlying structure, with a series of islands, each hosting buildings, structures, forests, etc. Flora in this neighborhood is blown up in scale and the center is an artificial topography hosting the icon.

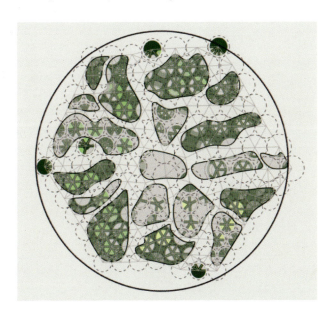

At the center is the AMSLM. It is a space that brings together, as it extends over the archipelago, and provides a sense of direction; a floating obelisk. The floating terrains, with the museum at the center, bring in an additional organizational layer on top of the organic one at the ground level.

## CENTRAL ICON: THE ARCHEOLOGICAL MUSEUM OF SYNTHETIC LIFE AND MEDIA

A Mobius-like form with lights and folding surfaces to unite both the mineral and the biological. The museum brings forward synthetic life and media, as it's traced back to their geological foundations: the mineral basis for the virtual life we inhabit.

The museum will host works of art and culture that happen within the boundaries of a connected narrative of geology, media, life forms, and intelligence.

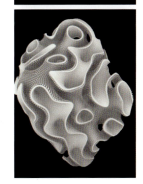

An island that has a clear geometrical form floating and includes a hyper-exclusive set of functions and services limited to certain communities. It is organized around a central tower within a generative urban layout.

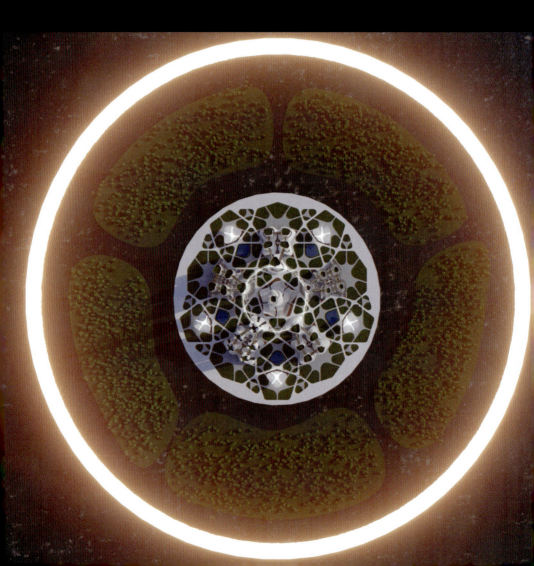

The neighborhood consists of ᴛɪᴠe clusters, where each cluster is made of five interconnected buildings, hosting a different program. A pentagon layout governs the spatial organization of Rei.

## CENTRAL ICON: QUANTUM TWIRL

Rei's central icon is a light strip-based tower that floats above the ground and guides the formal organization of the neighborhood. The Quantum Twirl tower encapsulates a vision of the fusion of the immersive internet and quantum computing, just like the neighborhood suggests. It celebrates a refined aesthetic and a vision of technological sophistication.

The tower floats within a ring of light that connects the neighborhood's cluster to the skyline.

## URBAN MORPHOLOGY

Rei's urban configuration is based on 4 layers: the outermost being the lagoon, then a rotating floating light ring where art installations and urban sculptures are placed, followed by a ring of water, then a ring of islands where the lands for sale are offered, water again, and finally a circular nucleus that hosts the city.

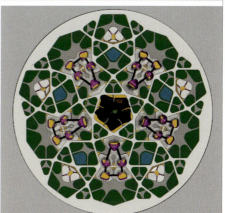

The geometrical base of Rei is contrasted with its organic form. Clusters are connected within themselves, at the level of each building, and on another level, all clusters are unified with a ring of light floating around the central tower.

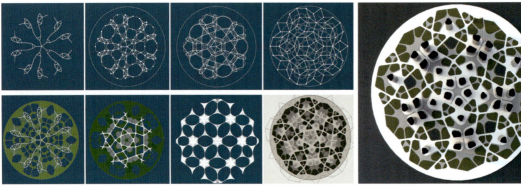

# NEIGHBORHOOD
# 9. SENA

Augmented Forests, virtual chlorophyll, technobiophilia, and the evolution of forest cities. Eco-nomics are literal. Sena is the forest neighborhood of the Gamium world, positioned within a crater, at the center of an island towards the northeast of the Gamium world.

Sena is a take on virtual urbanism as it merges with artificial nature to create a unique aesthetic. Sena is a place of high abundance. It is geometrical and 'natural'.

## CENTRAL ICON: THE TOWER OF LIFE ASSEMBLAGES

Spatial Intelligence is embodied here in digital assemblages, a computational space of automated formation processes. At the center of SENA, it sits as a beacon to what the neighborhood represents in its underlayer. A virtual attempt to recreate liveliness in a forest context.

The tower of life occupies the center, conceptually bringing to the foreground material assemblages as the basis of intelligence and life itself. It is an icon of automated assemblages and machinic design.

Virtual chlorophyll is perceptually valid. Clinical patients who attend virtual nature through VR wearables demonstrate signs of increased relaxation.

The forest, a vital element of life, is reduced to its aesthetics and perceptual qualities.

Technophilic environments take command.

## URBAN MORPHOLOGY

The urban morphology is based on a gradient circle packing as its underlying structure. Each circle hosts a building or a cluster of structures creating various moods, all within a forest context. Moving outward, the circular plots get smaller, and therefore, the structures they host do too.

Terrain manipulation is key to creating a subtle sense of place and direction, in addition to unique placemaking.

As the urban form gets more intense at the center, the spatial layout is 'naturalized' by aggregation-based architectural elements and an open terrain ground floor. The forest floor becomes the urban floor.

For increased spatial legibility, the neons flow as a second layer of organizational structure, leading to walkable or conceptual connections within the city fabric.

Into the future, as Sena is inhabited, a new flora species shall emerge— the blooming trees of QR-codes. As every surface is an information interface, leaves become the new QR codes.

# NEIGHBORHOOD
# 10. NOA

Noa is the Gamium Community neighborhood, one that is open to future collaborative design strategies. It is an experiment for a collage city for the metaverse. Along the scales of planning, from the most top-down to the most bottom-up, Noa is the neighborhood with no predefined urban morphology.

The neighborhood is left at the "Ground Zero" state, a terrain that follows the planning layout of the Gamium City-world, yet has all the rest open to experimentation; Noa is only bound by the rules and economy of the platform.

Through the neighborhoods, it was intended to experiment with various morphologies, planning strategies, and design aesthetics. At the strategic and planning level, if Genesis is the most top-down, Noa is the extreme bottom-up.

# LANDS

**Within the virtual, lands are virtual real-estate assets. The lands are modeled within a hierarchical clustering approach where different land types have different scarcities, and neighbors while optimizing positions, views, and proximity from wanted locations.**

Lands within the Gamium world correspond to neighborhoods. with a total land count of around 40,000 lands for the whole city, thus a rough estimate of 4,000 lands per neighborhood [ 10 neighborhoods ].

While all neighborhoods will be in the lagoon, lands can occur on the islands, underwater, on the terrain, or on floating structures.

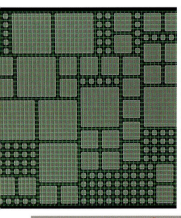
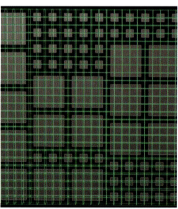
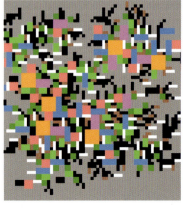
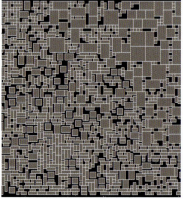
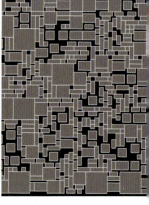

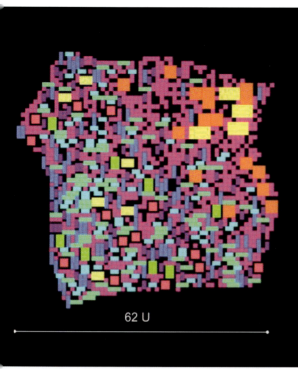

Land Size
Percentage

Land Type
Percentage

Land Target

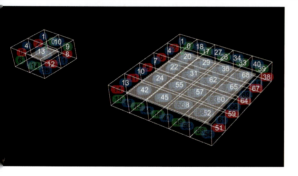

Lands range in size and have a rectangular form, of combinations of the following pool of integers: 1, 2, 3, and 5 units. Each unit is 16 meters.

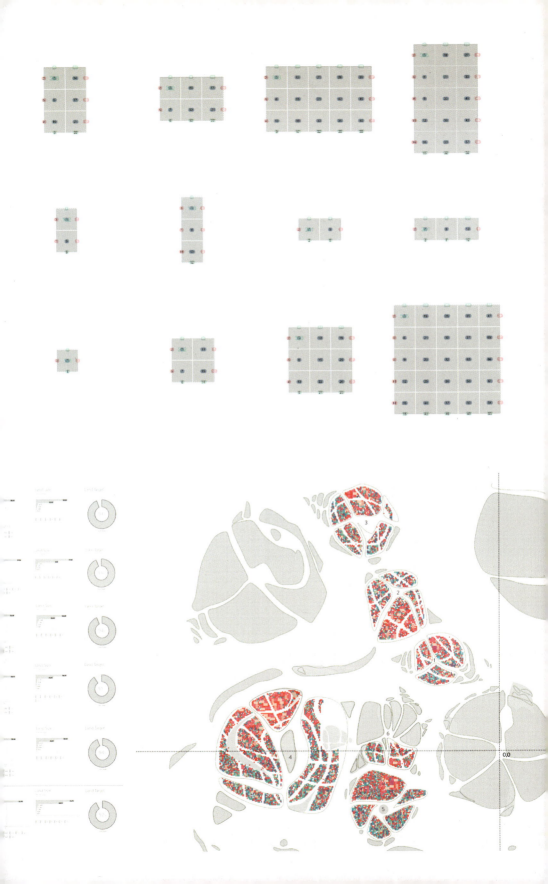

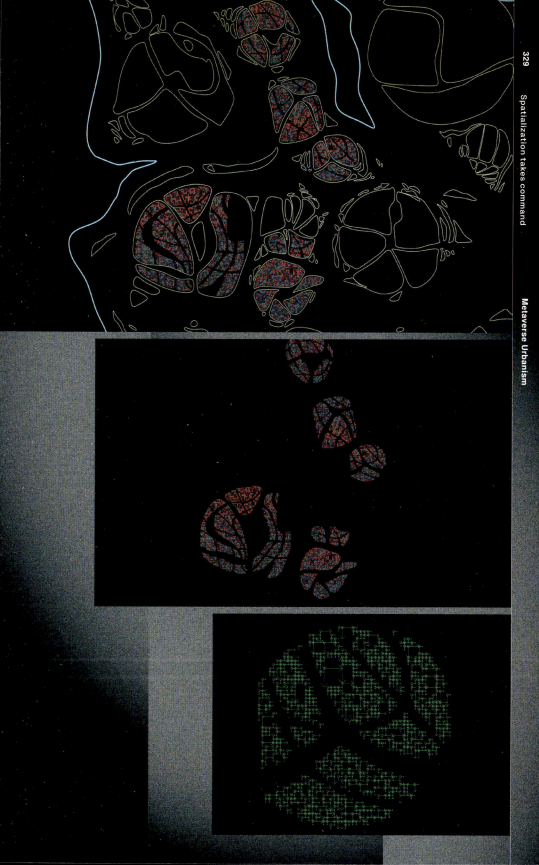

# DAO SPACES

The Neighborhood DAO spaces are experiences
that are characterized by each neighborhood as
catering specifically to its community.

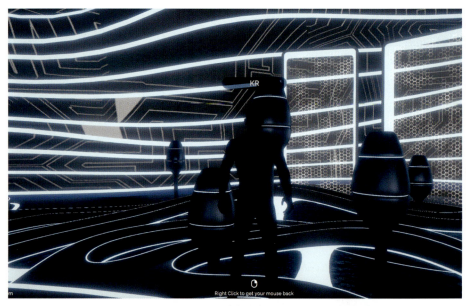

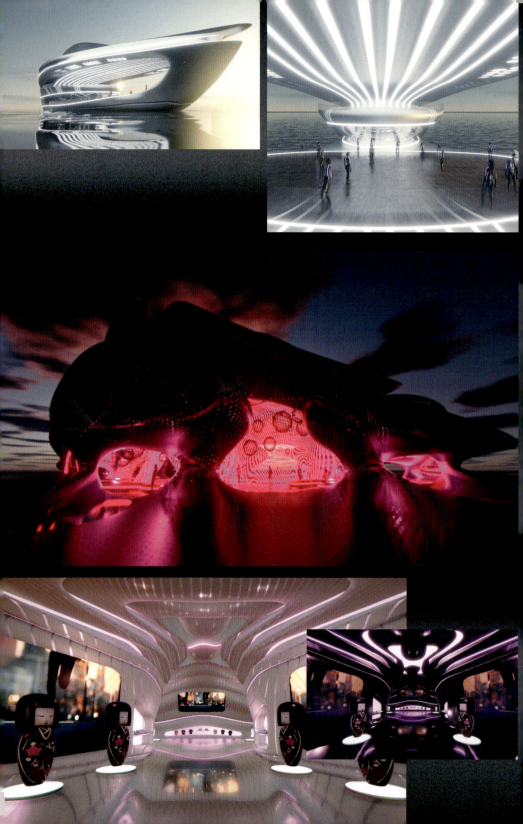

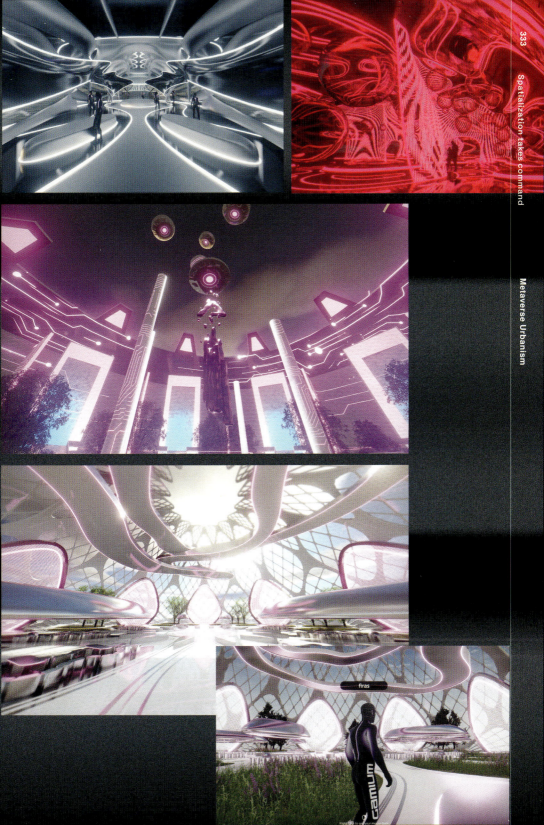

# REFERENCES

NOTES ON THE FUTURE OF
URBANISM, THE INTERNET,
AND LIFE AS WE LIVE IT

METAVERSE URBANISM

By weaving together a range
of topics, the book takes
readers on a journey through
the evolution of the Internet,
and its next generation - The
Spatial Internet- and explores
the current technosphere and
terminology necessary to
comprehend the metaverse. It
creatively delves into unique
social, cultural, technological,
economic, and emerging
urban phenomena, and
ultimately provides a
comprehensive guide to
designing and building
metaverse urban
environments.

The author draws upon their
knowledge of architecture,
urbanism, and spatial design
to present the metaverse, not
as a distant, abstract
concept, but as a tangible
reality that will revolutionize
how we live, work, learn,
socialize, and play. A seminal
work at the intersection of
technology and urbanism, and
the future of the built
environment, and life as we
live it.

$39.95USD /35,00EUR
ISBN 978-1-63840-147-6
53995 >

ACTAR
A

FIRAS SAFIEDDINE

9 781638 401476